No Ordinary Love

Dear Bethany,

Hope you
enjoy the Book!
Remember its
fiction!!

love
Mary Klempay

No Ordinary Love

By

Mary Dempsey

1stbooks – rev. 3/13/00

ABOUT THE BOOK

Keara Fitzgerald, a married woman with an intoxicating mix of sex and manipulation, spends her days maneuvering through a web of lies and passion: all the while fighting the urge to drink. Keara orchestrates everyone to cover for her, even Taylor, her teenage daughter. As she enters the torrid affair, not only does it reshape the face of her marriage, but her entire identity as well. Nick Bartoli, her husband's business partner becomes her latest obsesion.

Dedicated to the loving memory of Kathy Cannon, my token straight friend who never judged.

Part One

San Diego

I was standing in the doorway of the hotel room, my heart vibrating in my chest like I was next to a mega watt speaker blasting disco music. It was one of those awkward moments when you just had sex for the first time and you think it was great but you don't know if he was all that impressed with your deep throat skills .

"This is the first and last time, Keara. Your husband, after all, is my best friend and partner. I feel awful." Nick said with a huge sigh.

Reality check, thank you.

"But Nick, I've never ever cheated on David till now, you drive me wild. Tonight was incredible. Don't tell me you didn't feel it, too. I truly love you."

Big panic attack was happening across my chest and my stomach was in major knots. If I didn't see him again, I would definitely fill up the tub and get a fresh razor and slash away!

"Bye, Keara," he said, forcefully gripping the doorknob.

I flew out the door. I had to pick up my seventeen-year-old daughter, Taylor, who I supposedly was with attending the Lollapalooza Concert for the last sixteen hours. I can't believe I had dragged her into this mess.

Yes I can. I'd ask the devil for his help to get Nick.

I had to pretend I was at a drug infested, muddy moshing, heavy metal rock concert, me who was sixty days sober and a Sinatra fan. I had just spent the last sixteen hours making love, saw the play "Tommy", ate Chinese food, licked Ben and Jerry's coffee fudge almond ice cream off Nick private parts by candlelight and made love again and again. Then Taylor called saying the concert was over and wanted me to get her. She sounded like she was just coming down probably on coke all day and drinking, following her mom's footsteps.

As I was heading toward the address on the paper in front of me, I could see her sitting on the curb, her head between her legs in my headlights.

"You're late." Taylor groaned.

"Get in the car. We have a lot of work to do. You have to tell me in detail about the concert, plus I'm freshly showered and smell like soap. You look and smell like shit. What the hell happened? How am I going to look like you in twenty minutes?"

"I'm so sick." she muttered, "but I had the greatest time. You should have been there Mommy. You're a D.J., after all! I got to go in the mosh pit and Brad was there. He got me totally stoned and drunk. Two girls got crushed to death in the parking lot."

Mmm maybe I should share this with my AA group.

I was running out of time. I would be facing David in less than twenty minutes fresh as a daisy and walking in with Miss Manure 1994. That's it! I screeched my 86 convertible black Mustang to a halt in front of the park, which was completely uphill, perfect for rolling down it which in the daytime countless tiny tots did just that. Now it was my turn to have a crack at it. There was just enough light from the moon, just a touch of dampness and lots of grass and dirt for me to roll in. It was now two a.m., I prayed for no cops to drive by. How in the world would I explain this? I knelt down on all fours. Taylor just shook her head from the car. On the count of three I went for it and rolled around, laughing out loud to myself. After about three times of this, it was no longer fun. I wondered if I did this kind if thing in my childhood.

My therapist had suggested I was sexually abused because I can't remember a thing, not even a simple pleasure or loving moment that combined with being a full-fledged alcoholic by age seventeen. Obviously, I'd be in therapy a very long time. Back to reality, I needed to be more dirty and sweaty, the nerves would kick in when I would see David's face, so that would take care of the sick part. I took globs of dirt and started pouring it on my head and taking my finger tips, combed it through my thick hair. Now for the sweat.

"Taylor, I need you to drive the car home. I'm going to jog along side till I get nice and sweaty."

I got a really evil look with this suggestion.

"Please," I begged.

She crawled over to the driver side acting like at any moment she could heave. She pulled away from the curb at a nice pace. I anxiously looked around for Men in Blue, still could not explain this event to them, jogging beside my mustang at two thirty in the morning while my daughter who was coming off her high was driving the car.

Please God let this go perfect and I'll be good. Well I'll give it a good shot.

Good. I was getting sweaty as we started to turn the corner.

"Taylor pull over, I'll drive now just in case he's up and looking out the window."

Another evil look from her but let's face it, if it wasn't for her I wouldn't have been able to spend sixteen glorious hours with the man of my dreams, Nick Bartoli, my best friend and now I could proudly say my lover. Even though he was probably banging his head against the hotel headboard right now saying to himself, I'm bad, wicked, and no good.

"Taylor, tomorrow we'll go shopping and I'll buy you whatever you want for being such a good sport and for lying to David for me. I know I owe you big time. Before we go in let's go over the bands once more."

"Mommy, how hard is Green Day or Smashing Pumpkins to remember?" she growled.

I walked to the front door full of confidence. I was sweating, dirty and sick to my stomach the same as Taylor. I had to shake Nick from my thoughts and concentrate on the concert and David. I could do this. After all I was sober now and cheating with a clear head.

As we stepped inside the hallway, Jack, the big black slobbering Great Dane, ran toward us, tail wagging, spit dangling from his jowls. Taylor always called him curfew dog because you could never sneak in. Jack waited by the door for whoever was out. He couldn't rest until everyone was tucked safely in their beds. I didn't care about the drool. I reached out and grabbed his face between my hands and planted a big wet kiss on him. I wanted to confide in him and tell him everything I had just been through and know when I was done he would love me as always.

"Keara, Taylor come and tell me about the concert. I want to know everything." David shouted from the bedroom.

Taylor announced she was too exhausted to stay up another minute and wearily dragged herself into the bedroom she shared on her visits to California with her half sister.

"David, I'm exhausted too. The music was horrendous. I'm filthy and sweaty from the worse day of my life. Never again. Taylor owes me big time. It was disgusting, all the booze and drugs and Taylor moshed. I'm too old for this stuff but as a D. J. I felt I should experience every kind of music. This music I will never play. I need to shower and sleep for two days."

"Keara", David said painfully, " We have to talk. Since you sobered up, I feel, you've shut me out of your life. You're either at an AA meeting or off by yourself in La Jolla writing in your journal or working at the restaurant. You don't give me two minutes of your time. If this is what it's going to be like, I'd rather see you go back to drinking."

"We'll talk, David, tomorrow, I promise. I'm sorry if I hurt you in any way. I am trying to cope with just frigging waking up and breathing and trying to act normal like everyone else when every frigging second I want to scream and run into a bar and throw a tequila down my throat. Not to mention we own a Goddamn bar and I have to work there and act like it doesn't bother me that everyone is getting shit faced while I sip my coke instead of snorting coke. Let's not say anymore. We'll talk when I'm not so tired and edgy."

I slipped into the bathroom and turned the shower on full force. Stripped off my grass-stained jeans and shirt. My body was beginning to feel sore from all the delicious lovemaking. I stood under the hot shower and thought about Nick and how much I loved him and how we would both act in front of David tomorrow. The steam was filling up the bathroom. If only when I got out there would be a glass of dry white wine on the counter. David was having a hard time with my sobriety. I was always high, funny and sexy. Never drunk enough to fall down. I hated sloppy drunks. Since I didn't fall down or slur my words, I never thought of myself as an alcoholic.

Because Nick used a rubber tonight, I really didn't cheat on

4

David. Denial, Keara, Denial.

Usually when I craved a drink like this I'd call Nick instead of my sponsor and he would give me a pep talk and make me feel like Mother Theresa. David wanted the old Keara back and would say just drink, you had the strength to go sixty days so you must have the strength to have just one. I guess that's why everyone in my AA group was divorced.

I wrapped myself in a big green fluffy towel and over moisturized my body from head to toe. After all, Nick was six years younger than me. I had to keep looking young. I'd dropped twenty pounds instantly when I quit drinking. Now I always had a bottle of spring water in my hand to replace the wine glass.

The only thing I worried about was my lips. I had chicken lips. Even all the outlining and lipsticks couldn't give them any false fullness. Nick loved big lush lips and all his ex-girlfriends had them. Tonight he hadn't kissed me once. I was kinda glad because of my self-consciousness about my lips but I was also hurt. I used to watch him make out with all his old girlfriends and couldn't wait for him to hold me, thrill me, kiss me. I guess two out of three ain't bad.

I slowly opened the bathroom door and poked my head out listening for sounds of everyone sleeping. I tiptoed into the bedroom and slipped under the covers. David instantly rolled over and pulled me against his chest holding me tight in his arms. I went to sleep thinking of Nick's solid thick hairy chest.

At seven thirty a.m., David yelled down the steps that Jenny was on the phone and was I jogging today.

"Of course I am, I'll meet her at the park at eight," I murmured into my pillow.

Jenny, my token straight friend, was my running partner and seven years older than me. She lived for her kids, house, garden, and husband in that order. She was the last person on earth I could confide in about Nick, but she got me to run three miles on the beach every day so I was grateful to her for my toned body. I was five foot six and one hundred twenty pounds with nice long muscular legs. The only thing I hated dealing with was my age, thirty-eight years old. I was scared of forty.

I pulled on my sweats and headed up the steps. The kids were still sleeping.

David was probably up since five and buying and selling stocks in his office/living room.

"Hi, how's your morning going? Are we rich or do we have to jump?" I said, trying to make my voice sound like the loving wife not a guilty one.

"The market is up and all my customers love me," he said cheerfully. He was one of those dreaded morning persons that I hated. It was bad enough I had to have conversation with Jenny before my coffee and Honey Nut Cheerios.

"How about when I get back we have breakfast together on the terrace?"

"I'd like that, and maybe a walk on the beach too." He anxiously bit on the tip of his pen.

I walked over to his desk and bent over and hugged him. "I'd like that too," I said convincingly.

Just then Jack, feeling left out, thinking he was a lap dog, jumped up on David's lap. I kissed them both and headed for the door and out into the California sunshine.

I couldn't wait to call Nick. The quarter in my jogging shorts meant more to me right now than a precious stone. He must be home now. I wondered what he had told Claudia. It was hard to believe that he still lived with his mother. She was an aging hippie still wearing tie dye. Claudia loved controlling Nick and of course hated me. She knew. She saw through all the fake business calls at all hours. Hated my mini skirts and thigh-high boots and black spandex dresses. I was so preoccupied thinking of Nick and Claudia, I practically crashed into Jenny.

I looked up and saw the park where a couple of hours ago in the moonlight I was rolling down the hill.

"Where do you want to jog, the street or the beach?" Jenny asked. She was about my height and weight with shoulder-length brown hair that had a dusting of gray in it. My hair color changed with the seasons. Since it was summer I was blonde and that also meant my blue sapphire contacts.

"Let's do the beach."

6

The quicker this is over with the quicker I can call Nick.

We ran down the path that led us onto the sand. It was starting to get crowded. All the sunburned tourists running after their toddlers. People who saved all year for this trip to paradise and I lived here all year round. I was still in awe of the fact that we decided to move to San Diego from New York and start our life over. That's why I loved David. He had the ability to adapt anywhere and to any situation. To one day be rich and the next poor and it didn't matter. Life was an exploration. He was a millionaire when I met him, lost it all, and now was climbing back. David definitely was a fighter.

So what was I doing with Nick?

"Keara, are you okay? You look worried."

"No, I'm fine. I was just thinking about Taylor. Today is her last day. We had the best visit. Taylor, really is my best friend. I'll probably be a mess at the airport. She's taking the red eye back to New York tonight."

The perfect alibi and she was leaving.

"Emily's leaving tomorrow for college," Jenny said with anguish. She was a great help with Kate and we got closer too. I still can't believe I have a three year old. We're driving her back to Arizona. I'll probably be gone a week."

We were now walking at a fast pace. Our exercise time was over. I hugged her slightly damp body, wished her a safe trip and sprinted off to the phone. I knew there were two behind the lifeguard stand. I figured it was a perfect location. I could see the beach if David decided to jog here and I could see the street if he drove by.

I dropped the quarter. I couldn't believe Nick could get me flustered at a phone booth. I shivered thinking of the pleasure he gave me last night. He was the most considerate lover I ever had. It was ringing and I was praying Claudia wouldn't answer.

"Hello," he answered in a raspy voice.

"Hi! Did I wake you? I just finished jogging with Jenny and thought I'd check in on you. Did you stay all night at the hotel? Are you okay with me calling you?" I asked breathlessly.

"Keara, I just woke up, slow down. I couldn't sleep. I had a

7

head trip about us, so I decided to just come home. Listen, last night at dinner I had a really great time. I was with my best friend. I loved hearing you laugh but I'm just too uncomfortable with the sex part. I don't know how I'm going to face David today. I just want us to be friends from now on, okay? I can't handle the lover part."

"Is that why you didn't kiss me last night," I said, holding back tears.

"Yes, kisses are for girlfriends, someone you have a future with."

"I can't talk now. I'm taking Taylor to the airport tonight. Now I have to go home to my husband and pretend our marriage isn't crumbling." Tears were now streaming down my face and I was trying to bury my head into the phone. " That I'm not in love with you, not to mention, I need a drink and I'm sick of sharing at AA. My life is a mess!"

One of the lifeguards was coming down to check up on me.
He's probably worried I'm going to kill myself on his beach.

"Keara, don't cry. If you drink, will that change anything? Look at the strength you have. What about your therapist, why don't you see her today? How about you bring Taylor to the restaurant and we'll have a nice dinner before she leaves."

I was hysterical now. I was having trouble breathing. I mumbled that I'd call back. As I turned around, the lifeguard was in my face.

"Break up with your boyfriend? Can I get you something, a tissue or some water?"

"How about a life raft or a hug, " I said, acting pathetic.
He was hot!!!!!!

He put his muscular arms out and wrapped them around me tight. He smelled of suntan lotion. His body was hard like a rock. All of a sudden I became uncomfortable.

"I didn't realize you rescued out of the water too."

"Damsels in distress are my specialty," he said with a smile. He had perfect white teeth, short curly blonde hair and fierce green eyes. Taylor would love him. I judged him to be about thirty. Too young for me. I was already cradle robbing with Nick.

"Well thanks for the hug. I have to get back home."

"Come by again, you can cry on my shoulder any time."he said, oh so cute.

I turned and jogged across the beach in shock. Okay, what just happened? Nick had told me he only kissed girls he had a future with and acted like last night didn't exist. Bust my bubble!!!

Then this Greek God rescues me. Now I was jogging back home to have breakfast with David. This had nervous breakdown written all over it.

Give the lady a Bloody Mary!!!!

When I opened the front door, David was lacing up his running shoes on the bottom step.

"Hi, I was just going to look for you. What took so long?"

"Oh, you know Jenny, she's upset with Emily leaving, so we talked extra today."

That just rolled off my tongue.

"Let's eat breakfast out. The kids are up and watching television. I want us to talk."

"Sure. Hi kids," I yelled up the stairs.

Taylor and Tabitha looked over the banister.

"Hi Mom," they both said in unison.

Taylor and Tabitha, half sisters but looked nothing alike. They were both Irish, Italian and Jewish. My first husband had also been Jewish like David. The nuns would be frowning on my choices but deep down that's probably why I married them in the first place. Both had chestnut brown hair and soft brown eyes. That's where it ended. Taylor was short, only five foot. She had thick long curly hair, large firm breasts but heavy thighs and rear. Her face was drop dead gorgeous. Tabitha at ten was already five foot four. She had an athletic body with long beautiful legs. Her hair was thin, straight and short. She still had a cute baby face.

David was anxiously pulling me out the door as I was waving goodbye. The phone rang and I stopped dead. My whole body froze. I was chilled to the bone with the realization that if it was Nick, it would take everything in me not to run up those steps, grab the phone and scream I love you in it.

Taylor was screeching over the banister that it was Nick for

9

David. I was paralyzed. I was so afraid David would be able to see every emotion I was feeling.

"Tell Nick I'll call him after breakfast," David snapped.

Oh God the jig is up!!

We walked to the Mustang in uncomfortable silence. I thought I'd be cute and jumped in over the door. David didn't look amused.

"I'm getting sick of Nick, Keara, we work with him all day, go to the gym together, have lunch and dinner together, seven days a week. You seem to be glued to his side lately and it makes me cringe how you wait on him, you act like his mother."

"David, are you jealous of Nick? He's a kid. No threat. You know I have a father complex".

Guilt was nipping at me.

"Maybe I am acting like a mother hen but he's so straight, never done drugs, doesn't drink, helps people with Aids, kind to animals, he's what I need in a friend right now. All my other friends are still drinking and getting high and my AA friends I'm still getting used to."

"What would you two like this beautiful morning," said the bagel clerk, all too joyful. Californians were way too cheery. In New York you'd be thankful they didn't spit in your coffee in the morning.

I ordered my usual. A whole wheat bagel with light cream cheese and a tomato with a sprinkle of lemon pepper and a black coffee.

I went and got us a table and waited for David to bring over the food.

He knew, I was sure, now it was turning into a game, one I couldn't afford to lose. Do I really love Nick like my heart was acting? Since I sobered up I wasn't attracted to David anymore. He was fifty-two with a body like a twenty year old. Tall, lean and agile with thick salt and pepper hair and endless energy. He had warm hazel eyes and thin lips like me. For ten years, our sex life was full of passion but I was always drunk or high. Being sober was the pits.

He placed the bagels down first then went back to get the coffees. Before he sat down he leaned over and kissed my cheek.

"I love you, Keara, you're the best thing that ever happened to me. I want you by my side forever. Don't ever leave me."

"I love you too, David."

I took a bite of my bagel and knew I wouldn't be able to eat. I was sick to my stomach. It was like I was a schoolgirl all over again. I wanted to be sitting across from Nick eating my bagel.

We drove home in thick heavy silence.

"As soon as we get home let's put on our bathing suits and head for the beach," I insisted. I was afraid he would want to have sex with me since the kids were out of the house. Crazy as it sounded, I couldn't cheat on Nick, so soon after our time together.

We pulled up in the driveway and I shouted, "Last one to the beach is a rotten egg."

I raced into the house and tore off my clothes. I pulled on my black spandex one piece suit and Nike black shorts and grabbed my Polo bear beach towel.

"Ready, let's go, slow poke."

"Don't you want your bottled water?"

"My security blanket, of course, might as well bring the chips and pretzels too and some fruit."

We skipped out the door and across the street to the beach like two young lovers. We spotted the kids sunbathing. Taylor on her back and Tabitha on her stomach, hands holding her head up reading a book.

"Hi kids, we have goodies in the basket," I shouted, putting Coppertone on my nose.

Tabitha immediately scrambled for the basket. Taylor sat up and announced that she had invited Nick down to the beach for her last day. She hoped that was okay.

She could have asked me for a BMW at that moment and I would have bought her one right then and there.

The butterflies started up in my stomach. David immediately became sour.

No one said a word. I had to break the silence.

"Who wants to go boogie boarding?"

"I do, I do!" Tabitha screamed with delight.

I wanted to be in the water when Nick arrived. Let them talk

11

first.

Tabitha and I were fighting the strong current, trying to catch one good ride in. I turned and glanced toward our blanket and saw him and David talking. Taylor was heading toward us with her neon board. She paddled out to us quickly.

"Hey, are you two losers? I haven't seen you catch one wave," she said with a smile.

"We're just waiting for the big one. We don't want to tire ourselves out with the small ones."

I reached over in the water and hugged her close. We didn't say a word. We didn't have to. She knew exactly what I was feeling. Forty-eight hours before the concert I'd spilled my guts to her and told her how I felt about Nick. She was a trooper. She agreed to go to the concert with one of my coke whore friends from the restaurant. She was so proud that I was sober that nothing else mattered.

"Mom, here's the big one," Tabitha squealed.

"Oh my God, ready girls, let's boogie."

The huge wave washed us all up to the shore. What a rush! Tabitha was up first.

"Mom, I see Kate and Lauren, can I go over there with them?"

"Sure sweetie, just check in with me now and then."

She took off like a playful pup after a ball.

"Taylor, let's get the guys. I feel a sand fight coming on."

"You really owe me, Mom."

"I know, I know."

As we approached them, I could feel heat rising into my cold cheeks. Thoughts of Nick naked in the soft glow of candlelight and our moans of ecstasy played in my head. I briefly wondered if David would spot the canary feathers protruding from my mouth.

We first shook our wet hair at them, then bent down and grabbed fistfuls of sand and quickly put it down their trunks. They started chasing us toward the water where it turned into mud slinging. David called a truce. I suggested chicken fights. Taylor and Nick against me and David. They won. We continued on playing like this for an hour. All the tension washed away. It was a slice of heaven day. I knew we would never have another day like this.

After the beach, we showered, dressed and headed downtown to the restaurant for Taylor's last dinner with us. She wouldn't be back till Christmas.

The restaurant was hopping. It was a huge sprawling space with cathedral ceilings and big bay windows that opened up into the street. We were directly across from the Convention Center. After a convention, thick crowds of people would flow into Tequila Bay and drink our famous Margaritas. In the back of the restaurant, past the open kitchen, was a nightclub. There, I'd become D.J. Keara.

Taylor sprinted over to the bar and flirted with Brad, the bartender. I started going from table to table making sure all customers were happy with the service. David went into the kitchen to check on things and order our meal. Tabitha sat down at an empty table in the back and started drawing on the paper cloth with the crayons we provided in a glass. Nick was in the manager's office going over bank receipts.

Lou, Nick's father, was also there. He was seventy something, long thin gray hair pulled back in a ponytail, deep blue eyes like Nick and always a devilish grin. Like Claudia, I'm sure, he had guessed what was happening between me and Nick.

Everyone in the restaurant must have noticed. When I was with Nick I seemed on cloud nine and beside David I was in hell. You could have an IQ of a plant and pick it up.

I noticed Taylor nursing a rather large Margarita at the bar. I hoped the two meetings Taylor had attended with me would sink in sometime soon. Nick and Lou strolled over and plunked down beside her. Brad poured Lou a Cabernet and Nick his usual cranberry juice. I walked over, picked up a lemon from the condiment tray and squeezed it into Nick's drink.

"Taylor, you are going to be sick on that plane," I said, trying to act motherly. In the old days I'd be right beside her draining my glass dry.

"Mom, you know I hate flying. This is for my nerves."

Just then David popped up like a magician had just pulled him out of a hat.

"Let's eat, everybody. It's getting late and Robert has prepared a delicious feast for us."

David put his arm around me and steered me toward the table that Tabitha had worked so hard on decorating.

Dinner was quiet. I was slipping into depression and I could see Taylor was too. David kept looking at me and Nick. Lou and Tabitha were keeping one another entertained playing tic tac toe. I couldn't guess what Nick was thinking. I wanted to curl up in his lap with his arms around me. He was a weight lifter. His arms were solid muscle, big and strong like Popeye's. Just looking at them made me feel safe and warm.

It was finally time for the airport.

Taylor and Tabitha hugged goodbye. Tabitha was staying behind with Lou and having dessert.

Boy did I need a drink or a joint.

David and Nick waited in the car while I walked her in.

"Thanks for understanding me, Taylor, and helping me out. I'm sorry I'm so fucked up."

Taylor hugged me tight. "I'm so proud of you Mom. I know being sober is the hardest thing in the world for you. If you really love Nick, go for it but be careful, he has no money or future and you're too old to start struggling Mom. I can't see you living on peanut butter and jelly sandwiches."

We both giggled.

"I know what you're saying Taylor. I hate peanut butter and jelly too. I love you, Taylor."

"I love you, Mom," Taylor sobbed uncontrollably and then quickly turned and ran towards the plane.

My heart and head were exploding together. I would love an Absolut on the rocks with a twist. I could just walk over to the bar and order one and maybe David and Nick wouldn't smell it on me. I looked up and was face to face with Nick. I was about two feet away from the bar.

"Thinking about having a drink," he said in a clear voice.

"How did you know?"

"I'm your guardian angel. I know these things."

He hugged me.

He's such a giving friend. I'd throw myself in front of a bullet to save this man.

"Let's go before David comes in and breaks us up or worse tries to break my face," he said with a smile that melted me.

"I have an AA meeting tomorrow night. I'm getting a token. Please come. Eight-thirty at the church on twelfth street."

"I'll be there."

David was pacing nervously by the car. He ran over to me and hugged me.

"Are you okay?"

I started crying again. I just nodded my head.

I wanted to die.

* * *

The next morning I woke up with my arms around Jack. I could hear David chatting away on the phone. I tossed on my gray jogging bra and gray shorts. I laced up my Nike running shoes and bounced up the stairs.

David was just finishing up the call.

"Do you want me to run with you?" he asked, full of hope.

"I need to clear my head. How about I call you from town and you meet me for coffee?"

"Great, I'll finish up my calls and be ready when you call." He was so anxious to please me.

I ran down the steps and out the door into the sunshine. It felt good pouring all over my body. I jogged swiftly. I made it to the phone booth in record time. I was huffing and puffing as I dialed. Please God let Nick answer. Thank You.

"You sound distracted. Did I call at a bad time?"

"No, its not a bad time. I have to go down to my dad's plant and help him straighten out some problems down there. Things are starting to get out of hand there cause I'm spending too much time at the restaurant. I'm going to have to spend more time at the plant."

"What about cutting out some of your volunteer time at the animal shelter?"

"That's too important to me. It keeps me grounded. It feeds my soul to take care of those cats and dogs."

"How about I take over some of your responsibilities at the

restaurant? Why don't we meet there tomorrow morning and you can go over with me all the stuff you do? I'd meet you today but I have to get ready for my big night. Are you still coming?"

I saw the lifeguard coming toward me with a coffee in his hand.

"I'll be there. What's the time again?"

"Uh, hold on a minute." I held the phone down by me side as the lifeguard handed me the coffee.

"You look like you could use a cup of coffee."

"Thanks, you're too good to me."

"At your service, your highness," he said with a toothy smile. "There's milk and sugar in the tower. Come up when you're off."

I just nodded and put the phone back to my ear.

"Hi, sorry about that."

"Who was that?"

"When I hung up from you yesterday, I was pretty hysterical, the lifeguard kind of noticed and was being brotherly."

"So you're picking up the lifeguard now?"

"Shut up. Meet me tonight at eight-thirty and let's go out afterwards and celebrate."

"Okay, I have to go now. My mom is calling me downstairs."

"I think I'll go for a swim and see if Mr. lifeguard will save me. I don't think he'll have a problem giving me mouth to mouth."

"Keara, what are you starting up?"

"Ok, just kidding, see you tonight. Love ya."

He was so devoted to his parents. Both of my parents were dead but even when they were alive I was the daughter from hell. Too bad they couldn't have seen me finally clean and sober. I know this time I could make it.

"Hey, you didn't even drink your coffee," the lifeguard said with a hurt expression.

"I'm sorry but thanks for thinking of me."

"You're having an affair, aren't you?"

I turned crimson.

"My first if that means anything."

"If you ever want to talk I'm in my tower," he shouted over his dark tanned shoulder as he climbed the steps to the booth.

Was he coming on to me? Did guys come on to me before and

16

I just didn't notice in my drunken stupor? If Nick saw him would he be jealous?

* * *

I spent the day getting my nails done and shopping for a new outfit for tonight. I wanted to knock Nick's socks off. I bought some school clothes for Tabitha out of guilt but finally it was time to leave the mall and face the music. David and Tabitha were waiting for me to come home and have dinner with them before my meeting.

I arrived home to the sound of Kenny G playing softly throughout the house, fresh flowers everywhere, a candlelight table and beautiful wrapped presents. Even Jack had a big bow around his neck.

"Hi guys, what's all this?"

Both Tabitha and David spun around from the stove and ran toward me.

"This is your special night. We wanted to show you how proud we are of your accomplishment." David smiled, his face beaming with love.

"Mommy, open your presents. Mine first." Tabitha shouted, jumping up and down.

I sat down on the vinyl swivel chair that the previous renter had left for us. Jack always bit chunks out of every piece of furniture. So I stopped buying it years ago. Our last place had no tables and chairs. We ate on the floor, picnic style every meal.

I opened Tabitha's gift.

"Tabitha, I love it. I really need it too." It was a glass milk bottle with a cow face etched on it, filled with milk bubble bath. She knew I adored cows. I reached out and hugged her.

"Here, I bought you some new clothes for school. Why don't you go try them on."

"Thanks Mom, I love you." She grabbed the clothing bags and took off for her room.

David handed me a small silver wrapped box with silver ribbons curled on it.

He's so nice. Why don't I love him like before?

I opened the box to find a pair of thick gold star earrings.

"Try them on. Tonight's your night to shine," he said lovingly.

I took off my hoops and placed the stars in my ears. They covered my whole lobe. They looked expensive.

"David Fisher, are you crazy? These are too extravagant. I thought we had to watch our money."

"Don't worry about it. I wanted you to have something special for your big night. I'm proud of you, Keara Fitzgerald. I love you so much," he said, his eyes filling up with tears.

I just held him. I couldn't say it back. I knew I was going to have a breakdown.

"After the meeting tonight a bunch of us are going to the coffee shop to celebrate my sixty days. So I'll probably be late," I blurted out. Fear was gripping my entire body.

"How late?" David muttered, watching my face intensely.

"Don't start acting like you're my father and setting a curfew. I need to talk to these people. I'm going nuts. You have to give me space," I snapped, pulling the petals off the daisy in the vase.

He immediately backed down. "I'm sorry, Keara. I'll take Tabitha to the restaurant. I need to straighten things out down there. I'll call Nick. I need to go over the books with him and the advertising."

I'm going to pass out.

"I have to get ready. Let me know when you are leaving."

I decided to take a long hot shower. Maybe I could wash away my fear and confusion.

I was rinsing out the conditioner in my hair when David peeked his head in.

"Tabitha and I are leaving. I couldn't get a hold of Nick. No one knows where he is. I even called the shelter. If he calls tell him to meet me at the restaurant. Good luck tonight."

"Thanks David, don't work too hard tonight," I yelled over the curtain.

With the slam of the front door, I leaped out of the shower like a ballerina. I had the whole house to myself. In an hour I would be sitting next to Nick. Everything was going along nicely.

Somebody up there loves me.

I arrived at the meeting feeling like I was on fire. My blonde hair was fluffed out like a lion's mane, my nails neatly manicured

18

a dark maroon, my new black dress was extra short, and my black suede thigh high boots hugged my thighs just right. My Fendi perfume which I generously applied, floated around me like a cloud.

I sneaked up behind Heather. She was a tall, tanned, athletic, blonde haired, blue eyed California girl. Heather was twelve years younger than me.

"Boo."

Heather turned and hugged me. "Oh, I'm so proud of you. I can't wait to give you your token," she said excitedly, hugging me again.

"Thanks. I'm so nervous."

"Do you have a date afterwards? You look totally fabulous."

"Very funny. Uh, I did invite Nick. He's been so supportive and has been there a hundred percent pouring down the black coffee and countless walks," I said, trying to appear nonchalant.

"How ironic since he was pouring tequila down my throat on our date. It was after that date that I decided to go sober," Heather said bluntly.

"Heather, Heather, that was the opening of my nightclub. I was stoned and totally wasted. That night doesn't count." I grabbed her hand and pulled her into the meeting.

I had set Heather up with Nick for the opening of the club knowing he had a crush on her. She wanted to make her ex-boyfriend jealous. I was the one who became jealous. It was then that I told him I loved him and that if he took her out again I would take a baseball bat to his headlights. He never called her again and she hated him because she couldn't figure out why the sudden disinterest. She never suspected me since she thought David and I were perfect for one another. Now we shared a common goal of staying sober and also the same sponsor.

William, the secretary of the meeting just called out Heather and my name to stand up and give our speeches. I looked up and saw Nick sneak in and take a seat in the last row.

I need a brown bag to breathe into, I'm gonna pass out!

Heather was going on about how wonderful and strong I was, meanwhile I thought I was going to throw up. I looked like I was still on coke. I was fidgeting, tugging at my dress, twisting my hair

19

and running my hands over my suede boots. My heart was pounding so hard, I was sure everyone could hear it. It was now my turn.

"Thank you Heather, thank you Kelly, my sponsor, and thank you everyone in this room for all your love and support. I made a career out of partying for twenty-three years now. These past sixty days have been the hardest in my life. I have read that the first step toward change is recognition. Up until today I haven't been able to say this, my name is Keara, and I'm an alcoholic. Thank you."

I pressed the token into my palm till it hurt, and sat down. Everyone applauded. I looked across into Nick's eyes. He was beaming. I melted.

I was going to have to leave David.

After the meeting, I went around hugging and thanking everyone as swiftly as I could. All I could think about was my getaway. I knew Nick was in the parking lot and I had to lose Heather. My ulcer was starting to act up.

"Call me tomorrow, let's go to a women only meeting on Wednesday," Heather told me as I ran out.

Women's meeting on Wednesday, mmm, I can see Nick again.

He was sitting in the parking lot with his motor running. I opened the passenger's door and slid in. I immediately buried my head in his chest as he held me in those strong arms of his. We were silent for about a minute.

"I missed Melrose Place to be here tonight."

My laughter turned into a giggling frenzy. All the tension of the night was melting away. Nick started driving toward the beach. I put my head on his lap and he draped one arm over my shoulder. We drove in silence.

He pulled up beside the rocks and turned off the engine. I picked my head up off his lap and reached for the snap on his jeans.

"No, Keara."

"Not even a just friends blow job."

"No. You need to put your energy into something creative. It can't work with us. Why don't you think about a mediation class or yoga. It's getting late. I better get you home before David calls out the National Guard." He started driving back towards the parking lot.

"Oh, that reminds me, he was looking for you to meet him tonight at the restaurant."

"I figured he might. I went to Office Depot and bought some stuff so I have an alibi. I hate this sneaking around. I can't do this anymore, Keara."

"Oh Nick, you are so pure. I need just a little of it to rub of on me. Let me take a guess where you'll be stopping tonight. Billy's, right?"

"Yes, he's dying of Aids. I volunteered to walk his dog. I'm thinking of adopting it when he dies."

"What is it?"

"A pug."

"Your dog will eat it."

"I'll keep it inside. I can't think about it anyway. I really got to know Billy. He's really special." A tear raced down his cheek.

I reached over and hugged him. "I love you Nick Bartoli," I said as I jumped out of his car.

I sprinted over to mine to head home and let the lies begin.

David was up and watching an old movie on the television.

"How was the meeting?" he whispered, gazing into my eyes.

I sat down next to him on the floor since we had no living room furniture.

"Great! Heather gave me my token and gave a gushy speech about me. Then a bunch of us went out for coffee and talked about the joys of being sober. I met two new friends tonight, Carol and Maryann. They're like my age and have been through a lot."

"Are they married?" David asked, clicking the mute button on the remote control.

"No, they are both divorced."

"Don't you know anyone in AA who's married? Isn't there a couple we can get friendly with together?"

"Not that I know of."

I was laying the groundwork for Carol and Maryann. They were completely made up. They were going to be my way out at night to be with Nick. I was evil. I was starting to enjoy this game. Would I collect the $200 and pass go, or go directly to jail. I was rolling with the dice.

"Let's go to bed David. I want to get up early and jog."

"I'll jog with you. You know, Keara, we need to spend more time together. So, what time do you want me to wake you for our jog?" he asked, scooting Jack off the bed.

"David, please, let's discuss jogging when I roll out of bed in the morning," I snapped, kissing Jack on the face.

* * *

I was just about to plunk my quarter in the phone when I felt a tap on my shoulder. I spun around to face the lifeguard hunk.

"Good morning," he said with a warm smile.

"You caught me, I'm going for my morning fix."

"So, you're a phone addict."

"Yes, I give good phone," I said, flirting outrageously.

"Call me up at the tower. I'm listed. I'd love to hear from you."

That's all I need, another guy to complicate matters more. Why am I flirting with him? I don't even know his name.

I dialed Nick's number. My stomach felt like someone lit a small campfire in it.

"Hello." Claudia answered.

"Hi, Claudia, It's Keara. Is Nick up yet? I wanted to ask him some computer questions," I said too nervously.

"I'll get him," she growled.

"Hello."

"Hi, Nick, I guess you can't talk. Meet me at the restaurant in an hour. I have to practice spinning some new records and do some reports. I thought you could teach me your computer stuff. Did you see Billy last night?"

"Yes, he was doing better. I'll show you the banking I do on the computer. I'll meet you at the restaurant and then I have to take off for my dad's plant. See you in an hour," he said in a business like manner.

Why couldn't Nick get his own phone? What is wrong with him? What is wrong with me? I must be having a nervous breakdown.

I jogged home, peeled off my clothes and jumped into the

22

shower. As I was lathering up my hair with strawberry shampoo, David came in the bathroom.

"Are you going somewhere?" he asked, thrusting aside the beige shower curtain.

"Yes. I'm going to the restaurant. I'm behind on my reports and I need to practice my spinning. Plus I want to do the mail too."

"I'll come too. I need to check on things there anyway. Nick never seems to be there. I couldn't find him last night anywhere."

"David, can't I have a little space. Let me go down first and get the office together without you up my ass. Come down around dinner."

"It's my restaurant too, Keara. I'll go there whenever I want to," he snapped

I pulled the curtain out of his hand and drew it closed. "If you come with me now, I'll flip out," I growled.

"What's this all about? Why are you doing this to us? We worked together perfectly in the past in New York."

"Get out and let me shower," I screamed. I was shaking. I needed a drink. Vodka, gin, tequila, anything. I wanted it to be flowing in my veins again. I missed my best friend, the bottle.

I threw on a black t-shirt, jeans and a baseball cap over my wet hair, and ran out the door. David tried running after me, but I was already turning the convertible onto the highway.

I was climbing the steps to the restaurant when Carlos, our manager, met me half way.

"Keara, David has called a hundred times for you already. He said as soon as you get here for you to call him."

I just rolled my eyes and kept on walking toward my office. I plopped down on the chair and put my head across my arms on the desk and cried.

Nick gently tapped on the door and walked in.

"Carlos has David on two. He wants to talk to you now," he said softly as he massaged my back.

I picked up my head and grabbed for his hand. It was warm and the touch sent automatic heat through my whole body.

Someone shoot me now.

"I'll pick him up. Do you mind leaving while I talk to him?" I said, still crying.

"No problem. I'll be in the manager's office. Just buzz me."

He turned and shut the door behind him. I took a deep breath and picked up line two.

"Hello, David."

"Keara, what took you so long to pick up? What is going on with you?"

"David, I'm so tired and confused. I should go to New York for awhile. I want to be with Taylor and my friends. We need some time apart. I don't know if we should stay married like this."

Oh my God, I'm getting close to saying the D word.

"Keara, don't do this," David cried. "I'll do anything. We'll go for counseling. I'll give you your space, anything, just don't leave." He was sobbing now.

"David, I have to hang up. I'm meeting Carol and Maryann for a meeting. I want to drink. I'll see you tonight and we'll talk then."

I hung up the phone shaking. My marriage was going down the drain. I was starting to milk the Carol and Maryann lie already.

Big Bird has Snuffleeupagus, I have Carol and Maryann.

I picked up the phone and dialed Taylor.

"Hello," she mumbled.

"Taylor, what's wrong?"

"Oh Mommy, Adam broke up with me. He thinks I am a liar and a cheat."

We both started giggling uncontrollably at that statement.

"Tell me what happened."

"Brad wrote me, and Adam was in my room when Daddy gave me the letter. Adam grabbed it and read it out loud. Daddy is such a dick. How does he give me a letter from Brad with Adam sitting right here? I turned white as a sheet and started shaking. Adam just threw the letter at me and left. I've been crying on and off."

"Me too. I think I want to leave David. I need to see you and my friends, come back home and get grounded."

"Oh Mommy, hold on, I got a beep."

Taylor was following in my footsteps a little too close. It was scary to see a younger version of me.

"Mommy, it's Adam. I gotta go. I want you to come to New

24

York real soon. I really need to be with you, Mommy. It'll be good for us both. Bye."

I hung up still shaken. I buzzed Nick and started crying again. I needed a drink. A dry martini would do the trick. Nick came rushing into the office. I stood up and reached my arms out to him. We hugged silently.

"Let's get out of here," he whispered. "I"ll tell Carlos I have a business meeting in Hillcrest and I'll leave in about ten minutes. You leave now and meet me at the Batting Range in Mission Valley. Do you know where it is?"

I could only nod my head. The tears wouldn't stop flowing.

I started feeling better as I was driving. It was sunny and warm. I had the top down and the music blasting. Chaka Khan was singing "Through the Fire". It should be my theme song. The words, "For a chance to be with you, I'd gladly risk it all," were becoming more and more real to me.

I pulled into the lot and turned my motor off. I put my head back and closed my eyes. I held my father's dog tags in my hand. I'd been wearing them on a silver ball chain around my neck since he died.

Please Daddy, I know you're up there. Please, please help me.

I woke up to Nick caressing my hair.

"Want to play ball?" he asked quietly.

"Sure. I never played before though."

"I thought this would be perfect for you to get all your anger out here. You'll be too tired to think of drinking when you're done."

After the batting cage, we played for blood on the air hockey table and exhausted our supply of quarters Kung Fu fighting at the video games.

"Nick, let's have lunch together," I proposed. "I don't want to go home and face David."

"I'm going to have to get back to the office. David will be looking for me,"Nick said wearily. "Plus, I have to take Harrison to the vet."

"Who's Harrison?"

"Billy's pug. He has a crush on Harrison Ford."

He had his keys out and was about an inch away from putting

his key in the lock.

I put my hand over his and stopped the key from going in.

"Please Nick, let's get sushi and hit the beach. Just for an hour," I begged, stroking his arm.

"Okay, I'll get the sushi. Meet me at Shell Beach by the sea lions."

I wrapped my arms around him and squeezed him tight. Then, I slipped a twenty out of my back pocket, stuck it in his palm and raced over to my mustang. I was having an adrenaline rush. It was like doing drugs again. Cheating was definitely a high. Is that why I did it? Was Nick my replacement, my new crutch? Instead of a shot, snort or a toke, all I had to do was meet Nick and that made me high. What would my AA group say about this? My life and mind were unraveling.

My stomach started screaming, Mylanta, Mylanta. I quickly scanned the beach to make sure none of David's friends were around. Out of the trunk, I took the brightly colored Mexican blanket and my writing journal. I pranced down the steps onto the beach and took a secluded spot by the rocks. The waves were softly crashing all around me. A warm breeze was blowing on my face and through my thick hair. I took off my sandals and dug my toes into the soft warm sand and closed my eyes.

"Sushi delivery for Ms. Fitzgerald."

"Right here, boy."

"Boy, I said boy." Nick laughed and launched into a hilarious imitation of Fog Horn Leghorn. I pulled my knees to my chest and threw my head back and laughed and laughed. Now he was doing Porky Pig. He was adorable.

"Do Eek the cat, Eek the cat," I chanted.

"It never hurts to be nice," he said, sounding just like Eek.

Nick plopped down beside me and handed me a plate of California Rolls and a coke. I was in heaven. Beach, sushi and Nick, what more could anyone ask for?

"Where are you going to say you were all day?" Nick asked seriously. "I'm starting to get nervous."

"I told David I met some new women at AA, a Carol and Maryann. I didn't really. I made them up so I could get out at any time. I'll just say I called them and spent the day at meetings with them. I keep a list of meetings in my purse."

Now he'll never trust me. He has to see me as a big fucking schemer.

"I'm not good at all this cloak and dagger stuff, Keara. I want to help you all I can but I don't want David after me. I've never been with anyone married before. Gee, I've only been with about six girls my whole life."

Oh my God, I've slept with more women than he did. Great a bi-sexual married woman. I'm his worst nightmare.

I put down my half-eaten plate of sushi and hugged my knees to my chest.

"I won't bother you again. I'm sorry I love you," I said tearfully.

He reached over and hugged me. The love that welled up inside of me was so strong and pure. This couldn't be wrong.

"Keara, you're married and have a kid. I can't break up your marriage. I couldn't live with myself. You can't keep going from one to another. You have to learn to stand on your own two feet. Be by yourself and learn who you are. Take care of yourself for once."

I was sobbing once again, head buried in my arms. I looked up. Tears were spilling all over my face.

"You better go, Nick. I'll be all right. I'm going to stay here for awhile and write in my journal."

He rose slowly and brushed the pieces of rice off his jeans.

"I care about you Keara. I'll always be there for you. You're my best friend."

He brushed his hand over my hair and was gone.

I laid on my stomach and buried my head in the blanket and cried myself to sleep.

Good thing I had no mascara on today.

I woke up to a pounding headache. I picked up the sushi container and coke can and threw them in the bin nearby. Then headed up the steps to look for a phone. I called the eight hundred number and David answered.

"Hi. I had a rough day. I'm at the beach in La Jolla. Want to bring a picnic basket and we'll beach it and watch the sunset?"

"I'll be right there.

"I'm by the sea lions. Oh, and bring me a sweatshirt, please."

I hung up and wearily climbed back down the steps. One leaves, one comes. I picked up my journal from the blanket and headed for the rocks. Maybe if I see it in black and white, I'll be able to put the pieces together. See the light. I thought of Nick doing Eek the cat and smiled. David didn't even have a clue who Eek was or Fog Horn Leg Horn. One was a boy, one a man. I automatically rubbed my dog tags together making a clicking sound.

Help me Daddy. I'm drowning.

I only squeezed out about a paragraph in my journal. I found myself sketching the lazy sea lions. A strange calmness came over me as I drew. It was so satisfying. David came up beside me and broke the spell.

"Here, put this on. It's getting chilly."

I held up my arms and he pulled my navy blue sweatshirt over me.

"Have you been here all day?"

"No. I called Carol and Maryann. They live together. We all went to a meeting right here in La Jolla. It was intense. They left and I decided to write in my journal and call you. I'm sorry, I'm such a mess."

I am too much.

The tears started gliding down his cheeks.

"I love you, Keara. We can work this out. Let's go to a marriage counselor. Let's go away together."

I hugged him but couldn't muster up any feelings. David was so sweet and I was a monster.

We eased down onto the blanket. The picnic basket had all kinds of goodies spilling out.

"What does Tabitha think is going on?" I asked David.

"I don't know what she's thinking these days. You're never home. Things are upside down. She won't open up to me. When are you going to start mothering her again?"

"I don't know, David. I'm a mess. I can't be a mother now. Tabitha's strong, she'll get through this. I don't know about me."

"Let's eat and watch the sunset," David said softly, as he started to unpack the basket. He placed on the blanket, Brie and Fontina cheese, french bread, grapes, vegetable sandwiches, two small Calistoga waters, a small bud vase with a yellow rose tucked in it, napkins and pickles. He also pulled out a small white bag that was sealed with a heart sticker and handed it to me. Inside were two heart shaped truffles with white icing. My favorite. He thought of everything.

"Oh David, what a feast. Thank you."

He reached over and kissed my cheek.

"You only deserve the best," he said with sincerity.

After the beach, we walked through town till we spotted a Starbucks. We slipped inside and ordered two coffees. I felt like we were on a date. My mind did keep wandering back to Nick from time to time. I sensed that David was watching me carefully for any sign of me spacing out. When I was with David now, I had to concentrate on not blurting out Nick things, like what we did or said. I tried to recall when my life was simple with no lies.

Wish I had some Amaretto for this coffee.

"We better go," I suggested. "This coffee burned a whole in my stomach. I have to go home and go to the bathroom."

"Are you okay? You've lost a lot of weight, Keara. Do you want to leave your car here and I'll drive you?"

"No. I'll be all right. Can you take Jack for a long walk when you get home? We've been neglecting the poor baby."

"I've been neglected too," he said with a wink. "Maybe you could take care of me a little tonight."

My hands curled into fists at my side.

"I don't think we have had sex since you sobered up," he continued. "From twice a day to zero. What do you expect me to do?" he grumbled, running his hand through his gray hair.

"I expect you to be a little more understanding of what I'm going through."

I jumped into the driver's seat and slammed the door.

"See you at home," I snapped and took off like a rocket.

Houston, we have a problem

I awoke the next morning to the sounds of David getting

Tabitha ready for school. He was quizzing her on math as he was filling her lunch bag with fruit. I'd gone right to sleep last night so I wouldn't have to face either of them. I felt so awful hardly seeing Tabitha. But right now, I just wasn't up to being a mother or a wife. Being sober was so strange. I didn't know who I was or what I wanted. I did know I would like a drink. A Bloody Mary with some fresh horseradish and an olive and a celery stick. Now that's a wake up call.

Maybe I should be calling my sponsor this morning and not Nick.

I heard the door shut. I knew he was walking her to the bus now. I quickly got up and started my morning routine search for a quarter. Found one in my purse. I pressed it to my lips. I needed help. Serious help.

I pulled on my jeans and tossed on a white t-shirt and laced up my sneakers. I threw my makeup in my leather shoulder bag.

David opened the door and we were face to face. I stood frozen in place.

"Going somewhere?" he challenged, his eyes unreadable.

"I decided not to run this morning. So instead I'm going to La Jolla. You know, have some breakfast, go for a walk and do some journal writing.," I lied, trying to will my legs to walk toward the door.

"Sounds like a full morning. I guess you don't want company," he grumbled, watching me carefully.

"No. I need this time alone. I'll call you," I said softly, as I opened the door and made my escape. A sense of shame descended on me as I started the Mustang.

I called Nick from the road and told him I was delivering breakfast. Claudia was working, so the house was ours. Just before I turned up his street, I applied some mascara and lip gloss. I decided tomorrow I would change this hair color and eye color. Maybe that would make me feel better.

I dashed up the steps and rang the bell. Zeus was barking in the back yard.

Zeus was half wolf and half shepherd and enormous. Nick opened the door and smiled. I felt my breath quicken.

30

"Come in," he said quietly, taking the bag of bagels from me.

"I didn't know what kind you liked so I ordered a variety," I said nervously, twirling my hair.

"Relax Keara, I'm just finishing up a letter on my computer. Do you want to come upstairs to my office or watch TV down here?"

Zeus was hurling himself against the glass sliding door. He desperately wanted in.

"I'll come upstairs. I'm afraid your dog will bust in and eat me."

"He's really a sweetheart. I don't know why he's acting crazy today. Maybe a cat got him all riled up."

I followed him up the steps and into his office. He had a huge L shape blonde wood desk with a computer on one end and papers scattered around the middle. The rest of the room was crowded with boxes of files and under the window was a fax machine. The walls were bare.

"I built this desk myself. Do you like it?" he asked, his blue eyes bright.

"It's great," I said, trailing my fingertips along the edge of the desk.

He was seated behind the desk and moving his mouse. I mentally made a note to buy some cute things for his desk. I came up behind him and swivelled his chair to face me. I climbed on his lap and put my arms around his neck. We hugged not saying anything. I let the silence hang between us for a couple of minutes. Suddenly, we heard a faint knock on the door downstairs and Zeus was barking.

"Are you expecting someone?" I whispered, my heart pounding wildly.

What if it was David? What if he followed me here? I'm dead meat. Nick was already on the stairs. The color was drained from his face. I tried to lean over the banister without being seen. He opened the door. It was a little girl and she was calling him Uncle Nick. How cute. He gave her a bagel and told her to wait in the kitchen for him. He leaped up the steps huffing and puffing. He didn't look like a happy camper.

"That's my niece," he whispered. "I have to take her back home. She was at a sleep over in the neighborhood. Wait about ten minutes after I leave, then leave and make sure you shut the door hard and check it to see if it's locked."

He disappeared down the steps. No goodbyes. No see you later. He was probably freaked by the knock too, thinking it might be David.

I can't believe this happened as I slowly made my way down the steps. I decided to go out in the yard and pet Zeus. He was sitting quietly staring at me. I'd bond with his dog. Brownie points.

As I slid back the glass door, Zeus stood up on his hind feet and jumped at me knocking me down. He ran over top of me and towards the door. The door was slightly ajar. The stupid kid probably didn't slam it hard enough. Zeus slipped his paw between the door and flipped it open and ran. I started coming apart. Nick would never forgive me if something happened to his dog. What if Claudia came home? I scrambled to my feet and flew out the door. He was a couple of feet ahead of me sniffing a tree.

"Here Zeus, come here boy."

He looked up and took off up the street. Thank God I had my running shoes on. I raced after him. I felt my face turning crimson. I also felt an asthma attack coming on. There was no way I was going to catch him.

Just then I saw two Mexicans in a gardening truck turning the corner. I ran over to the truck and in tears begged them to let me in the truck to catch my dog. They didn't speak a word of English. I just opened the door and climbed in and pointed toward Zeus. We drove up along side of him. Jack loved traveling in the car. I figured he might too. I opened the rusted door and yelled for him to get in with us. I thought the Mexicans would have a heart attack. He leaped into the front seat panting heavily. There definitely wasn't room for all of us.

The driver got out and went to the back of the truck. He came back and handed me a yellow piece of rope and motioned to me to put it on the dog and get out. I put the rope around Zeus's neck and we started our walk back home. We were both breathing heavily. I needed my inhaler. As I was approaching Nick's street, I nervously looked around for any nosy neighbors or Claudia.

I pushed Zeus back in the yard and scolded him for giving me a mini nervous breakdown. I slammed the door hard and got the hell out of there.

I decided to go to Tequila Bay and get some work done. I was really behind. The restaurant was a joke now. No one was showing up. I was always running around with Nick and David was throughly confused. Which meant the employees were most likely robbing us blind.

I entered through the delivery door and went straight to my office. I was determined to get the carton full of reports finished but first I'd better call David. I slowly punched in my number getting ready for round two to start,

"Hello," he answered flatly.

"Hi. I'm at the office. La Jolla was great. Now I plan on getting all caught up. What's happening with you ?"

"I'm finishing up my calls and have to do some filing. Is Nick there? I have to talk to him."

"No Nick isn't here," I said sarcastically. "You know he's probably at the shelter or with Billy."

"I bet you he is gay that is why he is always over there."

"Billy is dying of Aids. Nick is a volunteer. That is so sick , David, twisting something good like that."

"Sorry, I forgot Nick is your hero. Is he the volunteer of the month down at the shelter?"

"Shut up, David. I'm not in the mood for this fight."

"Do you have a problem with me coming down there now," he grumbled.

"Don't be ridiculous. Look I have to go. I don't want to argue anymore."

I disconnected him and called the airlines. It was obviously time for me to go to New York. I wanted to be surrounded by my friends. I needed support and it sounded like Taylor really needed me.

For the next hour, I called everyone I knew to tell them I was coming in and would explain everything when I saw them. I felt like I was putting my nervous breakdown on hold for a week.

33

Maybe one of my friends would have an answer. Maybe Nick would join me.

Maybe I should just kill myself now.

As I started typing the reports into the computer, Nick and Lou came through the door.

"Hi guys," I said, eyeing Nick. "What's up with you two?"

"What happened to your arm?" Lou asked, putting down his briefcase and bending closer to the desk.

"Oh, I guess I slammed it into the file cabinet. Actually Nick is beating me cause I'm so behind on my reports. Tell him Nick."

"Yeah, that's right. I slammed the bitch," he said in a tough guy Brooklyn accent.

We all giggled but there was an uneasy feeling in the air.

"Nick, I'm having trouble on Maria's sheet. It's not adding up. Can you help me?"

He came around behind me. My heart had already speeded up and my mouth was getting dry.

Lou excused himself and took off for the manager's office.

"What's the problem?" he asked, softly in my ear.

I turned around and kneeled in the chair and hugged him. He felt so warm. I was instantly transported to heaven.

I moistened my lips. "I made arrangements to go to New York tomorrow."

"Just like that, you're taking off. What happened and what did happen to your arm?"

He was holding it in his hand examining the bright black and blue bruise. My present from Zeus.

"It's a long story. It has to do with Zeus and Mexicans but don't worry everything is okay," I smiled. "Look, I need to go to New York now. I need to be surrounded by my friends. I love you. I want to leave David. I want to drink. I don't know who I am, what I want. In other words, I am a fucking mess. Maybe if I take a break from being around you, I'll be able to think clearer. Do you understand anything I'm saying?"

He shook his head yes and held me. I returned to heaven. I pulled away from his chest.

"I haven't told David yet. It'll probably get ugly when I do. I

34

want to see you tonight. I have to be with you just one more time before I fly to New York. Don't disappoint me. Please say yes," I begged, looking into his warm blue eyes.

"How are you going to get out? David's going to go nuts when he finds out about New York."

"Don't worry, I'll get out. Meet me at two at the Lucky's supermarket in my neighborhood. It's open twenty-four hours. I'll be in the parking lot."

"You're going to be able to get out at two a.m., two o'clock in the morning."

He picked up his briefcase and lingered in the doorway.

"See you tonight," I said, in a low tone and started typing the report into the computer. When I looked up he was gone. Thank God. Any minute I felt like I was going to rip off all my clothes and bend over the desk and beg him to take me right then and there. Boy did I need a drink. A shot of whiskey with a beer chaser would be nice. David would probably be here any minute. I'd kill for a Valium right now. How could I do this straight? How the hell was I going to get out at two? Obviously, I'd gone completely insane. All the drugs had finally caught up with me. I was nuts.

As I started making progress with the reports David popped in the office.

"Well aren't you the busy little bee," he said, reaching over the desk to kiss my cheek.

"As Sister Mary would say, "Idle hands are the devil's workshop."

"I have something to keep your hands busy with." David smiled crookedly.

"I bet you do. Is that a pickle in your pocket?" I said, licking my lips.

We both laughed and let our guard down for the moment.

"What happened to your arm?"

"Oh, I don't know. Most likely Jack"

"Where's Nick? I saw his car in the parking lot."

"He's having lunch with his dad. Why don't you join them? I really have to get this done. When you come back, please bring me some water. I'm not hungry. I ate in La Jolla."

There was no way I could eat today. Not only did I have to tell David about New York, I had to get out at two in the morning to be with Nick. The adrenaline was pumping.

Face it Keara, you're an adrenaline junkie.

I wearily placed the last report in the file. It was time to take a break and tell David about my upcoming trip. I sauntered into Carlos's office. David and Carlos were going over the liquor inventory. There was quite a difference since I quit drinking.

"David, when you and Carlos are done, would you like to go out and get some coffee? I need a break. I'll wait for you at the bar."

"I'll be right there, Keara."

I sank onto the bar stool. A drink would give me the courage to do this. A nice Absolut on the rocks with a twist would certainly take the edge off this day.

"Hi Brad," I smiled. "Just a club soda with a twist, please."

Taylor had a mad crush on him. He was thirty-two, an artist, long sandy blonde hair, big brown eyes and perfect muscular arms. He had a following of girls every night to watch those magnificent arms pour.

"Have you heard from Taylor?" he asked, as he squeezed a lemon into my glass.

"I talked to her today. She always asks for you. She'll be back Christmas."

"Keara, let's go." David called out standing by the door.

I hopped down from the stool and immediately shifted gears into overdrive. My heart started racing. Stomach was burning. I felt like I was going to crash and burn. I put my hand in his and we walked out the door.

"The place is a mess," he grumbled, gripping my hand. "I think everyone is stealing. I need more controls. I don't trust Carlos. I haven't been spending enough time here. Oh by the way, I called Tabitha. She's doing her homework. She wants us to bring her home a hamburger and fries."

We entered Coffee Mecca and ordered two black coffees. It was a funky coffee house with old beat up sofas and chairs, a pool table in the center and a wooden table on the side with a roll of paper attached to it for people to draw.

We plopped down on a worn green velvet couch. Annie Lennox was playing softly in the background. She was singing "Would I lie to you." Was my guardian angel trying to send me signs?

"David, we have to talk," I whispered, raking my nails through my hair.

"I don't like the sound of this," he scowled, placing his coffee on the badly scratched table.

"I made arrangements to go to New York tomorrow. I need to get a break from our marriage. I'm hoping to find answers there. When I come back, I won't jerk you around anymore. We'll either stay together or we'll divorce. That's why I must go now. It can't wait another day or we'll both go insane."

"I'm stunned," he muttered, his face white as chalk. "We're talking divorce. What the hell is happening here? Is this, cause you are sober? What did I do? Help me Keara. What about Tabitha? Maybe you should have a drink. I want the old Keara back. The one who loved me and our life together. We were a great team."

I threw my arms around him. "I'm sorry David. I'm so sorry," I whispered into his ear.

Maybe my plane will crash tomorrow and take me out of this misery.

We walked back in heavy silence. My chest felt like a water buffalo was standing on it. We entered the restaurant and it was hectic. A Convention had just let out. I immediately went behind the hostess stand and started taking names. David started bussing tables. This was perfect. For the next three hours we'd get slammed and I was too busy to think about Nick, New York and two a.m..

David and I worked in perfect harmony together.

Why am I rocking the boat. I'm going to drown. I can't swim.

I drove home with the top down. I was hoping the chilly night air would slap some sense into me. David was driving along side of me. He looked so gloomy. I felt like a heartless cruel bitch. Plus the night wasn't over. I still had to get out at two. Suicide was crossing my mind. Drive one hundred miles per hour straight into a palm tree would be easier than what I had to do. Heaven help me.

We pulled up together in the driveway.

"You're telling Tabitha about your trip," he hissed. "Say your goodbyes tonight."

I grabbed the bag with the hamburger and fries in it out of my trunk.

"I'll tell her now while she eats. Why don't you take Jack out so I can talk to her alone."

David opened the door. Jack came charging at us like a bull. Spit went flying everywhere.

"Okay, boy," David said gently, petting Jack as he hooked his black leash onto his black nylon collar. He walked out and slammed the door. I headed up the steps. I might as well add worst mother of the year to my list.

Tabitha was asleep in front of the television. Instead of having a mother coming home drunk every night, now she had a mother who just didn't come home. Maybe David was right. I should just drink. Everything was great when I drank. Now everything was crap.

I knelt down over Tabitha. She was such a sweet child. Never a problem. I started stroking her hair and whispering her name. She opened her eyes and gave me a big smile. My heart was aching.

"Hi pumpkin. Are you hungry? I bought you a hamburger and fries. I'm sorry, I'm late. The restaurant got slammed and Daddy and I had to work."

She sat up and rubbed her eyes and reached for the bag.

"That's okay Mom. I did all my homework. Then Jack and me watched a movie. Can I have some ketchup and a soda, please?'

I jumped up and went into the kitchen, grateful for the stall. She was so precious and I was a snake. Was Nick really worth putting my family through this?

I walked back into the living room confused, depressed and suicidal. I knelt down beside her and handed her the coke and ketchup.

"Tabitha, we need to have a girl talk," I confessed, twirling my hair around my index finger. "As you know, I'm having a hard time not drinking anymore. That's why I haven't been around much.

I'm very confused and I feel different without drinking. I know this is hard for you to understand especially now that Daddy and me seem to be fighting all the time. I just need time and space to get everything together. I'm going to New York tomorrow to spend some time with Taylor and my friends. I can't explain why. I feel like I have to go but I hope you understand and forgive me for not being the best mother right now. You know I love you very very much." I reached out for her and we hugged a long time. I kissed her gently on the cheek.

"It's okay, Mommy. I'll take care of Daddy for you while you're there," she said quietly, munching on a fry. "I'm glad you're not drinking anymore."

I squeezed her hand. "I love you so much," I murmured in her ear, suppressing my tears.

During our mother and daughter bonding, we didn't hear David bring Jack back in the house. Jack dove on top of us grabbing the remaining pieces of hamburger and fries. It was like we were stampeded by elephants.

"David help." "Daddy help." We both cried out, rolling around while Jack was going crazy from the smell of the food. David pulled Jack away and enticed him into the kitchen with a treat.

Tabitha had drool dripping from her hair.

"Let's go to the bathroom and get you cleaned up,"I said, pulling her up off the floor. "It's time for bed too."

I draped my arm around her and tried to act like Leave it to Beaver's mother. I have to find time to watch more Nick at Night. Tabitha loved those old shows. The mothers on those shows weren't recovering alcoholics or having affairs. I was more like Melrose Place.

It was after midnight when David and I were finally under the covers. Jack was stretched across the bottom of the bed snoring gently. I had to time my exit. It was a good thing I didn't eat dinner because I would definitely be throwing it up now. Fear engulfed me. I had to keep him talking for an hour and then somehow find a way to leave.

I need the help of Harry Houdini for this one. If you're up there Harry, please help.

We talked about Tabitha, Taylor, New York, the restaurant, alcohol, our past and divorce. I got up to pee around the divorce talk plus I had to check the time. One forty five. It was time. I slid back under the covers.

"Why do you think you want a divorce?" David challenged, his face so intense in the soft light of the room.

"Okay, for instance, here it is two' o clock. If I was single, I could get up and go for a ride to Seven Eleven for some coffee and not have to answer to no one. Just get up and leave."

"So try it. Get up and leave now. You can go out every night this late as long as we stay together. Be a Seven Eleven groupie. Just don't say the "d" word."

I flipped off the covers and swung my legs over to the floor.

"Fine. I'm going to take a ride now. I'll take Jack with me for protection. We can bond."

Nice touch, Keara.

I grabbed the keys off the bureau. My heart was beating so fast. I didn't think I'd breathe. I had to struggle to keep from vomiting.

"Want anything while I'm out," I whispered , standing by the door.

"Just you when you come back," he said seductively, pulling the covers up to his chin.

I called to Jack to go for a ride and we both ran like bats out of hell.

I took David's car because Jack didn't like the mustang. David's car was a big luxury gold town car. His father had given it to him when we were down on our luck. It was comfortable and roomy. Perfect for sex.

Jack was pacing back and forth in the back seat. My nerves were raw. I was ready to explode as I entered the parking lot looking for Nick. He blinked his headlights at me.

I pulled up beside him. Jack stuck his head out ready to bark and recognized Nick. His tail started thumping against the back seat and he drooled in my hair.

"Let's go for a ride in this car," I suggested, gripping the steering wheel so hard I felt like I could have snapped it off.

He opened the passenger's door and slid in. The radio was playing Bonnie Raitt's song "I Can't Make You Love Me." Was this another sign? Jack immediately charged over to greet him with a heavy supply of drool.

"Why did you bring Jack?" he muttered, pushing the dog back to sit.

"Who goes out at two in the morning without protection?" I shrugged. "Don't worry he promises to keep our secret. I trust him. Where should I drive to?"

"Go up two more streets and make a left. There's a deserted road there."

"Were you here before with someone else?" I asked sarcastically. "Should I park in your spot?"

"No, I checked it out while I was waiting for you."

The tires crunched on the dirt and gravel. I turned the car off but clicked back on the radio. I scrambled from under the steering wheel and crawled into his lap.

"I'm going to miss you so much," I whispered. "I'm in pain already."

"I'll miss you too," he said softly, as he tugged on my sweatpants. I picked up my hips and let him slide them off. I pulled off my sweatshirt. I was completely naked, sitting in David's car with a Great Dane breathing in my hair.

You're totally nuts, Keara. You're over the edge. How are you going to drive to the airport tomorrow in this car?

As soon as he entered me I forgot all about David, New York and being in the car. I instantly became airborne. I was flying like someone injected clouds in my veins. We were playing among the stars for about an hour.

"Oh my God. It's almost four," I shrieked. "I have to go."

We unlocked our arms and I grabbed for my sweats. Jack was sleeping in the back.

I raced back to Nick's car in the supermarket parking lot.

"Call me Nick. I'll be at Kylie's around nine tomorrow night. Here's her number."

I placed the paper in his palm, folded over his fingers and bought his fist to my lips.

"I love you," I confessed in a whisper, taking his hand and rubbing it against my face.

"I'll miss you," he said, his eyes getting misty.

He opened the door slowly. You could feel the pain in the air where just a few minutes ago was joy. I watched him put the key in his door.

I was toast. Where the fuck would I say I went? I was driving like a mad woman. I felt like there were aliens in my stomach trying to eat their way out. Could I say I got abducted by aliens? How far could I push David?

I cruised into the driveway. Jack was excited to be home. I was about to wet my pants. I crept into the hallway and placed the keys on the table. Jack took off upstairs for his water bowl.

David flicked the lights on. It was curtains for me. Where are the aliens when you need them?

"Where the hell did you go Keara?" he snapped. "I've been a nervous wreck. I thought you were in an accident."

"I told you I wanted to go for a ride and have coffee and Jack had to pee," I said loudly, tugging on my sweatshirt.

"Do you think I'm a fool?"

I reached for him and gently pushed him towards the bedroom.

"Let's not ruin our last night together."

I nudged him into bed and laid on top of him. I tried to black out Nick from my thoughts. My life depended on this act, I told myself. I hate what I'm about to do but there was no getting around it. There were no clouds this time.

I drifted off to sleep thinking about how mechanical the sex was with David. I felt like a robot that was programmed. When I was with Nick I didn't even feel like I was on earth. Most important, I didn't have to fake it.

The next morning I woke up emotionally exhausted. Jack was curled up beside me. Poor dog was probably confused about last night. Mommy was with Uncle Nick and Daddy. Can you bark whore? I rolled over and scratched his belly. If I left David, who would get Jack?

"Keara, are you up," David asked loudly, from the hallway.

I leaned up on my elbows. "I'm up and need coffee," I

42

grumbled.

David swept in and pulled me up in his arms.

"I'm going to miss you so much.. We have never slept apart," he said, his voice cracking.

If he cries again, I won't be able to bear it.

"David, why don't you get us some coffee and bagels and we'll have a nice breakfast on the terrace."

I detached myself from his embrace and headed for the closet. I had to pack. I stretched my arms up and grabbed my L.L. Bean bag. It was a little bigger than an overnight bag.

"I'll be right back. Do you want anything special?" he asked weakly, holding back his tears.

"Surprise me," I said softly, afraid to turn and look at him. I started tossing all my clothes on the bed, to see what I wanted to take.

This felt so strange, going back to New York, where I had a reputation for being totally off the wall. Everyone knew how much I loved David and that I'd never even looked at another guy. Now I was going back, an emotional wreck from cheating.

I heard David pulling out of the driveway. My heart immediately started pounding like I'd just finished a race. It knew I wanted to call Nick and say goodbye again.

I leaped up the steps to the kitchen and picked up the cordless phone. I punched in his number standing by the window. I started doing my daily chant of, please answer, please answer.

"Hello," he mumbled.

"Hey, sleepy head, late night," I said, laughing into the phone.

I thought you'd be up in the clouds already," he said, clearing his throat.

"You took me in the clouds last night, today I'm taking a plane," I whispered, watching for David's car to pull up. "I'm going to miss you."

"I'm going to miss you too. I'll call you tonight at Kylie's around nine."

I walked into the kitchen and slowly replaced the phone in the cradle.

My heart was in pieces. After last night, I knew Nick could

give me his just friends speech till he was blue in the face but I knew the truth now. Instead of going to New York, I should be going to Oz to see the wizard for some brains.

While you're there, get a heart for David because you broke his, Keara.

David was pulling in the driveway as a wave of shame washed over me. I was emotionally drowning. Just end it with Nick and save your marriage and your sanity, I kept telling myself.

"Keara," David yelled up the steps. "Help me."

I bounced down the steps and took the hot coffees from him. He had bagels, scones and a dozen yellow roses in his arms.

"Here's your surprise," he said, handing me the roses.

I had set the coffee down and reached for the roses. I shoved my nose in them.

"They're beautiful and smell wonderful. Thank you."

I leaned over and kissed his nose.

"I'll go put these in water."

Breakfast went over smoothly. Now I had to shower, leave a note for Tabitha, pack and make it through the ride to the airport. The airport would be a nightmare. I'd better look for the Mylanta now.

"Keara, when you come back, let's start over. Maybe we should move to a new city."

"Let's use this time to get our heads together," I said, my voice choked with pain.

I didn't know what I was saying. I just knew I had to get out of the car and on the plane fast before I had a breakdown.

"Bye, David. I love you," I said, pulling apart from him and jumping out of the car. I grabbed my bag from the back seat and took off.

The airport was a blur. I was still shaking when I sank weakly into my seat and buckled up. Everyone probably thought I was a nervous flier. I knew I looked a mess too. My hair was wild from the convertible ride. My eyes were red and my face was ghostly white. I closed my eyes and didn't open them till New York.

* * *

I walked off the plane completely frazzled. I was raking my

44

manicured nails through my hair when I spotted him. It felt so good to see an old friend. I hadn't seen Vince in four years but we'd kept in touch. In the old days when I used to party, we were a great team but it was strictly a platonic friendship. He was a couple of years older than me, Italian, dark curly hair, dark eyes and connected.

I dropped my bag and flew into his arms.

"God, it's good go to see you," I said loudly. "I look a mess and my life is a mess. Help!!

"I can't believe you called me," he said, picking up my bag. "It's been a long time. Let's go eat and you can fill me in."

We ate at the Friday's by the airport.

"So, Keara, let me get this straight. You're in love with some young guy who still lives at home with his mother and has no real future."

"Oh God, do you have to put it like that? He's so sweet and wonderful."

"What about David? Is he so evil and nasty?"

"No. He's sweet too. Oh, Vince, that is why I'm here. I'm so confused."

"What happened to the greatest girl D.J. on Long Island? The Keara that had her own fan club. I still carry around the newspaper article that just praises you endlessly."

"I still D.J. but I'm sober now. I'm too tense. That was the party girl, Vince. That's the girl David wants. Nick sees me as a person. He wants me to turn my creative energy into something that will be good for me."

"Didn't you use to draw all the ads for the club yourself? They were incredible. You could be Keara the Artist now."

"I love drawing. I drew some sea lions the other day and it made me feel really good. Oh, God, it's great to see you. You're the best, Vince."

"I know, that's what all the girls say."

He dropped me off at Kylie's house before nine.

"You're the best. Stay with David. He's a good man," Vince whispered and reached over and kissed my cheek. "Stay in touch."

As I headed up Kylie's driveway Vince's words echoed in my head. Stay with David. Meanwhile, all I could think about was

Nick's call.

I rang the doorbell and instantly heard two dogs barking like crazy. Kylie opened the door and we both screamed and hugged while the Pit Bull and Lab jumped and barked at us.

Kylie was Jewish, thick blond hair, sparkling green eyes, tiny, lush lips and ten years older than me. She had three older kids and a husband who no one paid attention to. I loved her kids.

We climbed the steps to the living room still clinging to one another and laughing. Kylie's house had an aura of craziness around it.

Spencer and Alexis, her two daughters, were on the couch. More screams and hugs. Her son, Greg, popped his head out into the hallway. He had a party going on in the basement. You could smell the marijuana drifting up the steps.

"Hi, Keara, still sober?" he asked, with a sly grin. "Want to party with us."

"No, Greg, I'm really straight now," I replied laughing. "Listen, Greg, I'm expecting a call from someone named Nick. Come and get me, okay?"

"Sure, Keara," he shrugged and stumbled back down the basement.

When he was in the Navy in San Diego we used to party hard.

"Keara, I have a date tonight," Alexis said, "but tomorrow we'll go to the flea market and talk."

She kissed me on the cheek and took off down the steps. Alexis had come to visit me in San Diego a couple of times. Every time she came we would just get stoned. Her visits were fattening. She was Taylor's age. I'd watched her grow up since she was two. Alexis was a bigger version of Kylie.

It was just Spencer, Kylie and me on the couch. Her husband was upstairs watching the television. The dogs were biting one another ears and tumbling into us and the furniture.

No one seemed to notice them.

Spencer was the oldest child. She was twenty-seven, thick beautiful auburn hair and emerald green eyes. She lived in Washington and drove five hours to see me.

If was after nine. My stomach was churning and I couldn't stop playing with my hair. We were in the middle of ripping guys apart when one of Greg's friends came up to raid the refrigerator.

"Kylie, ask him if anyone called for me," I asked anxiously, rocking back and forth on the couch.

"Michael, did anyone call for Keara?"Kylie asked.

"Yeah, some guy Nick, about half an hour ago," he answered, stoned out of his mind.

I leaped to my feet.

"I'm going to kill Greg," I hissed, as I bounced down the steps two at a time.

I opened the basement door. The smell of smoke, pot and beer hit me at once. I was afraid I'd get wrecked just being in the room. I ran across the room and jumped on Greg. I started strangling him. The joystick fell out of his hand.

"Keara, what the fuck, I'm in the middle of a game," he mumbled, thrashing on the couch.

"I'm going to fucking kill you, Greg. I told you I was waiting for that call, you fucking loser."

It didn't take long for me to lapse back into my New York tongue. You didn't talk like that in San Diego. Everyone there was so fake and fragile. Not to mention in fear of being sued.

"Where's the fucking phone?" I snapped, letting go of his throat.

One of the stoners handed me the cordless. I dialed and handed it to Greg.

Ask for Nick for me or I'll kill your Iguana and eat it for breakfast," I screamed, pointing at the glass aquarium his reptile was lounging in.

Greg was twenty-five, jet black hair, baby blue eyes, a real charmer and a pot head.

He handed me the phone and lit up a joint.

"Hi, Nick," I said with a sigh of relief. "I just found out you fucking called from these pot heads. This is a crazy house. I miss you. How are you?"

I ducked into the hallway for privacy.

"I'm fine. I can tell you're back in New York."

"Oh, fuck this and fuck that already right, a real New Yorker.

47

Listen, I miss you, I don't think I told you that yet. I'm so happy to see everybody here but I want to be in your arms. What are you doing?"

"I'm going to try and catch up on some sleep. I've been working overtime at the shelter. I miss you, too. Call me tomorrow when you get up. I have to go down to the restaurant now."

"I'll call you around seven your time, make sure you answer. Goodnight, Nick."

"Goodnight, Keara."

I pressed the off button and threw the phone on the couch and raced up the stairs. Spencer and Kylie were going to have to scrape me off the ceiling. I was so high just from hearing his voice.

We were sitting around giggling and watching the dogs play when I realized I had to call David. Time to come down from my high. I immediately got depressed.

"Hello," he mumbled.

"Hi David, you sound awful. What's wrong? How's Tabitha?"

"She is at a friend's. Come back, Keara."

"David, get it together. I just got here. Please stop. This is why I didn't want to call."

"I'm sorry, Keara. Please call me tomorrow when you get up. I'm going down the restaurant now. Tell Kylie I said hello. Goodnight."

You better ask the wizard for some courage, forget the brains, you need to tell David the truth.

Spencer and Kylie were waiting for me in the living room. They were each on a couch under a blanket. I sauntered over to my couch and slid under the covers that were laid out for me. We talked into the night. I was feeling lost. What was I doing here? Would I find the answers to any of my questions?

I wanted a drink but pushed it out of my head. This was the first time my friends were seeing me straight.

Between Greg's friends coming and going all night and the dogs barking, there was little sleep. I woke up with a gray cat on my chest. Kylie was up and folding the blanket on her couch. She was dressed in running shorts and a sweatshirt.

"Let's run, so we can call," she whispered, picking the cat up in

48

her arms.

She had a boyfriend but couldn't talk about him in front of Spencer. Spencer was sleeping soundly.

It was raining and cold. San Diego was probably warm and sunny now.

We were drenched as we ran into a Friendly restaurant. There were two pay phones in the entrance.

"This is where I beep him every morning,"Kylie said, still breathing hard from the run.

I pulled the quarters from my pocket. Kylie was busy punching in numbers.

"Hello," he answered in a sleepy voice.

"Hi," I said, my teeth chattering.

"What's wrong? Are you cold? Where are you?"

"It's pouring here. Kylie and I are out jogging. She's on the other phone with her boyfriend. I'm tired and cold. There was no sleep in her house last night. Why do you sound so tired?"

"I was at the restaurant late and then I stayed up all night with Billy. I saw David last night, he was very cold to me. When are you seeing Taylor?"

"Later. Don't worry about David. He is just grumpy that I am here."

"Sounds like things are going well with you."

"Yeah, it feels good being surrounded by old friends. I miss you terribly. My heart feels so heavy. How's Billy ?"

"He's hanging in there. Harrison is so cute. I love the way he snorts. Have fun with your friends. Call me tomorrow. . I miss you."

I hung up and turned around to see if Kylie was off her call. When I was on the phone with Nick, I was in complete oblivion. Kylie was looking at the rain, arms folded across her chest.

"How was your call? Mine was a ten. He told me he missed me," I said beaming. I felt like I could run the New York marathon right now and win.

"I'm meeting Christian after work for drinks," she said flatly, as she was stretching getting ready to run again.

We headed back out in the cold rain. I was still on my high.

Nothing mattered.

"I think Christian is seeing someone else. He's single and hot. I can't be with him every night."

"Did you ever think of leaving your husband?"

"I can't leave now. You saw how crazy my house is. Alexis and Greg are living there. All the animals. I can't walk away besides Christian has never mentioned that he'd want to be together if I were free."

"I want to leave David but I'm so afraid. Nick will never leave his mother's side. He's never been married and he wants kids. I've been there done that. It would never work."

We both lapsed into silence on the last leg of the jog. Both lost in our own heartaches. My high ended and I was feeling the cold.

Kylie braced herself against her front door. "Ready to enter my insane house?" she smiled and pushed open the door.

The smell of wet dogs immediately drifted up my nostrils. Alexis was standing on the steps, kissing her boyfriend goodbye. Spencer was in the kitchen, making breakfast for Greg's friends. Greg was pacing back and forth in the living room on the cordless phone. The Lab was humping the Pit Bull. The cat was eating eggs off of someone's plate. Kylie's husband was still upstairs watching television. What was his story?

"Keara, look at the dining room table," Spencer yelled out. "You had a delivery while you were out."

There was a dozen yellow roses in a round glass vase with yellow and orange ribbons tied around their base. I sauntered over and opened the card. They were from David, of course. I had to call him now. I had a clear head but was totally lost. Drinking was so much easier. I could hide.

I spent the day with Spencer and Alexis. We went shopping. Shopping cured everything. I bought a pair of sand colored boots and a pair of black suede heels.

Alexis and Spencer both agreed that I should stay with David. Forget Nick Bartoli.

When we arrived home, I had a couple of minutes to make phone calls before Taylor was to pick me up.

I called David first.

50

"Hello," he grumbled.

"Is anything wrong?"

"I just came from the restaurant. I caught Maria stealing and had to fire her. Nick was there too but of course I had to do it. He just walked away. I can't stand him. He's such a wimp!"

"Calm down, you sound like you're going to have a heart attack."

"There's a lot going on down there. I just want to walk from it."

"I have to go David, Taylor will be here any minute. Relax, everything will work out."

I picked up the phone to call Nick. He answered on the first ring.

"Hi. I miss you so much," I said in a silky murmur.

"Keara, we have to talk. When you come back, we cannot see one another anymore," he said sharply. "Do you understand?"

"Nick, what is going on? Why are you saying this?"

"Look, we were wrong to do what we did. David's my partner, and things have become very tense between us. I can't face him anymore. Plus my father sat me down and told me I was scum."

There was a lump in my throat the size of Florida. I didn't think I could speak.

"Nick, I love you. I'll leave David when I get back," I said, my voice choked with pain.

"It won't work, Keara. We're from two different worlds. I have to go see Billy now. Bye, Keara."

I slammed down the phone and threw myself on the couch.

"What's wrong Mommy," Taylor screamed out, running up the steps with Alexis and Spencer close behind..

"Nick just broke up with me," I shrieked, trying to catch my breath. I worked myself into an asthma attack. Taylor rose off the couch to get my purse. It had my medicine in it.

I want to go to the store and buy a big bottle of Tequila and even drink the worm.

The medicine took effect and I was breathing normal again. It felt like there was not a tear left inside me. Razors were slicing at my heart right now.

51

She linked her arm in mind and helped me into her blue little car like I was a hundred years old. Nick's call had definetly aged me. I touched my face expecting to feel the lines from the stress.

"Okay, tell me everything," she said softly, patting my hand. "We have to be at Adam's house in a half hour. Are you gonna be okay? I just got back with Adam, you know. You can't be nuts at his party tonight."

"Don't worry, I'll pull myself together. I won't embarrass you." The tears were now pouring down my face. I knew I must have looked like Alice Cooper.

"It's really over with Nick. I love him so much, Taylor."

"Mom, it would never work out. He wants kids. Your tubes are tied. He could never support you in the style you're used to. He doesn't even have a cool car. If you're going to have an affair, he should at least be filthy rich."

"Pull over, I need to fix my face," I sobbed, tears spilling all over my makeup bag. "Taylor, you don't understand. He made me believe in myself and made me feel like a person not a party girl or a possession. He gives me strength not to drink."

"Do you want me to call him?" Taylor asked, putting on an Ice Coffee lipstick and fluffing her hair. She was beautiful.

"No, I'll call him tomorrow morning. I think I'm going to cut my whirlwind tour short and go home. I need to see him face to face."

"You have so many friends left to see yet. Does the word suicide mean anything to you?"

"I'll kill myself if I don't see him now. I can't enjoy this trip anymore," I grumbled, as I blotted my red lipstick on a tissue. "There, how's my face?"

"You look beautiful, Mom, but you've been blonde a long time. When are you changing the color and eyes?"

"When I go back. First thing for sure. This color is bad luck now. I'm not having fun."

"I like it when you're a red head and have green eyes. I want to get contacts," she said, starting up the car.

The party was at Adam's parent's house. It was his sister's birthday. They had a big sprawling ranch house across from the

52

beach.

Adam was standing on the porch waiting for us. He looked like a model from GQ magazine.

There was a lump in my throat, a knot in my chest, and an alien in my stomach.

Should I tell Adam's parents that my boyfriend broke up with me and to hide all their sharp objects because I was suicidal.

"Keara, you look great," Adam smiled and reached for my bag. "Taylor you look beautiful."

Taylor was wearing a black silk pajama type pants suit. She looked crisp, cool and elegant. I had a long sleeve black tight spandex shirt tucked into a tan suede mini skirt with long fringe hanging off it. A cowgirl look. When I walked it reminded me of a car wash swishing over the windshield.

Taylor and I fought for years over my taste in clothes. I had a great body, why not flaunt it. Nick used to tell me to stop using my sexuality to get things. To stop hiding behind it. Nick, uh oh, I could feel the tears starting to come.

Taylor had taken me around the room and introduced me to everyone. I found a chair in the corner away from all these strangers and began sipping a coke. Everyone looked happy. I swiped a tear that was rolling down my cheek. Oh no, Taylor was walking my way with a cute young guy on her arm.

"Mommy, this is Jeff. He was sober for four years. He's Adam best friend," she smiled and turned back into the crowd.

"Hi, Jeff. I'm Keara," I said softly, shaking his hand, glancing at the glass of whiskey he had in his other hand.

"I started drinking again," he said nervously, reaching for a cigarette. "Mind if I smoke?"

"No, I'm okay by it. Why did you start again?"

"After being sober for four years, I felt like I could handle drinking again. That I could be in control."

"Are you?" I asked, twirling my hair.

"Yes, I'm in total control," he said in a clear voice, running his hand over his long black ponytail.

Taylor was sauntering back over again with Adam on her arm.

"Taylor, can you show me where the bathroom is?" I smiled

graciously and excused myself past Jeff and Adam. We went arm and arm up the steps to the bathroom and closed the door.

I closed the lid to the toilet and sank down on the seat. "Taylor, I can't make it," I cried, putting my head in my hands.

"Don't cry, Mommy," she muttered, stroking my hair. "It'll be alright."

"Can you make up a story for me. I have to lie down. I can't go back down there. I'm sorry, I'm such a mess." I was shaking and sobbing now.

She led me to a small room with a single bed against the wall. My bag was by the side of the bed. We were spending the night here.

"Wait here," she whispered and ran out of the room.

I pulled out my sweats from my bag and slowly undressed. Taylor came back holding a big Winnie the Pooh stuffed animal.

"Here, sleep with him. He always makes me feel better."

I reached for him and started sobbing into his head. Taylor sat on the bed holding me.

"Don't cry, Mommy. You're the one who tells me guys are dicks. They're not worth our tears."

We both started giggling and I wrapped my arms around her.

"Now get some sleep. Tomorrow we are going to school. You're going to meet all my friends. I'm so happy that you are here."

"I love you, Babes."

"I love you, Mommy," she whispered, pulling up the covers and kissing my forehead.

Who's the mother here?

I woke up to puffy eyes and a pounding headache and chest. All I could think of was to go home and see Nick. I wanted a whiskey. I could be in control too.

Taylor stumbled into the room half-asleep. "Mommy, time to get up," she grumbled. "We have to go to my house. Don't worry, Daddy's gone. I have to shower and get ready for school. You can call David and Nick from there."

We pulled up to my ex-husband's house and made a mad dash for the front door. It was bitter cold and raining out. The weather here sucked.

She went into the shower and I called David.

"Hello," he murmured.

"Hi. Are you sleeping? Do you want me to call you back?"

"No. I'm up. I haven't been sleeping well. I got some sleeping pills but they don't seem to work on me."

"I'm not feeling well. I think I will cut my trip short and change my ticket for tomorrow."

"You will," he shrieked.

"It's been so crazy, rushing from place to place. It's just too much for me. Plus the weather is so bad. I'm cold. I'll call you later with my flight information. Bye."

I hung up and started to tremble. I slowly punched in Nick's number.

"Hi," I whispered, rocking back and forth on Taylor's bed. "I'm coming home tomorrow, Nick, we have to talk."

"I'm sorry if I ruined your trip," he said quietly. " I was sick to my stomach all day yesterday."

"I cried all day yesterday," I said, choking back tears, once more. "I can't live without you, Nick. You're my soulmate." I burst into tears.

Taylor was rushing around the room looking for something to wear in the piles on the floor. Her room looked like a department store exploded. Clothes, jewelry, curlers, makeup, flowers and shoes were scattered everywhere. Every inch of the floor was covered

"Mommy, it's your turn to get ready. I can't be late for school."

"Give me a minute."

"Can you sing "Stray Cat Strut" for me. You know I feel better instantly when you sing it. Please," I begged, pacing back and forth.

He sung softly into the phone. I immediately relaxed and my tears dried up. My love for him was flowing through my veins. I hung up floating.

"I think it's going to be okay," I screamed, jumping up and down.

"Mommy, get in the shower before I fucking kill you," Taylor snapped.

55

We raced over to her high school and came to a screeching halt in the parking lot. Taylor was the queen of her school. She came and went as she pleased. The principal and teachers seemed afraid of her. Her friends were all princesses with Jeeps and BMW's.

Stray Cat Strut played in my head all day.

Taylor and I went back to her bedroom from hell to get ready for our big night out. Taylor started sifting through the piles for something to wear. I decided on my black suede vest and shorts and my black thigh high boots. She picked out a shimmering silver mini dress. We both went through the ritual of looking beautiful.

"What time are you leaving tomorrow?" Taylor asked, curling her lashes.

"I have a seven o'clock plane. Will you be alright to take me?"

"Yeah, Adam will drive. I'm getting wasted tonight."

"That's nice dear," I said sarcastically, pulling on a boot.

We pulled up at Club Voodoo and strolled to the long line waiting to get inside. Everyone in line looked like zombies or vampires. The club was dark and funky. The bars all had scorpions or snakes encased in them. In one room, a girl was giving buzz cuts in a barber chair. There was a different D.J. and different music in each room. We picked the disco room.

Jeff was at the bar doing shots of tequila. Adam pulled me out on the dance floor. Taylor joined Jeff at the bar doing shots. The music was so deafening. I knew I'd never be able to hear Nick sing again. Adams started grinding up against me and had a hard on. How sick was that?

"Adam, I need a coke," I screamed into his ear and joined Taylor and Jeff at the bar.

"Taylor, Adam is fucking sick, you know," I screamed into her ear.

She shrugged. "Buy me a drink, Mommy."

"I think you've had enough. I have to find a phone and make some calls."

"Take Jeff's cell and call from the ladies room."

"Jeff," she yelled, "give my Mom your cell."

He pulled the small phone out of the pocket of his baggy black pants. Jeff had the look of a drug dealer, tall, thin, dark and sleazy good looks.. I had to admit though, I liked his silky black pony tail.

"Here Mom," he said, his dark eyes unreadable as he placed the phone in my hand.

Was I excited by the phone in my hand or his touch?

This is a weird fucking place and night.

I worked my way through the bizarre crowd and into the ladies room. The bathroom had about two feet of toilet paper and paper towels on the floor. Beer bottles, cigarette butts and half empty drinks were scattered on basins and the floor. There was graffiti written on every inch of the walls. Everyone was pasty white and wearing black lipstick. I know if I said Bettlejuice three times, he'd appear.

I found a small unoccupied corner of the room where I could press up and call. These creatures of the night didn't even notice me. I called David and left my flight info on the answering machine. He must be out with Tabitha. I then called Nick, praying he's there. Yes.

"Hi. I can't talk long. I'm on someone's cell in a pit of a bathroom. I'll be home by the afternoon and I'll go straight to the restaurant. Please be there."

"I'll be there all day. I have a lot of book work to do."

"I can't wait to see you, Nick."

"Keara, a lot has happened since you been gone. Things have to be different."

"I can hardly hear you, Nick. I'll see you soon."

I pressed the end button and turned around as Taylor stumbled into the room.

"Taylor", I said loudly, "over here." I slipped the phone into my shorts pocket and grabbed her by the arm.

"Mommy, I think I'm gonna be sick," she moaned, swaying at my side.

I asked the anorexic girl with a couple of nose rings if we could go ahead of her. I took Taylor in the stall and held her wild mane back as she threw up. Memories flooded me of my time spent with the toilet. I put my arms under her chest and lifted her up. I carried her to the sink and washed her face with a wet paper towel.

"Taylor, do you see me in AA? Do you want to go that route?

Quit now. I wish I had."

I pushed her hair away from her damp face. "Let's go back to Adam's house." I took her arm and draped it over my shoulder. We fought the crowd back to the bar. Jeff volunteered to take me back in his red corvette. I must be suicidal because I say yes.

Jeff did a couple of lines of coke first before he squealed away from Club Voodoo. We flew down the country roads. I was feeling a bit reckless and wicked.

"Are you in control of your coke habit too," I grinned mischievously, running my hands over my thigh high boots. I felt seventeen again. Fast car. Hot guy. Drugs. Danger.

"What habit, a couple of lines here and there is not a habit. I've hit bottom before, it's not going to happen again," he shrugged, lighting a cigarette.

I guess I'm not the only one in denial.

We arrived at Adam's house miraculously in one piece. Jeff did more lines before we entered the house.

"Keara, I tucked Taylor in bed already. She's sleeping peacefully,"Adam whispered, standing at the bottom of the steps.

"Thanks, Adam. I'm going to stay up and keep Jeff company. I have a feeling he's not tired. It rhymes with tired though."

"You're a funny lady," Jeff smiled, his eyes dancing.

"It's funny girl. What's this lady bullshit. Come on Jeff, let's make some coffee and play cards. This girl will beat your ass at gin."

"Goodnight you two," Adam said over his shoulder as he padded barefoot back up the steps.

We drank coffee and played gin till the wee hours of the morning. He was wired from all the coke. I was wild knowing I would see Nick soon. Was Nick my drug of choice now?

"Jeff, do you think you can drive me to the airport? I don't want to bother Adam," I asked, as I laid down my cards. "Gin."

"Bitch," he muttered. "Yeah. I can't wait for you to leave. I can't win a game."

"Give me a couple of minutes to freshen up, change and say goodbye to Taylor." I picked up my bag and marched wearily up the steps as the sun spilled through the blinds. Hopefully I'd be able to sleep on the plane.

I slowly pushed open Adam's bedroom door. Taylor was on her stomach, one hand over the side of the bed. Adam was on his back, gazing at me with his cool green eyes. Six years ago he worked for me as a busboy. I had a successful nightclub in New York where I was on stage every night dancing and spinning records. I was another person then. Drunk. Wild. Reckless.

"Adam, Jeff is taking me to the airport," I whispered leaning over Taylor. I kissed her on the forehead. She rolled over and painstakingly opened her bloodshot eyes.

"Bye, Mommy, I love you," Taylor moaned, trying to shade her eyes from the sunlight filtering in the room.

My heart was sinking fast as I went downstairs. Jeff was leaning against the porch door, a cigarette dangling from his lips.

"I'm ready," I mumbled, handing him by bag.

"Are you okay, Keara?"

"Yeah. The vacation is over and I have to go back to the real world. Trouble is I don't know what that is anymore. I came here confused and I'm still confused."

We slid into his cold white leather seats and roared out of the driveway.

"Are you gonna be okay?" Jeff asked, reaching his hand over for mine.

"Yeah, as they say in AA, one day at a time. I hate being sober. I wish I could drink and wake up and everything would be like before."

"What was before like?"

"Before was when I was happy drinking every night with friends, laughing and partying. I loved my husband and my life."

"Things will get better. You just got sober. You have no coping mechanisms."

"What's that," I sniffed, an unexpected tear starts making it way down my cheek.

"In the old days you just drank when you couldn't cope. So it went away. Now you can't do that and have to face the problem. You should start meditating. Go to more meetings," he suggested, as he pulled up to the curb in front of American Airlines. "What about your painting? From everything I gathered, you have talent. This Nick guy just sounds like another addiction for you. Stop distracting yourself. Do something for your own good."

"You should think about going to a meeting again and take Taylor," I said softly, kissing his cheek. "Thanks for the ride and advice. If you ever come West, look me up."

* * *

We spilled out of the gate like race horses. David was standing behind the rope with a bunch of wild flowers in his hand. His face was full of hope and love.

Okay, I can do this. I just have to put myself into a soap opera character. Take One. As San Diego Turns.

"I missed you, so much," he whispered in my ear, hugging the wind out of me.

I took the flowers and he took my bag. We walked hand in hand out of the airport.

"Are you tired? Hungry?" he asked as we strolled into the warm California sunshine.

"I slept on the plane, so I didn't eat." "Let's go to the restaurant. I'm starved ," I blurted out, twisting my hair.

Sadness clouded over his face. He seemed dazed and confused.

"You win. We'll go to Tequila Bay." He reached into the glove department and pulled out a small silver wrapped box. "Here's your welcome home gift."

"Thanks," I said weakly as I tore opened the silver foil. Inside was a beautiful silver chain with a purple heart dangling from it. On the heart was a tiny silver angel laying across the top.

"David, I love it. Put it on me, please." I wrapped my arms around him and kissed his cheek. "You're the best."

He tenderly placed the chain around my neck. "You're my angel."

There was still some tension lingering in the air.

"I have a gift for you too," I said, unzipping my bag and pulling out a navy blue rectangular box. "Sorry it's not wrapped."

He opened the box and a smile danced on his lips.

"Juggling balls. I always wanted these," he exclaimed and started tossing the colorful balls in the air.

60

"Juggling is supposed to relieve stress," I smiled, fingering my new heart.

Our eyes locked and we both started giggling as he headed for the restaurant. I spotted Nick's car as we parked in the lot. My heart started beating wildly. My mouth went dry. I had liquid heat pouring through every inch of my body. I guess I did trade one addiction for another.

We walked through the entrance and it was slammed. A convention had just let out.

"No time for jet lag," I mumbled as I slid off my jacket.

I picked up a pad and pencil and started taking down names. I estimated at least a twenty minute wait.

David headed for the kitchen.

I could see Nick out of the corner of my eye. He was making Margaritas at the bar. Lou was sitting at the corner of the bar, taking it all in.

I grabbed the iced tea pitcher and started refilling glasses. The waiters all look drained of color. I seated the next couple in Jane's section. She came running over to me, her eyes bugged out like a scary monster.

"Keara, I can't take this table."

"Don't worry, I'll take it for you."

Now I could take their drink order and finally get to go to the bar and see Nick. David was safely in the kitchen. Coast was clear.

"Can I get you something to drink?" I asked sweetly, pen and paper in hand. They ordered Margaritas. Yes. This was my lucky day.

I strolled up to the bar. "Two Margaritas, bartender, and make it snappy," I laughed, tossing my head back.

He was just pouring a glass of red wine. Would I love to be draining that glass dry.

"Welcome back," he smiled, flashing his pearly whites. "This place is a madhouse today."

"I brought you a present," I said in a low tone. "We have to hug in the office later or I'll explode."

Our fingers lingered over the Margarita glasses. Electric currents were traveling through my body and scorched my brains.

I felt Lou's eyes burning a hole through me.

Fuck him.

The pace slowed down on the floor and I retreated to my office. I slid into my chair and propped my feet up on the desk. The phone started ringing and snapped me out of my trance.

"Hello, Tequila Bay," I said sharply, hooking all the paper clips together on the desk.

"Is Nick there?" a female voice asked.

"Who's calling?" I asked, a cold sweat started to break out all over my skin.

"Dawn." she said impatiently.

"What company are you with Dawn?"

"My house. Look we have a date tonight. Could you please put him on."

My heart had already shattered on the floor into a million pieces. My hands were trembling as I put her on hold. I didn't think I could breathe. I needed my inhaler. I rose slowly and walked as if in a trance to find Nick. David was involved in a meeting with the cooks. I smiled weakly at them as I pass by. Nick was in the manager's office counting money when I stumbled in.

"Line two is for you," I snarled, twirling my hair around my index finger. Wanting to rip out every hair on my head and run screaming from the room.

"Who is it?" he asked, not looking up from his counting.

"Dawn." I snapped, hands on my hips. "She says you two have a fucking date." Tears glazed across my eyes and my breathing became rapid. I ran out of the room and down the hall and back into my office. I slumped down on the floor into a ball of pain and tears.

I need a drink. Fuck, I need a bottle.

"Keara, don't do this," he muttered, bending over me and wrapping his strong arms around me.

"Is this why you broke up with me when I was in New York?" I sobbed, holding onto him for dear life.

"Keara, listen to me." He grabbed me by the shoulders and shook me."Georgia came in a couple of days ago for the advertising and set me up on a blind date with David's encouragement. You see, David confronted me about you, when you were away. It wasn't a pretty scene. I had no choice."

"What did David tell you?"

"He doesn't like it that I'm your best friend. He doesn't think it's healthy."

"I don't care what he fucking thinks."

"But I do. So let's just cool it for now. I'll take this Dawn out and everyone will be happy."

"Just get out," I screamed hysterical. "Leave me alone." I doubled over with stomach pain.

He brushed away a tear from his eye and walked out the door.

I crawled over to the desk and punched in Georgia's number. Georgia came in weekly and did our ad for the newspaper. We all loved her.

"Hello," she answered cheerily.

"Georgia, I fucking hate you," I exploded. "How could you set Nick up and who is Dawn?"

"Calm down. Tell me what is going on."

"Why did you set Nick up?"

"He's not dating anyone so I just thought I'd play matchmaker. Dawn's one of my clients. David thought it was a good idea too. What's the big deal?"

"I'm in love with him," I blurted out. " Are you fucking blind?"

"Keara, I had no idea," she said shocked. "I'd never hurt you. We're good friends. Don't worry, she's really trashy, anyway."

"Well isn't that comforting? I have to hang up. I'm going to be sick." I slammed down the phone and ran to the bathroom. Jane was in there reapplying her makeup.

"Keara, are you okay?"

"No. I have to throw up," I said, kneeling over the toilet.

"Let me hold your hair."

"Thanks," I cried as I lost my lunch in the bowl. She helped me up and over to the sink.

"Should I get David. I saw him by the bar talking to Nick."

"Please," I whimpered, sliding down onto the floor. "I'm really sick."

David and Nick both came barreling through the door.

"Keara, are you okay?" Do you need a doctor?" David asked,

63

crouching down beside me, feeling my head.

Nick was standing by the doorway with a pained expression on his face.

I bit my lip till I could taste blood. "David, please take me home. I need to go to bed."

He tossed his keys at Nick.

"Nick, please bring my car around. I'll carry Keara. She doesn't look like she can walk."

"Keara, what happened?" David asked, wiping my forehead with a wet paper towel.

"I guess everything just caught up with me. Must be exhaustion," I smiled weakly as he picked me up in his arms.

* * *

I woke up the next morning with a crushing pain in my chest. It felt like during the night a wild animal had ripped my heart out. All I could think of was Nick kissing that Dawn goodnight. My eyes started swimming with tears.

"Keara, you're up," David smiled, rushing in the room. Are you crying?"

"No. My eyes are just irritated from sleeping with my contacts in."

"I have an appointment later but first let me get you breakfast in bed. What's your pleasure?"

"Mm, I'd like an egg in the cup and some tea, please."

"I'll have to go to the store. The refrigerator is bare, not even a bone for Jack. Are you going to be able to D.J. tonight?"

"Of course, the show must go on." I pulled the covers up to my chin and closed my eyes. As soon as I heard the door shut, I shot out of bed and raced up the steps. I checked the driveway to make sure he was gone. I grabbed the portable phone and called Nick.

"Hi," I said weakly, twirling the ends of my hair.

"How are you? I was so worried."

"I'm okay. I still feel a little weak," I said softly, playing on his emotions. "My chest is still hurting."

"I had a horrible time last night. I couldn't even carry on a conversation. I was so worried about you."

"Will you see her again?" I sniffed, rocking back and forth.

64

"No," he growled.

"Will you be at the party tonight that I'm working?"

"I can't. It's my Mom's birthday."

"Can we get together tomorrow? Let's spend morning, noon and night together. Please say yes. Just this one last time."

"David would go crazy looking for me besides I promised Billy. He needs me more than ever. He could die any day now. We shouldn't start up again."

"Nick, our last night together was pretty special."

"You're a wicked temptress."

I looked out the window and saw David's car turning the corner. My heart started racing.

"Nick, I'm feeling dizzy. I have to lie down."

"How are you going to DJ tonight?"

"I'll be all right. I just feel nausea. I'll call you tomorrow morning to confirm our date. I love you."

I hung up the phone and scrambled downstairs. I dove into bed and pulled the covers up and closed my eyes.

I heard pots and pans clinking upstairs. David was putting together a breakfast for his loving wife. Guilt twisted like a knife in me. How was I going to eat when my stomach was on fire?

"You're breakfast is ready," he said softly, holding a huge wicker tray filled with goodies. Under his left arm was a stuffed black cat. He placed the tray at the bottom of the bed and handed me the kitty.

"I got this kitty to watch over you while I'm at my meeting."

"Thanks, I love it," I exclaimed, hugging it to my chest. " It's so cute. I'll name it Midnight."

"Let's have a real family night tonight before you have to work," he suggested. "When Tabitha gets home, let's have a picnic on the beach and maybe an early movie. How does that sound?"

"Great," I replied, nibbling on a piece of dry whole-wheat toast.

I spent the rest of the day dying my hair to a dark auburn shade and I changed my contacts to emerald green.

Tabitha came home from school and we had a warm reunion .I'd been too sick the night before to see her. She liked her Ren and Stimpy baseball cap I'd picked up for her in New York. The rest of the day was spent as David had suggested. Family picnic and movie. I moved through the day like a robot. Thoughts of Nick programmed in my head. I couldn't delete the file not even for a minute.

I was anxious to work tonight. It would be an easy party. Older people. That meant a lot of fifties thru seventies music.

I selected a light green lycra dress to match my new eye color and hair.

We kissed Tabitha goodbye and left for the restaurant.

"David, why are you driving so fast?"

"I just called Carlos. He told me Nick hasn't been by all day. He knows about the party. You'd think he'd be there setting up."

"It's called communication. You could have called Nick and told him you weren't going to be there till later. Just relax. The party will be perfect."

David immediately started barking orders when we arrived. I jumped on stage and started practicing. An older woman heavily made up, approached the booth.

"Are you Keara?"

"Yes," I smiled sweetly. "Can I help you with something?"

I knew she'd be the one responsible for paying me.

"Here's a list of songs that I would like you to play tonight and some announcements."

I gazed at the list. "I have all these records."

"Oh, wonderful. Is there anything else you do besides spin?"

"Yes. I get a conga line going, a limbo contest, dirty dancing contest and if you like I do a mean Tina Turner impersonation."

"My husband loves Tina Turner."

"Okay, don't worry about a thing. Your party will be perfect."

"Thank you, Keara."

David rushed into the room and motioned for me to come to the edge of the stage.

"Everything is a mess. We have convention people piling up in the restaurant. The kitchen is behind. I'm afraid I can't watch you perform. I don't know where the hell Nick is either."

"Don't worry about the party. I can take care of it."

Two hours into the party, I began to feel drained. I just finished

66

a conga line and a limbo contest. I couldn't even think about doing Tina. This was not a good time for depression. I buried my face in the stack of records and looked for my next selection. A stray tear crawled down my face.

"Hey D.J., you need a break?"

I spun around.

"I know how hard it is for you to work sober. Here's some gummy bears and a coke. A nice sugar high for you."

"Oh Nick, as always your timing is perfect." I quickly wiped the tear away with the back of my hand.

"Were you crying?"

"No, it's the fog machine. It makes my eyes water."

"You are such a liar, Keara. Come here and hug me."

"Where's David?"

"He just fired George so he's playing bartender."

"Nick, I promised the crowd "Proud Mary". Do you want to do Ike? You've seen me rehearse it a million times."

"Sure, let's do it, Tina."

The crowd loved us. I rode the high for the rest of the evening. Nick had disappeared after our number together. It didn't matter. I felt his presence deep in my soul.

* * *

I woke the next morning with my skin tingling. I propped up against the pillows on the bed and pinched the bridge of my nose. First things first. I had to call Jenny and resume my jogging.

We had a good run and said our goodbyes a couple of feet from the lifeguard tower. We confirmed our run for tomorrow. I watched her jog away before I pulled out the quarter. Tension was clawing at my stomach.

I turned to make the call. The lifeguard was standing watching me with his hands on his hips.

"Hey, what's with you?"

"You don't come by in ages. Then you show up with different hair and eyes," he said good naturedly. "Are you incognito?"

"I thought I'd be more intriguing as a red head."

"Are you still having your affair?"

"Are you a reporter or a lifeguard?"

"Want to have a drink sometime?" he asked, digging his toes in the sand.

"I'm an alcoholic. I spend my nights talking about how I wish I could have a drink. Thanks anyway," I smiled sweetly and plopped the quarter in the slot and punched Nick's number in. The lifeguard sauntered off the beach. Nick was on the other end.

"Nick, can you meet me?"

"Meet me at eleven in Carlsbad at the coffee shop with the fire pits," he grumbled.

"What's wrong?"

"Billy died last night. This time I need a hug."

"Oh, Nick. I'm sorry. Are you taking Harrison?"

"Yes and No. I talked Fiona, my secretary at my dad's plant, into keeping him."

"Well, let's have a mini vacation today. We both need it."

I ran home like I was being chased by bulls.

When I entered the house I didn't know if the sweat dripping off me is from the run or the fear in having to confront David. I'd love a Mylanta now. On the top step, my mouth went dry. David met my gaze with his hazel eyes.

"How was your run?"

"Great. Do you want me to get breakfast?"

"No. I'll go. I need the break. I've been on the phone all morning."

"I'm going to take a shower while you're out," I yelled over my shoulder, bouncing down the steps.

So far so good.

I dressed in black cut offs, black tights, black t-shirt and black boots. I looked liked ninja cheater. Desire started stirring up in me thinking of meeting Nick. I sat on the edge of the bed lacing up my boot and daydreamed of his long fingers touching my breasts. My skin was becoming hot like I had a fever. Stop. I had to go upstairs and have breakfast with my husband.

Cool down Keara, or you'll blow it.

I raced upstairs and was greeted by a slobbering Jack. David had chased him off the terrace and made a picnic.

"Let's eat, Keara," David smiled as he smoothed out the corners of the Mexican blanket.

I sat down cross-legged opposite him. Breakfast consisted of bagels, scones, coffee and fresh fruit. There were beautiful pink tulips in a pitcher in the middle of the blanket.

"What a treat," I said happily, sipping my coffee. I reached over and squeezed his hand.

"I had a good morning so far. I made five grand."

"So you won't mind if I go shopping," I smiled wickedly, picking at my blueberry scone.

"Don't you want to save some money so we can buy a house again?"

"Of course, I do, but I've lost so much weight, I need new clothes. I thought I'd spend the day shopping."

"I'm going to take Tabitha and play tennis at the club later. Why don't you meet me there and we'll work out together?"

"What time?" I asked, trying to keep my voice calm.

"How's five?"

"That's perfect. I want to go to a meeting tonight too." I rose up slowly and bought the dishes into the kitchen. David followed me and wrapped his arms around me.

"Have fun today. Buy something sexy."

I kissed him on the cheek and took off. I dug in my purse for a Mylanta tablet. My stomach would feel better soon but not my heart.

I raced to the mall and bought the first outfit I saw on the mannequin. It was a black pleated mini skirt and a white cotton shirt with a black puffy heart in the middle. That was probably the color of my heart. I destroyed the receipt so David wouldn't see the time. I had to pretend it took me all day to find this perfect outfit. I threw the bag in the trunk and went flying down the highway.

Nick was sitting by the fire sipping tea. I stood for a moment taking in the sight of him. It made me high. He looked up from his mug and the corners of his mouth turned up in pleasure. I strode over and plunked down on his lap.

"Let's get the hell out of here," I said in a silky murmur, rubbing my hands all over his body.

"Leave your car here. I already got us a room."

"Where?'

"The Best Western on the beach. It has a fireplace too."

"I'm totally excited," I shrieked, pulling him to his feet. I was a teenager again.

We spent the afternoon caressing and exploring every inch of each other's bodies. He was better than any drug I have ever snorted or swallowed. He took me to a level I didn't know existed. The room was thick with the smell of sex and the heat of passion.

I disentangled myself from Nick's muscular's arms and slipped from the bed. My skin was raw from the past five hours of lovemaking. Did we make love or was it just sex? Did he love me or was he just horny?

"I have to meet David and Tabitha at the club," I muttered, snapping my black lace bra back on. "I'll be back here by seven-thirty. Let's do Sushi."

"Sounds good. There's a Sushi place right on the strip here. I'll meet you there.."

I finished dressing and sat on the bed playing with his chest hair.

"What will you do while I'm gone?"

"Probably take a nap, shower and get ready to meet you."

He was sprawled out naked on the bed with his hands behind his head. I felt he was absorbing my every thought and move. An anxiety attack was about to embrace me. Was he having a head trip?

I jumped up and blew a kiss goodbye. It was time for my other life.

Unexpected tears came to my eyes as I was heading downtown. I couldn't take this much longer. Lies. Deceit. Guilt. I wished I could pull over and find a bar and get trashed.

When I arrived at the club, Tabitha and David were playing tennis.

"Hi, guys," I shouted, twirling my hair.

"Keara, go put your jogging clothes on. We're almost done."

"Hi, Mom. I'm beating Daddy," Tabitha exclaimed, running over to kiss my cheek.

"You go girl," I laughed , picking up my gym bag and heading

70

for the lockers.

I dressed slowly. How was I going to run? Every part of my body was sore, especially my legs. My vagina was throbbing. I was drained of all energy plus depression was setting in.

My mind drifted to picturing Nick curled up and sleeping like a baby back in the room. He was a baby. Still living with mommy, depending on daddy for money. I needed a man to empower me. Neither David or Nick qualified. Maybe it was time for me to begin depending on myself. I'd always been taken care of, first by my parents, then my ex and now David. I had never been alone. I had always depended on others to fulfill my dreams. I had to muster up all my strength to rise off the bench and go jogging.

"Ready for a run along the water," David asked, putting away his racquet.

"Mommy, I won," Tabitha said triumphantly, grinning from ear to ear.

"Congratulations, baby. Here's five dollars to play the video games."

"Thanks, Mom," she said excitedly and ran down the steps into the game room.

David and I decided to jog through the Seaport and down by the bay. There was a cool breeze blowing. Perfect for jogging.

Perfect if you didn't have sex for five hours and felt like any minute you were going to pass out. Oh Keara, Keara, Keara.

"How was shopping?" David asked, pulling off his shirt and tucking it in the waistband of his shorts.

"I had a great day. It took me all day but I found an adorable outfit after trying on a million different things."

"What else did you do?"

"The shopping completely exhausted me. I went to the food court and had some rice and vegetables. Then went over to Starbucks for dessert and coffee. Then sat at one of those tables inside by the ice skating rink and watched the skaters and wrote in my journal.

The lies were just rolling off my tongue. I didn't even know where they were coming from.

"Where would you like to have dinner tonight?" he asked,

watching me carefully.

"I can't. While I was at the mall I called Carol and Maryann. We are all going to a meeting. I really need one since I haven't been to any in awhile."

"You must stop depending on meetings! I know you, you made up your mind not to drink anymore and you won't. So why do you keep going?"

"You're wrong, David. I need these meetings. I'm not yet strong enough to do it alone."

"I spend my day and night alone. We're not a couple anymore. This AA is a cult thing."

"Don't be ridiculous," I snapped, coming to a stop and walking back to the gym.

"Everyone in your group is young or divorced. You run around as if you are also single."

"I need meetings right now. End of discussion."

"You can never discuss anything without getting emotional."

"I'm not discussing it anymore. Keep it up and I'll flip out right here."

"When should I expect you home tonight?"

"Shut up David or I won't come home at all," I hissed as I got off the elevator and headed for the showers.

I took a scalding hot shower hoping to burn off all the layers of shame. I dressed, did my hair and makeup and got ready for round two.

I walked over to the elevators. Tabitha and David were sitting in the chairs there. The door opened and we all entered like we were going to the gas chambers. Tabitha was biting her nails and David's jaw was clenched tight.

The door opened and we crept along to our cars in thick heavy silence. I hugged Tabitha goodbye. David had an aura of hatred around him. I weakly mumbled a goodbye in his direction. He wouldn't look at me.

I cruised down the highway. The top was down and the music was blasting. I pushed David and Tabitha out of my mind and let thoughts of Nick drift in.

I was about ten minutes late. He was already at the Sushi bar

72

sipping tea. I slid in the chair next to him.

"I'm starved," I said dramatically, bugging out my new green eyes. Why don't you order for us both?"

He poured me a cup of green tea and ordered tons of Sushi.

"So, what did you do when I was gone?"

Nick started singing softly "All By Myself". He knew all the words. When he was done he went right into "Stray Cat Strut". My favorite song in the whole world. He had my complete attention. I hung on his every note like a star struck groupie hanging with the band. If it was possible, I was more in love with him than ever. Tears welled up in my eyes.

"Are you okay?" he whispered, squeezing my hand.

I dabbed my eyes with my cloth napkin. "Yes. I just love you so much Nick. I don't know what to do."

"How about relaxing and just being my best friend for now."

I nodded and picked up my chopsticks and dove into the Sushi.

Nick sung silly songs in every cartoon voice from Daffy Duck to Pepe Le Pew all through dinner. My heart belonged to him.

I followed him back to the hotel. We drifted into the room. He flipped a switch and the fire instantly came on. We held one another in the soft glow of the room. It slowly heated up with our flames of desire. We ripped at one another's clothes like they were ignited. He started licking me where the fire was burning out of control. I started gasping for air like my lungs were filled with smoke. I screamed out his name and collapsed on the bed. Nick joined me on the bed and we became one in the blaze, our passion burning into the night.

Around midnight, I slipped out of bed and dressed hurriedly. "I have to get going," I whispered leaning over and kissing his cheek.

"Keara, I have something I must talk to you about."

"Does it have to do with having the best time ever today?"

"We did have a great time. We also said it would be the last time."

"So, what are you saying?" A cold numbness came over my whole body.

"I need a normal relationship. You are married. This is a no

73

win situation."

"You can't deny we have something special together." Tears rose automatically in my eyes. "I couldn't bear it if you were with someone else."

"Keara, come over here and hug me," he said, stretching out his arms. "Don't get crazy."

"Leave me alone. This is so fucked up, Nick," I screamed, gripping the door knob. A wave of pain crashed over me as I ran into the darkness.

I drove home in a haze of confusion. The flames of desire were ashes now but the flames of hell burned brightly.

* * *

The next morning I dragged myself out of bed and into the bathroom to inspect the damage. Wow. The addiction to Nick was more damaging than alcohol. Eyes were all swollen and red, face blotchy, stomach queasy, heart broken.

I splashed cold water on my face. A chill passed through me and it wasn't from the ice water. This time it seemed like Nick and I were really through. A tear escaped down my cheek. Uh oh, I couldn't start this again. I quickly dressed and donned a pair of dark glasses and a baseball hat.

"I'm going jogging with Jenny, David," I yelled up the steps.

"Hurry back, Keara, I have a surprise for you," he smiled lovingly, waving goodbye as I ran out the door.

Jenny would kill for her husband to be like David. Any woman would. Why did I rock the boat? Everyone knows the grass isn't greener.

"Keara, what's with the glasses," asked Jenny, as she jogged up to my side.

"I slept in my contacts last night and my eyes are slightly infected and sensitive to the light."

"Oh, I thought you had gone Hollywood on me."

We both giggled and the mood of the jog was light and breezy. When it was over we talked about the upcoming holidays. I told her I wanted to paint. I also had a couple of DJ jobs coming up. She would be busy baking, of course.

Without realizing it, I ended up by the lifeguard tower and

phone once again.

"Hey, no phone call today," the lifeguard called out, strutting toward me.

"Not today," I mumbled, chewing on my lip.

"What happened?"

"It's over," I muttered, my voice cracked on over.

"Let's go for coffee tonight and talk."

"I'm sorry, I wouldn't be good company right now. I'd rather have coffee with you when I'm sane."

"Some of my best friends are crazy."

"Thanks but I'm not ready yet," I said sadly. I gave him a quick hug and jogged off down the beach. My mind flooded with a dozen images of Nick. My heart was so heavy I didn't think I could carry it another step.

David was leaning against the Mustang's trunk when I turned down the street.

"What's wrong? Why are you here?" I asked, total fear taking over my body.

"I told you I had a surprise. You need a little fun in your life."

"What's the surprise?"

"You have to come with me to find out," he suggested, jumping behind the wheel of my Mustang.

"I haven't had coffee yet."

"No problem. We'll stop and eat breakfast on the road."

I hopped in the passenger's side and unsuccessfully tried to escape from thoughts of Nick.

The surprise was an hour of jet skiing on the bay. David had packed our bathing suits and the owner lent us wet suits. We played like two seals bobbing on the waves and diving for fish. It was fun, exhilarating, pure pleasure. Thoughts of Nick were left behind at the dock.

We peeled off our wet suits and headed for the outdoor cafe across from the dock. We plopped down on white plastic chairs and ordered Virgin Marys. There was a Jazz band playing in the courtyard. David knew how to spoil me. The sun, the ocean and Jazz, who could ask for more in life.

"Happy," he asked, sipping his drink.

"Yes, thank you," I smiled and squeezed his hand across the table.

* * *

I had to go down to the restaurant and practice my spinning for the upcoming party. Being a DJ sober was the hardest thing in the world for me. In the past I had always had a couple bottles of wine before I entered the booth.

As I was hauling my crate of records to the booth, Nick walked in. My heart stopped.

"Let me help you," he said, rushing over to grab the crate.

Thanks," I mumbled, trying to keep calm. .

"Getting ready for the big party?" he asked, brushing off pretend dirt from his jeans.

"Yeah. Are you bringing a date?"

"No, I'm not bringing a date," he said mimicking me.

I threw my arms around him not caring who was watching and hugged him. I felt my face flush with pleasure. His touch sent electric shocks all through my body.

"I missed you, Nick," I confessed in a whisper, not letting go of him.

"I missed my best friend."

"I've doubled up on my meetings."

"You have to dig deep and remember the reasons why you chose to be sober."

"You always make me feel better, Nick."

"How are you and David getting along?"

"The same. He hates that I'm still going to AA. I don't want to be a DJ anymore and he wants me to work more parties. He would probably love it if I went out drinking."

"Have you tried to meditate? What about painting?"

"I did sketch a few things. Would you like to see them?"

"I'd love to. There is the cutest dog down at the shelter maybe you could come down there with me and sketch him."

Just then Lou walked into the room with a disapproving look on his face.

"Hello Keara, ready for the big night?" he asked, stroking his chin.

"You know me Lou, always ready."

"Nick, let's go to lunch now," he ordered, turning his back, leaving as quickly as he entered.

He nodded and trotted after Lou.

The angel on my shoulder told me to forget him. My marriage just seemed to be getting back on track. David was beginning to trust me again. They wanted me to be secretary of the AA meeting. Things were pretty smooth. The Devil on the other shoulder told me Nick and I belonged together. Fuck my marriage.

I needed a drink. Seeing Nick again made my insides feel like Jell-O.

Tonight's party was being given by a group of rich retired men who threw monthly parties at different locations. They had a following of long legged, silicone injected blondes. I hated these parties in which everyone ended up drunk and sloppy but I couldn't complain about the money. For a night's work, three hundred dollars in cash.

I decided upon my black velvet short Betsey Johnson dress. It was tight fitting and showed every curve. I skillfully applied my makeup, curled my thick auburn hair and generously spritzed on Fendi perfume.

"I'm so nervous about spinning tonight."

"You're the best DJ, Keara. I don't know why you're so nervous," David frowned. "Tabitha forgot her favorite bear. Do you think I should run it over to the sleep over?"

"No, she's a big girl now, you might embarrass her. Anyway, David, I wanted to talk to you about something. I want to retire from spinning. I'm too old to be up on stage."

"Don't be silly. You look like you're in your twenties. No one has an ear like you for music. You're the only DJ that can keep a floor going all night, Keara."

"Thanks for the vote of confidence, but we'll see. Did you get Taylor's plane ticket yet?"

"I took care of everything today," David replied, jingling the keys. "Come on let's go."

"Is there anything special you'd like for Christmas?" he asked, keeping his eyes on the road.

"Maybe a big sketch pad and some charcoal."

"What is the charcoal for? Is it because you know you've been bad."

"Guess I can't pull the wool over your eyes. Yes, give me a big lump of it."

Thoughts of Nick and the party were swirling around in my head. My nerves were screaming for a drink. I was tying the black velvet strap around my ankle for about the tenth time. I had on my F.M. shoes tonight, a.k.a. fuck me shoes, black velvet heels that tied around my ankles in a bow. These shoes aroused Nick.

Inside the restaurant was a state of chaos with the last minute preparations. I spotted Nick across the room tying black and white balloons to the railings. David immediately took off for the kitchen and I climbed into the DJ booth. I started playing some Jazz to warm up before the craziness began.

As I was pulling a record from it's sleeve, Nick approached the stage, with a six pack of spring water for me.

"Thought I'd bring you your security blanket," he said softly, handing me the water.

"Thanks. I wish it were vodka."

"No you don't. Wait till the end of the night when everyone is acting stupid. You'll be in complete control and happy."

"I just can't wait till this is over and then I'll be happy," I grumbled, placing the six pack under my record crate. "David's coming you better go."

Nick sauntered over to the door to start greeting everyone as they started trickling in.

David came to the edge of the stage. He had a six pack of water under his arm. I bent down to grab it from him.

"Thought you'd might be needing this," he smiled, straightening the bow on my ankle.

"Thanks. Looks like it's show time."

"Break a leg, Keara."

He flowed into the crowd and started mingling. He knew how to work parties, getting new accounts for the market. David was always wheeling and dealing. It was the New Yorker in him. He could never be the laid back San Diegan.

The party turned out to be a huge success. The tunes I selected matched the group's energy. My DJ booth was busy through the night with requests, job proposals and lots of flirting. David and Nick, both kept their eyes glued on me all night with green clouds of jealousy hanging over them. Lou sat at the bar all night not missing a trick.

I had talked Nick into a night of Christmas shopping and a movie. A just friends get together. I used my invisible pals as my alibi. Kylie had one of her friends call my answering machine pretending to be Carol inviting me out. I just couldn't be good.

Nick bought us tickets for the movie. I was excited. This was like a real date. I couldn't wait to sit beside him in the theater. Hold his hand during the scary scene.

"Let's get candy," I suggested.

"I'll get in line . What do you want?"

"Gummy Bears. I'll go to the bathroom while you're in line."

I freshen my makeup and tossed my head upside down to fluff up my hair. As I was crossing the lobby, I saw Nick talking to Kristen, one of our waitresses. I slipped past them and into the movie. It was one of those multiplex theaters, hopefully she wasn't seeing this movie.

I was sitting in the last row biting my fake fingernails when Nick entered. He had a sour expression on his face. He plopped down beside me.

"Do you think she saw you?" he snapped, handing me my candy.

"No. I was careful."

"She's at the movie next door but we should leave soon. I'm too upset now."

This was definetly turning into the date from hell. I could feel my face flushing with frustration.

"Let's just get out of here," I hissed, tossing about ten gummy bears in my mouth. I needed the sugar high.

"I'll meet you outside," he said gruffly, jerking his head around, scoping out the theater.

He didn't see the solitary tear that escaped down my cheek. I left the theater dazed and disoriented. How did it get so fucked up so fast? .

Nick was waiting for me outside. I could see he was filled with anguish and self-loathing. I felt like I was going to throw up the gummy bears.

We walked wordlessly to his car. We slid into his cold leather seats and drove off. He parked somewhere in the back lot. He turned off the engine and faced me. His forehead was creased with a look of concern.

"Kristen probably saw us together." He slammed his fist down on the dash-board.

"Nick we were just going to a movie," I mumbled, blinking back tears.

"I don't need the restaurant gossiping about us".

I pressed my index fingers to my temples. I felt chilled. I started to shiver.

"Are you okay?"

"What do you think? We haven't seen one another in a long time. It started out tonight so great at the mall. It was like old times hanging out and being goofy. Then, poof, it was over," I cried, burying my face in his chest. "I know you, you'll never meet me again."

He started the car. "I'm sorry, Keara. Let's take this as a sign that we can't sneak around anymore."

I stumbled out of his car not looking back.

* * *

I woke up feeling groggy and did a quick mental review.

Uh huh, that's why my heart is in pieces on the floor. A breeze might as well blow it away. I certainly don't need it anymore

"Good morning, Keara, I already made us breakfast. It's outside on the terrace," David said cheerfully standing in the doorway.

A thought crossed my mind of slicing his throat and removing his vocal cords.

"Come on get up. Let's have a nice breakfast and then we'll all go the airport."

"I need some strong coffee and two Excedrins before I can function," I mumbled.

80

David and Tabitha chatted excitedly about Christmas over breakfast. I sipped my coffee and let the realization settle in that this was my life.

We piled into the Mustang and headed for the airport. I couldn't wait to see Taylor.

"Keara, did I tell you about my lunch with Nick the other day?" David asked loudly over the music on the car radio.

I reached over and lowered the music. "No. Tell me about it."

"We had a couple of beers and he told me his ex-girlfriend is calling him and asking him out again.

"Who, Jessica?"

"She wants to go out with him for New Year's."

"Is he going?" I asked, trying to keep my voice calm. An explosion erupted in my head, heart and stomach. I was starting to sweat.

"He doesn't think he'll go cause she really hurt him once. He still has feelings for her. Did you ever meet her? She's really hot. She came in looking for him the other day."

I felt like I was going to throw up breakfast. I had to sit on my hands so David wouldn't see them shake.

If he spends New Year's with her, I'm taking my life. I had to work on New Year's. I'd be playing every sad song in the universe. Why was she so hot? Why couldn't she be fat and ugly? Oh God and she was probably young.

Shoot me now. I don't want to live.

We were standing at the gate of American Airlines. Tabitha and David were playing rock, paper, scissors. I was leaning up against a gray pole trying to focus on Taylor's arrival. I didn't want to spoil it by being taken away in a straight jacket.

She strolled through the gate looking cranky and irritable. We all jumped on her at once and did a group hug.

"I just got my period on the flight," she announced, fumbling through her pockets for her cigarettes. "I need to smoke plus I'm starved. Let's go to the restaurant. I need a burrito."

Taylor had a way of reading my mind.

David and Tabitha went to get the car while I waited with Taylor who smoked at the curb.

"Mom, you look awful. You're thin as a rail. What's up with you?"

"David, just told me about Nick's old girlfriend. She is trying to get back with Nick and she is hot. Nick never told mean any of this."

"You need a cigarette."

I never smoked. Everyone at AA smoked after the meeting. One addiction for another.

"Here take a drag. You need something to calm you down. Are you gonna fuck up Christmas?"

"No. I'll kill myself January second. Don't worry."

David pulled up to the curb and we jumped in.

"Do you really want to go to the restaurant?" David asked, frowning.

"Yeah. I want to see Brad," Taylor whined.

I thought for sure everyone could hear my heart pounding. I turned up the radio.

The restaurant was lively. I started to hostess so that my mind wouldn't snap. Taylor camped out at Brad's bar. David took off for the office with Tabitha. I knew Nick was around because I'd seen his car in the lot.

I strolled over to the bar and plopped down beside Taylor.

"Feeling better?" I asked, giving her a hug.

"Yes. Brad is making a special drink named just for me," she exclaimed, lighting a Marlboro Light. "Mommy, you look like you could use a puff." She held the cigarette up to my lips and I sucked on it. I felt instantly dizzy as I exhaled a stream of smoke.

"Hey, are you smoking?" Nick asked, coming up behind me.

I spun around on my bar stool to face him.

"Tell me about Jessica," I said, my voice cracking.

"She's walking in the door now." Pain flickered in his eyes.

They sat at the opposite end of the bar. She was petite with brown hair streaked blonde and about a pound of makeup on. She had a black tight dress on with white thigh high stockings and black high heels. Definitely trailer trash. A cheap slut. How could Nick have been with her?

"Here Mommy, take this cigarette," Taylor said, lighting it for me.

I inhaled deeply and blew the smoke towards Nick. I knew he was watching me out of the corner of his eye.

David was now walking toward me shaking his head. "Why are you smoking?"

"I'm an adult. I can smoke if I want."

"Taylor, let me have one too."

"Copy cat."

David lit up and started puffing away.

I wondered if I jumped off the Coronado bridge if he would too.

I liked smoking. It made me dizzy. I could now bond with Taylor. It kinda replaced having a drink at the bar. It was like I was still doing something that was bad for you.

"Let's move this party to a table everybody. The food is ready," David announced, pulling me off the stool.

As if I could eat! I wanted to sit at the bar and just stare at Nick and Jessica. Smoke a pack of cigarettes. Throw up and kill myself. In that order.

Nick joined us for coffee and dessert. Jessica had left. Taylor had gone back to Brad's section. Tabitha took off again for the office to play computer games.

"So, are you getting back with Jessica?" David asked, his voice filled with hope.

"No. I blew her off. I just can't start up with her again. She really hurt me at one time."

My guardian angel had just came by and lifted the five hundred pound weight off my chest. All of a sudden I could breathe freely again but I had to keep a poker face and act calm.

Ahh, I just experienced peace of mind. David just lost his.
* * *

Christmas Eve we closed early. I cooked all afternoon. Nick, Lou and Jane were expected over.

Before dinner, with the help of our guests, we decorated our tree. I loved watching Nick carefully select each ornament. I knew it had to be hard for him, knowing that all these ornaments meant something to me and David. As the angel was placed on top by David, I announced dinner.

83

"I made lots of desserts, too. So save room, everybody," I said proudly, holding a glass casserole dish with stuffed zucchini. I placed it down next to the plateful of burning candles.

"Mommy, what possessed you to be Susie homemaker," Taylor asked playfully, a big smirk on her face.

"Taylor, did I mention an elf dropped by and told me how bad you have been. You'll be getting no presents."

"Don't even go there, Mommy," she laughed wickedly.

After dessert, we surprised Tabitha with a calico kitten. She named her Tara.

"Okay Lou, Jane and Nick, I got you all a little something."

"Oh, Keara, I thought we said we weren't exchanging," Jane sighed, adjusting her glasses on her nose. They were too large for her small face.

"I know but I couldn't resist. Here, Jane, open this and shut up."

She tore off the red paper. "Oh, Keara, this is the perfume I wanted. Thank you, thank you so much. Now I just need someone to wear it for."

"Okay, Lou it's your turn." I handed him a silver wrapped box.

He opened the box to find a wine glass with his name etched on it.

"It's for the restaurant, Lou. Now you'll have your own special glass for your red wine."

"Keara, you do think of everything. Thanks."

"And last but not least, Nick. I made you something." I presented him with a rolled up paper tied in a gold ribbon.

He slowly undid the ribbon and uncurled the paper.

"This is incredible. I don't believe it. When did you do this?"

"Let me see it, Nick. Keara wouldn't tell me what she was working on," David said flatly.

David looked and shrugged. "That's nice."

"I called Claudia and arranged a time when you were out to sketch Zeus. He was a real sweetheart or I should say showoff. I think he knew I was drawing him. Look at his eyes."

"You should come down the shelter and draw the dogs and cats. We could give it to the people who adopt them as an extra bonus."

"Don't even think about it, Keara. You are booked solid with parties from now into the spring"

"I have to get going. I have to get up early tomorrow and cook," Jane said uneasyly. "Nick, Lou are you two ready to take me home."

She tucked her short thin brown hair behind her ears.

"One minute, Jane," Nick said. " I have to give Keara her gift. I'll be right back. I left it in my trunk."

He rushed back in holding a brown paper bag.

"Sorry, I didn't wrap it."

I thrust my hand into the bag and pulled out an octagon wooden box. It had a purplish color to it. The lid was glass, trimmed with the purple wood. It was divided into eight sections inside.

"I made it myself. It holds up to five years of AA tokens."

"This is so beautiful, Nick. Wait till everyone in AA sees it. You'll start getting orders."

"Sorry, but you have the one and only."

I had to pull up every strength in my body not to cry and hurl myself into his arms. There was a feeling of awkwardness in the room. Lou broke the spell.

"Come on, Nick, you heard Jane, she wants to go home and I'm tired."

"Yeah, I want to go to bed too, Santa will be here soon. Come on, Tabitha," Taylor said, giving everyone a peck on their cheeks.

I followed behind Taylor kissing everyone. I could feel my face turning crimson as my lips brushed Nick's cheek. My breath caught in my throat as I tried to speak.

"Go-od night everyone," I stammered, clutching my box close to my heart.

* * *

For the next couple of months, I stopped the madness. There was no searching for change. No secret plans to meet. No more lifeguard. I found myself drawing daily at the beach. I was getting more and more into creating images. I loved capturing the seagulls in flight, the sandpipers pecking by the water's edge. Being sober was getting easier. I was still smoking, though.

Meanwhile, David and Nick had decided to sell the restaurant.

They spent their days going over all the offers that came in. David talked a lot about moving away from San Diego. I couldn't imagine being away from Nick.

On Saint Patrick's day, I had to work a big party. I started feeling anxious during breakfast.

"David, I need some stockings for tonight and maybe a new lipstick. I think I'll go out shopping now, this way I can come home and have plenty of time to take a nap before the big event."

"Do you want a nap partner?"

"Of course," I chuckled, leaning over and kissing his forehead. "See you later. Want anything?"

"No. Just have fun."

Well that was just too easy. Should I be paranoid?

The next thing, I was knocking and ringing the bell at Nick's house. My body was one big pins and needles. I couldn't have been more wired if I'd done five lines of coke.

He barely got the door open when I jumped into his arms.

"Oh my God, Nick, I missed you so. I can't believe I'm here."

"Keara, calm down," he laughed, picking me up off the ground.

"You know what would calm me down."

"Uh oh, where is Keara? The evil temptress has returned."

"Come on, Nick, show me how much you missed me," I said excitedly, pulling him towards the bedroom.

"Keara, this isn't a good idea."

"Shh, no more talking."

We went at it like animals in heat. I stroked, he purred. He stroked, I purred. Clawing. Scratching. Biting. It was feeding time at the zoo.

We walked arm in arm to my car.

"Nick, we have to talk sometime soon. I know I've said this a million times but I've been thinking about leaving David again. I feel strong now. I'm okay with my sobriety. I need to be on my own for awhile. I won't even give you any pressure to date me."

"When did all this come about?"

"David is thinking about moving us to another state once the restaurant sells. I decided that I'm not going to go with him. I want to stay here. I can move in with Jane. Anyway, I'd love to talk

86

everything through with you. You have this quiet strength that you emit and it gives me courage. Can you meet me for breakfast sometime this week."

"I guess so."

"See you tonight. Make sure you wear something green."

* * *

The party was jumping. I had everyone on the dance floor twisting. Between my red hair cascading down my back and my emerald green eyes, I looked every bit Irish. I was wearing a green velvet low cut mini dress. I taped my breasts up for major cleavage.

David and Nick were sharing a laugh at the bar. The intoxicated host slipped three hundred dollars down my dress. The tape holding up my breasts was irritating my skin. I wondered if he felt the tape. Who cared? I had the luck of the Irish today. Incredible morning with Nick. Successful party. Cold cash. What more could I ask?

But my luck ran out the very next day. It started with the Mustang. I was headed downtown. I was planning to do some reports and hostess lunch. All of a sudden, the Mustang started acting funny. I didn't know a thing about cars. Just gas and go. I'd never even pumped my own gas.

I exited the highway and found a phone. My first impulse was to call Nick.

I called David and told him my location. Thank God I wasn't near Nick today. David was on his way.

I opened the trunk and removed my journal. Slammed it shut and hopped on top. I lit a cigarette and wrote in my journal till David pulled up.

They had to tow my baby away. It was the transmission. I was in a panic without the Mustang, my getaway car. I loved driving around with the top down. I didn't even bother to put the top up when it rained.

I slipped into the passenger's seat of David's car and threw my journal into the back seat. We arrived at the restaurant just in time for the lunch crowd. I grabbed a couple of menus and started seating people. David took off for the kitchen. Nick was hauling a huge trash can filled with ice to the bar. Lou was in his usual spot at the bar.

Jane sprinted over to me, a pitcher of ice tea in her hand.

"Keara, I have to tell you something. Promise not to freak out in front of everyone."

"Oh no, this is bad."

"Promise me you won't freak."

"Ok, ok, I won't freak. Tell me."

"Sara is trying to fix Nick up with her roommate. She just told me. Lou is behind it."

"Oh my God, I'm gonna freak. Get me a paper bag. I can't breathe."

"Stop. Get it together. You promised. Come on you have to hostess."

"Table for two?" I asked, trying to swallow the lump in my throat. I led them to Jane's section. Sara will never get another table as long as I live. I was filled with rage. Sara was a ditsy blonde waitress who I didn't like anyway. She's dead meat. I had to fire her without David getting suspicious.

I picked up the intercom at the front desk and asked Carlos to meet me here. Carlos, the general manager, was tall, dark and handsome. He looked like a young George Hamilton. I'd covered for him many nights when he was cheating on his wife. He owed me.

"Keara, what's wrong?" he inquired, tugging at his deep purple silk shirt.

"What's wrong? I'll tell you. I'm freaking out. I just heard about Sara. Tell me you don't know about it?"

He looked over his shoulder nervously. "She's a bitch, that one."

"You have to fire her. Think of something. She has to be taught a lesson. You have to send her home now. I can't look at her another minute," I hissed, shaking from head to toe. Suddenly, I was very cold.

"Don't worry, Keara, I'll send her home now. She'll be gone by the end of the week. I'll think of something."

"Thanks, Carlos. I love you."

I motioned to Jane to come over by my hostess stand.

"Carlos is sending her home now. He promises to get rid of the bitch by the end of the week."

"Good. I hate working with her. What are you going to tell Nick?"

"I don't know. Can you cover for me. I'm sick to my stomach. I have to go to the bathroom."

"Sure, go ahead. I only have two tables left."

I raced to the bathroom like my clothes were on fire. What a day. First, my car. Then this bitch. What next?

I crawled into the office with my arms folded across my stomach.

"Keara, you look awful," David said in a worried voice. "What's wrong?"

"I have to go home. It's my stomach, of course. I need to sleep. Can you get the car?"

He jumped up and grabbed his keys. "Nick, can you help her outside?"

David flew through the office door and down the corridor.

"Keara, how did you get this sick?" he asked, sliding his arms around me.

"Is there something you want to tell me?"

"Is that why you are sick?" he asked shocked. "Because of Sara trying to set me up?"

"Yes," I whispered, holding my head down. I was on the verge of tears.

As David pulled up to the house, I started throwing up. I had managed to open the back door and was puking in the driveway. The neighbors probably thought I was back to drinking.

David quickly swept me up in his arms and gently placed me on the bed. He wiped my face with a cool cloth.

"Should I call a doctor? You are so frail and thin, Keara."

"I'll be okay, David. It's probably from working late last night and the Mustang breaking down. You know I can't take so much stress."

"I'm going to go out and get you some soup, crackers and tea."

"Thanks. Please get some ginger ale too."

He kissed my forehead and was off. As I heard the car pull out

89

of the driveway, I realized I'd left my journal in the backseat. The third nightmare. I was going to be sick again.

I was stroking the kitty's head when he appeared in the doorway. It was all over his face.

"Keara, I know you're sick but I'm about to be too."

"You read my journal," I shouted. "That is so low."

"Low is having an affair with my partner," he exploded. "Why, Keara, Why?"

He slumped on the edge of the bed and put his head in his hands and began to cry.

"I must look like one big idiot. Everyone in the restaurant knows, I'm sure. Taylor probably does too, right?"

"Don't cry, David. Please don't cry," I begged, reaching out and touching his shoulder.

He jumped up.

"I'm going to kill him."

David made a fist and slammed it into the wall. There was a crackling sound. He made a hole about the size of a grapefruit.

"Stop. It's my fault. I came on to him. Kill me. I'm no good."

"No. You were vulnerable. You'd stopped drinking. He took advantage of you."

"I'll move out."

"So you can be with that wimp? You are not leaving me for him!"

He sat down beside me.

"We'll have to work this out, Keara. We are a family. I know I wasn't there for you when you stopped drinking and he was. I was wrong but what he did was pure scum."

"What?" I asked weakly, chipping off the polish of my thumb nail. I couldn't make eye contact with him.

He pulled me into his arms.

"I'll fly to New York and rent a place there. You'll move there immediately. I'll stay here with Tabitha till school is over. We'll start fresh in New York but you must never contact Nick again."

"It sounds crazy."

"I'll get a flight tomorrow. I'll take Tabitha. You do what you have to do to get ready to leave. If we stay here, I'll kill Nick and you too."

He was talking and acting like a mad man. I was scared.

"Okay, you win," I said wearily, sinking back on my pillow.

David sprinted up the steps to make calls and I went into shock. I was emotionally exhausted.

The next morning, I drove them to the airport. We drove along in thick heavy silence. There were polite goodbyes at the curb. As soon as their jet was airborne, I raced over to Nick's house.

A look of alarm spread across Nick's face as he opened the door.

"Keara, what are you doing out of bed? You look like you are dying."

"David read my journal. He knows."

Nick instantly paled. "What did he say?" He plopped down into a green bean bag chair.

"You don't want to know."

"Tell me."

"He said he was going to kill you."

I plopped down beside him. "He just took off for New York. He is going to get a place and send me there to live. I'll never see you again. That's the deal." I started to sob and crawled into his lap.

"What deal? Is he going to continue living here?" Nick massaged my back.

"Yes, till Tabitha is out of school. Don't worry, he's never going down to the restaurant again. The sale is about done anyway, as you know."

"Did you ever think of divorcing him?'

"I can't. He'd kill you if I tried," I cried out hysterically. Nick was holding me tight and stroking my hair. "This is it, Nick. We only have a few days left and then I'm gone for good."

We spent the next couple of days together. It was as if I was single and we were really dating. All the burden of getting caught was lifted. We didn't care who saw us. We went to the movies, walks on the beach, breakfast, dinner, a ferry ride. We were inseparable the whole week. A real couple. I had done all these things with David but with Nick everything was brighter. Nick

91

showed me life through the eyes of a child. We were both hoping to go over the rainbow. I didn't want to go back to Kansas.

What a world! What a world!

Our last night together we decided to dress up and eat at a fancy Italian restaurant. I suggested we give one another something of ours that we cherished.

We were sitting outside the restaurant in Nick's car. I wanted to exchange before we ate. I slipped my hand into the brown shopping bag and pulled out Barney. I fought back the tears.

Barney was my pink stuffed dog. He had a pot belly and red ears. Barney had slept beside my bed for ten years. He was my security blanket. He had also flown everywhere with me. He was my good luck charm.

"Here, I want you to have Barney. You know how much I love him. Now he'll watch over you. Please take good care of him," I said, trying to swallow the lump in my throat.

"I can't take Barney. He's your life!"

"No, you must. Oh, I have one more thing. Here's my journal. I want you to have it. You can read it and know just how I've felt about you all this time," I whispered, wiping away my tears.

Nick reached into his pocket and handed me a gold number eighty.

"This is from my tassel, when I graduated. It's my lucky piece and now it'll be yours," he said softly, tears splashing down his face.

"Nick, why couldn't we be together?"

"I think it's safe to say that the number one reason would be because David would kill me."

David and Tabitha came home the next day. They couldn't wait to tell me about New York. David had rented a cottage on Long Island, about ten minutes from Taylor. It was practically on the bay. Jack would also be going with me. David had leased a brand new black Jeep Cherokee for me to use there. He handed me my one way ticket. I would be leaving in three days. I couldn't believe that I was buying into this whole thing.

Why wasn't anyone yelling "April Fool".

I packed and cried, cried and packed. I went to Amber, my

hairdresser, and instructed her to chop off all my hair. I then dyed it honey blonde and changed my contacts to a deep purple.

My last night, I went to AA and received my nine months token from Heather.

Ever the drama queen, I confessed my affair to the group. I told everyone how my husband was giving me a second chance in New York. I received quite an applause.

I lit up a cigarette in the parking lot and was getting my keys out when I saw him. Nick was leaning against his car watching me. I threw down the cigarette and ran into his arms. We spent the next hour crying and hugging.

"Promise me, you'll find a way to visit me somehow. Promise me," I begged.

"I promise, Keara. I'll get there somehow," he said in a quiet voice.

We hugged one last time. I couldn't believe he never kissed me. That's all I could think of driving home by the beach. Top down. Stars shining over me. Gentle ocean breeze. He couldn't even kiss me goodbye! It took all my strength not to drive the Mustang into the fucking ocean.

Goodbye, San Diego.

Hello, New York.

* * *

Part Two

New York

The plane was about to land at JFK in ten minutes. I was wondering how Jack was doing underneath. I wasn't doing so well on top. How was I going to live without Nick, the beach, my friends, AA and the restaurant? East coast and West coast were two different worlds.

I slung my green LL Bean bag over my shoulder and headed down to baggage. My ears were still ringing from the landing. The depression had settled in every bone and was flowing through my veins. I went to the section where they would bring Jack out.

Joan Rivers was waiting there also. She looked so tiny. All my life I'd wanted to meet her. Now she was standing next to me in a pink Chanel suit. I wanted to tell her how much my parents loved her and how much I enjoyed her show but nothing came out. Two men finally carried Jack's cage out to the floor. He was all scrunched up. Joan walked over and peeked in.

"What kind of dog is that?" she inquired.

"A Great Dane," I said flatly, opening his cage to coax him out.

Just then Taylor, Alexis and Greg came bursting through the doors. I could tell they were all stoned.

"Joan Rivers," they all shouted at once. "Hi Joan."

She smiled back at them and said hello.

"Hi, guys," I said softly, hugging them one at a time. "Let's get out of here. I can hardly hear and Jack is a nervous wreck."

We helped Jack up into Greg's green Jeep. The plan was to meet at Kylie's and from there we would all go to my new place. No running out tonight and meeting Nick. No driving the Mustang by the beach listening to the crashing waves. No more climbing up on stage and spinning records. No more Nick.

Somebody fill up the tub and get me a razor, please.

Kylie and Spencer were in the driveway with big smiles and a water bowl for Jack. I jumped out of the Jeep into their arms. Jack lapped up the water like he was just rescued from the desert. Everyone raved over my new look but were concerned about my

95

weight.

It was time to go to the cottage that David had rented in Huntington Bay. I gave Taylor money to stop and pick up pizzas and drinks. Everyone got in their cars. I went back in Greg's with Jack. Greg was cool about the spit. The caravan started to my new location and life. There wasn't one palm tree. Worse. There wasn't even blue skies. It was drizzling, cold and damp.

I was sent to hell for my crime of passion. Just give me the scarlet A to put on my chest, already.

Greg made a left into a long winding muddy driveway. At the end, sat the cottage from hell. I knew David was angry but what was he thinking. The grass surrounding the place was waist high. Were we in Kansas? I wanted to click my heels so bad and be back in Nick's arms.

The outside of the house was screaming for a paint job. We entered through the porch, which was a slab of concrete with a broken down roof over it. The first room off the porch was the kitchen. It had no refrigerator and the floor had cheap white vinyl squares that were either chipped or broken. The rest of the house had dull stained wooden floors and all the walls were dirty white. The living room had a fireplace and a huge bay window. No curtains anywhere. Upstairs were two small bedrooms and a bathroom. The cottage was filled with dust and cobwebs. No one had occupied it for two years. The bathroom had a big old fashion tub but it was rusted inside. The shower looked like it had never been cleaned. The only piece of furniture was an old phone in the middle of the living room. It was the kind you had to dial with your finger.

Kylie and the girls were lighting candles and laying down blankets from Kylie's house in the dining room. Taylor was handing out pizza. Taylor, Alexis and Greg had also invited some of their friends over. Jack was nervously chewing on his new Mexican blanket. I had bought him one just before the trip. The smell of pot and greasy pizza was drifting through the rooms.

I slowly dialed David's number blinking back the tears.

"Hello," he answered, anxiously

"Hi. I'm here."

"Well, what do you think?"

"Were you on crack when you rented this?"

"It was cheap and I thought we'd have fun fixing it up together. The landlord said we could do whatever we want to do to it. He's bulldozing it down next year."

"Why wait," I said sarcastically, reaching for some hair to twirl but it was too short.

"What's all the noise? Who's there?"

"Everyone. I'll call you tomorrow. I'm exhausted and I have a house full of people."

"Don't worry, Keara. We'll turn the house into a palace."

"Sure, David. Goodnight."

I hung up the phone and wished I could join the party. I plopped down on the blanket next to Kylie and Spencer.

I talked everyone in the room into sitting in a circle around the candles, holding hands and chanting Nick's name. Since everyone was mostly high it didn't take a lot of persuading. Just then, the phone rang. Taylor jumped up and ran into the living room. It was Nick. Wow. I suggested they try Elvis as I sprinted out of the room to speak to Nick. Taylor hugged me and handed the receiver to me like it was a piece of gold.

"I'm so glad to hear from you."

"I said I would call."

"I know. I was just scared. I had all my friends chanting your name and then you called."

"Uh oh, you're not going to get a doll next are you?"

"Only if I don't see you soon."

"How's the new place?"

"It's awful. I'm in the middle of the woods. The place is a hell-hole. I hate it."

"I'm sure it's not that bad. I always wanted to live in the woods. Try and make the best of it. Why don't you write me and tell me all about it in a letter. Better yet, how about drawing me a picture?"

"Oh Nick, I don't know if I can make it without you," I whimpered, pulling off an acrylic nail.

"Keara, you have new challenges now. You'll make it. Don't

cry."

"I miss you so much, already."

"I miss you too."

This, of course, sent me into hysterical sobbing. "Call me tomorrow, Nick. Please."

"I will. Now go back in with Taylor and your friends and enjoy yourself. No more tears."

"I love you, Nick. Bye."

I hung up the phone and collapsed into a heap on the floor sobbing.

Please God, help me get through this. I'll baptize Tabitha. I'll go to church again. Please I'll do anything. Just help me.

Kylie came rushing in and flopped down beside me. She started rubbing my back.

"Come on, Keara, I'll help you get through this," she said softly, handing me a napkin.

I blew my nose into the rough napkin. "I really love him."

"I know you do. But he made no effort to stop you. Did he? He has no money and still lives with mommy. What's wrong with that picture? Whereas David is fighting to put you two back together."

"I know. I'll be alright," I mumbled, trying to muster up a smile.

We scrambled to our feet and went back to join the party. It broke up after midnight.

Taylor and Adam slept over. Their relationship was hanging on by a thread. Adam talked soothingly to me about how I made the right decision to stay with my family. Forget Nick. I snuggled up against Taylor. We were lying on top of two blankets. The hardwood floor was uncomfortable. Of course, I couldn't get to sleep all night.

I had the same chance of forgetting Nick as I had to be President.

The next morning, Taylor left for school and Adam for work. I eased myself off the floor and took Jack for a tour of the neighborhood. My mood was the same as the sky, black. There was going to be a downpour soon. Jack was still acting confused.

98

The move had aged him overnight. He was ten, which was very old for a Dane. They usually only made it to eight or nine. Jack was peeing at the stop sign on the corner when the sky opened up. The rain teemed down on us as we scurried to the porch for cover.

I lit up a cigarette as we stood on the porch watching the rain. A white van pulled up. David had ordered me a twin mattress to sleep on till ours was shipped. I had the delivery guy place it in the dining room against the wall. Kylie had given me some sheets, pillows and a comforter in a black and white pattern. I placed some candles around the mattress and on the window-sill. I lifted Nick's box from my suitcase and set it by the side of the bed. There. I had made a little studio. The phone shattered the silence.

"Hello, how is New York this morning?" David asked brightly, on the other end.

"It's cold and rainy," I answered in disgust, lighting a cigarette.

"Keara, do you have to smoke so much?"

"Yeah. There is nothing else to do. The weather sucks. This place sucks. I fucking hate it here. It's really ugly. You're punishing me, aren't you?"

"Calm down. The Jeep will be delivered by the end of the week. I'll be in next week to check on you. We'll go shopping,okay?"

"Okay. Look, I have to go. I need to go get breakfast. It'll take me awhile to walk into town."

"I'll call you tonight. I love you, Keara. Don't worry, everything will be fine."

"Yeah, bye," I said stiffly, dropping my cigarette in a styrofoam cup. It was half filled with coke from the night before.

I flopped down on the edge of the mattress and put my head in my hands. I felt like I was going to lose it. My head was about to explode into tiny pieces. My heart already had. Panic started rushing up inside me. The phone rang out again. My heart started beating wildly as I scrambled to my feet.

"Hello," I said, squeezing my eyes shut tight.

"Hi," Nick said in a low tone.

"I can't take it anymore, Nick. I am going insane," I blurted out in one breath.

"Take it easy. Take a deep breath and relax. Now tell me what's wrong?"

"Everything," I mumbled, lighting a cigarette and inhaling deeply.

"Keara, must you smoke. Please stop."

"I can't. If I don't smoke, I know I'll drink now. I'm feeling unglued."

"You're in New York. Take in a play with Taylor. Go shopping with Kylie. I thought you were going to start painting seriously."

"I just want to be with you, Nick"

"Keara, I have to get on with my life."

"You're seeing Sara's friend, aren't you?" I sobbed, lighting another cigarette from the old one.

"That's none of your business," he growled. "I have to go. I am running up my mom's phone bill."

"Why can't you get your own phone?"

"I will have it by the end of the week."

"You're expecting a call from her!"

"No. I think it's time I got my own number. Maybe, we should talk another time."

I flung myself on the twin mattress and cried myself to sleep. Jack curled up beside me chewing on his pink and blue blanket.

I spent the rest of the week surrounded by Taylor and friends. Taylor would drag me out every night. We played pool, went to the movies, had Sushi dinners and sleep overs. Stella, an old friend, came by during the day and we shopped. I bought navy blue plates and glasses with gold stars on them. Black and white towels. Silverware. Lots of candles. Kayla lent me her round wooden dining room table with four wooden chairs trimmed in blue. Kylie helped me pick out beige curtains with blue hearts on them for the dining room. My mattress was still in there. I was just living out of one room.

Kayla was stopping by a lot. She was my age. We met when I moved next door to her during my first marriage. We became fast friends. Cancer had ravaged her body. She wore a baseball cap at all times. Underneath was just some fuzz. She was down to eighty pounds and whiter than a ghost. Kayla always had a warm smile for me. She had a fighter's attitude. She was not letting this killer disease get her down.

My Jeep Cherokee finally arrived. It was black with beige interior. The first day I drove it, a spark from my cigarette flew off and burned a tiny hole in the passenger seat. The seats were felt. Of course, I had just given David my word that I wouldn't smoke in the car. I bought a paint set and found a color as close as possible and painted over it. It looked like it could have been a dried coffee stain. David was color blind, so I figured I could get away with it.

I stayed up every night writing Nick long letters. I wrote about ten pages a night by candle light. I sketched him some pictures of the house, too.

I found a phone booth by the supermarket that was only seventy-five cents for three minutes to California. All the other phones were either two dollars or three. I'd stop at the Laundromat and get ten dollars worth of quarters to call Nick.

Like a little kid with a shiny new toy, I spilt open the brown wrapper. I laid out all my quarters on the edge of the phone. Quarters and phone booths brought me great joy these days. I plunked my quarters in and called Nick on his new number.

"Hello," he mumbled.

"Hi. Did I wake you? I can't get used to this time difference. I'm sorry for calling this early but I couldn't wait," I said nervously, rummaging in my purse for a cigarette.

"I was up. Relax, Keara. I'm doing numbers for the restaurant. The sale is almost done."

"How's it going?" I asked, lighting a cigarette.

"You're still smoking?"

"I know, I know. I already burnt a hole in the Jeep."

"David bought you a brand new Jeep."

"Yeah. It was part of the deal. I love it. It's cool."

"Do you miss the Mustang?"

"No. I love the Jeep. I like being high up looking down on the other cars."

"I always wanted a Jeep."

"Get one?"

"I can't afford it. I put everything into the restaurant. We just break even on the sale. Plus, I originally borrowed the money from my Mom. I have to pay her back."

"I'm sorry, Nick, for the way things turned out."

"It's not your fault the restaurant turned out the way it did. It was losing money. We had to sell anyway."

"Did you get my letters and drawings?"

"Yes. I have been saving them in a shoe box to take down to our cafe and read them at breakfast. This way I can pretend you are there with me. I framed the sketch of your house."

This of course pushed me over the edge.

"Oh, Nick, that is so beautiful." Tears started to well up in my eyes.

"I miss our breakfasts," he whispered sincerely.

"Nick, are you still seeing that girl?"

"We had one date and I decided that was enough. I guess I'm not ready to date."

"It's hell being without you."

"Keara, you have to make the best of New York. You know I'm here for you always."

I was down to my last seventy-five cents.

"Nick, I have no more quarters left. Can you call me next?"

"When?"

"David will be here the weekend. So call me Monday morning. Seven your time, ten mine."

"No problem. Take care, Keara."

"Bye, Nick," I sighed, lighting another cigarette.

I staggered away from the phone, picturing in my mind Nick reading my letters at our cafe. I passed by Dunkin Donuts. Taylor and her friends were inside drinking coffee. It was still weird for me after all these years in California to run into Taylor in town. On one hand I loved it but on the other it made me aware I was in New York. Three thousand miles away from Nick.

"Mommy, get in here," Taylor yelled out into the street. "Why are you walking in the rain?"

"What does it matter?" I mumbled, raking my pink nails through my wet hair.

"Oh no, she just talked to Nick everyone. Suicide watch. She is going to fill up the tub now."

"Very funny, Taylor. David's coming to my studio this weekend."

"Oh Mommy, you'll have fun. Now, go home. Put on dry clothes and take a nap. I'll be over later and we'll do Sushi."

"Thanks, Taylor. Bye, Everybody."

Outside, the rain blended in with my tears. The cold penetrated my body but I felt nothing but heartache.

Will it ever go away? Please help me, Lord. Daddy, if you're up there, help.

* * *

I settled on my new black and white long dress for David's homecoming. As I was deciding on how many buttons to leave undone, the phone rang.

It was Kylie. She wanted to meet me at Friday's on Jericho turnpike right now. She sounded distraught. She would clue me in when I got there. I knew it was going to be about Christian, her boyfriend. Christian was half Spanish and half French. He looked like Jimmy Smits but with a French accent. Kylie was always catching him in some lie or situation. Then she'd have a mini breakdown and we'd talk on the phone for hours.

I spotted her white BMW and pulled up next to it. She jumped immediately into my passenger's seat.

"Thanks for meeting me," she said, her voice laced with pain.

"No problem. I don't have to be at the airport till midnight. What's up?"

"That bastard. I know he's over at Jana's tonight. I just want to catch him. See him with my own eyes. Then maybe I can break it off with him. Can you drive me to Jana's?'

"We are both in the same boat. That's why I'm not in San Diego. I'd be stalking Nick right now too. Where does she live?" I asked, driving toward the expressway.

"She lives out by the Hamptons. Thanks for doing this."

"Don't be silly."

We chained smoke the ride out there. We were about a block away from Jana's apartment when Kylie spotted Christian's Jaguar driving on the other side of the highway.

"There he is," she shrieked. "That fucking bastard. Don't lose him, Keara."

Her face looked like she just witnessed a violent murder. I looped the Jeep around and gave it the gas. The Mustang would be good for this chase. The Jeep was too clumsy.

"Pull up beside him," she yelled, fumbling for the button on the door to make the window go down.

We were side by side on the highway. Kylie was hanging out the window screaming fuck you at Christian. Christian had a shocked look on his face. He drove faster.

"Don't lose him," Kylie screamed, her whole body shaking like it was below zero outside.

He finally pulled over by his apartment building. We were right behind him. He stomped over to the passenger's side.

"Get out of the car, Kylie. We have to talk in private," he demanded, his fingers drumming on the window.

"No. Whatever you have to say, you can say it in front of Keara. You told me it was over with Jana. You're a fucking liar. I never want to see you again," Kylie hissed. "Let's go, Keara."

"Wait, Kylie, let's talk, please."

"No. I hate you, you fucking bastard. Let's go, Keara, now."

I flew out into traffic and headed back for Fridays. What a trip! Was this a lesson for me or what? This could have been me in San Diego with Jane driving, chasing Nick. My heart went out for Kylie.

"I don't know what to say, Kylie. I know what you must be feeling," I said softly, reaching out for her hand. She just sat there in a state of shock. "Do you want to go to the airport with me? Maybe you shouldn't go home like this."

"I'll be okay. I'm sorry about all this."

"Don't be crazy. I'm here for you."

I cut the engine and leaned over. I squeezed her tight. "I love you, Kylie. Call me."

I hated leaving her this way but I had to get to the airport. David would not appreciate my reason for being late. Chasing a married woman's boyfriend. Too close for comfort.

* * *

The weekend turned out to be fun. David found someone to cut the grass. We picked out new tiles for the kitchen floor. We even ended up with a new member in the family. A black and white long haired cat, about a year old. One of the girls from David's new office was taking him to a shelter. David couldn't let that happen so I acquired a new roommate. Jack immediately bonded with his new playmate. The cat wasn't really thrilled. I named him Bruce after Bruce Willis, whom I love.

The twin mattress was uncomfortable with two. Jack kept trying to sneak on too. There was not much sleep.

"I love you, Keara," David whispered, kissing my neck. "See, everything works out. This house will be beautiful once we fix it up. I'm going to get us tickets to Seattle. What do you think about Seattle?"

"I don't mind the rain," I said with sincerity, already calculating the miles between San Diego and Seattle.

After David left, I went back to my usual routine. Shopping. Hanging out with friends. Spying on Christian. Dinner with Taylor. Candlelight letters to Nick. Passionately sketching my surroundings.

Taylor graduated from High School on her eighteenth birthday. A miracle considering she never went to class or did homework. During the party her father threw at his house, everyone kept asking me if I was sick. I did look ghastly. When I wasn't smoking, I was brooding. I rarely ate because it always made me sick.

I went to see my ex husband's doctor who's been treating me since I was twenty. He prescribed Pepcid for my ulcer and some mild tranquilizers for my nerves. Gave me a diet to follow and set up some tests. Nothing for the broken heart, though.

David flew in one more time, bringing with him Tara, the kitten. She hit it off immediately with Bruce. Now Jack had two fur balls to chase through the house.

We purchased a white wicker set for the living room. A love seat, two chairs and a coffee table. We hung up the paintings he had shipped in earlier. Put up some lace curtains and threw down a black and white area rug. We picked out some colorful cushions for the wicker and some cute throw pillows. I was losing my studio.

"The living room looks great," David said excitedly, straightening the painting over the fireplace. "It's the first time in years we have something to sit on."

"You know the only reason we couldn't have furniture before was because of Jack eating it. It wasn't worth it," I shrugged, filling up the bay window with huge potted plants.

"Maybe we should have just gotten him trained, instead of not having furniture. That would have been normal."

"What is normal? Let's face it. We are just not your normal couple."

"Is there a mouse in your pocket? You're the crazy one. I'm just along for the ride."

"Oh really, what about birds of a feather flock together," I smiled wickedly, picking up Tara and kissing her head.

"How about we go to your studio and really get crazy."

As I was faking my orgasm, I heard Taylor's car in the driveway. David had just screamed out for real.

"David, I hear Taylor, get off."

I pulled up the covers over us just as Taylor barged in the door.

"Mommy, David, where are you guys?" she yelled, as the porch door slammed.

She entered my studio and stopped dead in her tracks. "Oh gross, get dressed or I'll throw up," she groaned, covering her eyes with her fingers.

"Nice to see you too, Taylor," I said sarcastically, as I grabbed my sweatshirt off the floor.

"David, thank you so much for the Rolex. It was the best birthday, graduation present. I adore it," she shrieked, running over and hugging him. "I love you."

"I love you too, Taylor. I'm so proud of you. Graduating without going to class. Now that is unique," David chuckled, ducking as Taylor threw a pillow at him.

"I went to class sometimes," she whined, playfully smacking him. "Listen you guys, I'm shot girl tonight at Duffy's Tavern. Be there. That's why I came by, to make sure you two are there. I have to get going. Adam is taking me to dinner before I start."

"We'll be there, Taylor. You can sell me Seven-Up shots."

"Next month is your year, Mommy. I'm so proud of you."

"Yeah, who would have thought I'd make it a year?"

"I did, I did," they both yelled in unison.

We did a group hug and Taylor vanished.

"I really miss Tabitha. It's been a long time since I've seen her. How is she holding up?"

"She's great. This weekend her friends are throwing her a big party at Emma's. She is really excited about coming to New York. She can't wait to see Bruce. She's hoping that Tara and Bruce get together and have kittens."

"Oh no, from crazy house to animal house," I groaned, reaching for my cigarette pack by the bed.

"She's been through a lot. If she wants kittens maybe we should let her have kittens."

"Sure and we can have fun watching the cats do it."

"You're sick, Keara, very sick."

"I know, I know."

David flew back to San Diego. The plan was for him to drive the Mustang with Tabitha to New Orleans. Then I would fly with Taylor and Adam to New Orleans to meet them there. Party for a few days. Then Adam and Taylor would fly back with Tabitha. I would drive the rest of the way with David. The only thing wrong with the plan was I wouldn't be able to call Nick.

I wanted him to visit me in New York. It would be perfect with David driving across country. It was a safe plan. I desperately needed to see him. Nick wouldn't give in.

Fighting back tears, I blew out the last candle. The vanilla scent drifted up into my nostrils. I just finished another ten page letter to Nick begging him to be with me. I was pathetic. I needed to get some sleep. Tomorrow I'd be leaving for New Orleans. When I returned, there would be no more studio. As I settled in bed with Jack, the phone rang. Maybe it was Nick, picking up all my vibes tonight. Maybe he finally realized we have to be together.

Am I the Queen of fantasy or what? Am I smoking crack?

"Hello," I mumbled, crossing my fingers, hoping to hear Nick's voice.

"Mommy," Taylor sobbed. "It's over with Adam. I hate him. He is not coming to New Orleans."

"What happened," I sighed, grabbing my cigarettes.

"I was shot girl tonight and just doing my job. Adam came in and thought I was with some guy. He pushed me into a wall. Then the bouncers were on top of him and dragged him out, kicking and screaming. I hate him."

"Were you with the other guy?" I asked, inhaling deeply on the Marlboro Light.

"Not really. This guy bought my whole tray of shots and tipped me fifty dollars. So I gave him a little peck. That's what Adam saw. The next thing I knew, he was out of control. You have to call him, Mommy. He is not going. I fucking hate him."

"Taylor, calm down. I'll call him and then I'll call you back." I dialed Adam's number.

"Hello, Adam. Sorry to call you this late but Taylor is hysterical."

"Did she tell you what happened."

"I thought I'd hear your side and maybe get a little sleep before the plane."

"I walk into Duffy's and there she is drunk out of her mind with her tongue down some guy's throat. So I lost it. I don't want her working there. I love her."

"How about we all go to New Orleans. You two can get back together there. New Orleans is so much fun and it's romantic too. Are you still going?"

"I want to go. She doesn't want me to go."

"I'll talk to her and everything will be fine tomorrow. See you at eight. Goodnight."

I called back Taylor.

"Taylor, he's coming, don't argue with your mother."

"I hate him."

"No you don't. You are going to have so much fun there with him. I promise you, you will thank me for this. Please make up. Now get some sleep. I love you, Taylor. Goodnight."

"Thanks, Mommy. Goodnight."

Taylor and Adam got back on track in New Orleans. They

drank, sang at the Karoke bars, and gambled to the wee hours of the morning on the River boat.

I had a warm reunion with Tabitha. We spent our days swimming and sightseeing. Our nights, strolling on Bourbon Street and shopping.

One of the reasons David probably picked New Orleans to meet was that we were married there. On the river boat, Natchez, going down the Mississippi River at twilight. My boss, David Forrest, whom I called Ranger, had given me away. After the ceremony, we took the wedding party to Bourbon Street and I got David a stripper and he got me one. We were wild, young, passionate and drunk. Both set of parents had vowed to disown us if we married. We had known one another only three months.

David was most likely hoping to rekindle some kind of spark from those days. I gave it my best shot but I knew it was flat. We kissed the kids goodbye at the airport and started out journey home. Who was I kidding on this trip? Trying to get back our love and passion. I was just trying to stay sane. Every time we passed a phone booth, images of Nick, spun around and around my head as we drove towards New York.

In Savannah, I stepped on a mound of red ants barefoot. There were thousands on my legs biting me before I knew what hit me. The next day, my legs were painfully swollen and I was feverish. I actually welcomed this different pain.

By Washington, I was better. We stopped by to see Spencer, Kylie's daughter. It felt good to be around someone I could exchange glances with and know no words were needed. We spent the night with Spencer and started for our new home, New York, in the morning.

"We're almost home. How do you feel about everything?" David asked watching me carefully.

I forced a smile. "I'm sure New York will be fun. All our friends are there. Taylor is so happy we are back." My eyes glazed with tears.

David's eyes widened. "I want to know what you're feeling about us? I feel you were not really here the whole trip."

Oh well, might as well milk these tears.

"I'm so sorry for everything I put you through, David," I said, my voice trembling. "I'll try to make you happy in New York."

David brushed away a single tear on my cheek. "Don't cry, Keara. We're together now, that is all that matters."

New York was hot, sticky and unbearable if you didn't have an air conditioner. David bought one for our bedroom. Our bedroom consisted of a queen sized mattress on the floor, two oak dressers, that Stella's friend lent us and a thirteen inch television. In other words, depressing and gloomy.

If I didn't take Tabitha to the mall or a movie, we were stuck in the bedroom from hell. I had to use my inhaler if I wanted to walk outside. The heat was suffocating.

I spent the summer swimming in a sea of pain. Kayla died suddenly and I didn't get to say goodbye. I had loved spending time with her again and renewing our friendship. Stella moved to Florida. I missed my life in San Diego. I was constantly fighting with Nick on the phone. Jack started having trouble walking and was having accidents all over the house. Tabitha broke her leg playing tennis. Taylor's fights escalated with Adam to calling the cops to break them up. Tara, our kitten, was pregnant.

"Keara, you're still hung up on Nick," David said flatly, propping his elbows on the pillow.

I was laying on my back, staring at the ceiling. The room was dimly lit by the half moon. There were no curtains on the windows.

"What makes you say that?" I challenged, my heart starting to race at the mention of Nick's name.

"Do you think I don't know you are crying yourself to sleep or that I don't see your depression. You never touch me. I can go on and on."

"I'm just depressed because of it's so hot here. The house is gross. Jack is dying. I can go on and on."

"Why can't you just admit it's Nick?"

"Okay, it's Nick. Are you happy?"

"Why, Keara? He is a loser. He lives with his mother. He has no money. What is the fascination with him? I don't get it," David grumbled, pounding his fist into the pillow.

"I don't know why. He always made me feel good. He treated

110

me different. I can't explain it."

"The only reason you are with me now is because he didn't want you."

"That is not true, David. We are a family. I picked New York. I didn't want him, I wanted you."

"Honest?" he asked, pulling me into his arms.

"I swear," I whispered, pulling his Bugs Bunny boxers off. "Fuck me, David."

I am nothing but a whore. I need a team of shrinks.

* * *

Summer was coming to a end. We were getting ready to fly off to Seattle. Tabitha was going back to San Diego to visit friends. Lucky dog. Taylor had broken up with Adam for the millionth time. Jack was chewing on a red checkered Mexican blanket. Our friends now sent them in for him. Tara's stomach was so swollen she looked like a float in Macy's parade. David was doing well at the firm. I had gained some weight and started to look healthy.

I was packing my hiking boots for Seattle when I heard the phone ring. I raced down the creaking stairs into the living room and grabbed the phone.

"Hello," I said, trying to catch my breath.

"Hello, remember me?" the voice asked on the other line.

"Oh my God, Ranger. How did you find me?" I shrieked, raking my frosted nails through my blonde hair.

His real name was David Forrest. He had given me away at my wedding. I used to teasingly call him Forest Ranger. Then Ranger just stuck. Fifteen years ago I worked for him as a receptionist. I came in stoned, snorted coke and always came back from lunch drunk. The reception area was like a three-ring circus. The customers loved me on the phone and in person. Business started booming. We started an affair. His cock was the size of Florida. He had no looks just major charisma. A born salesman.

"You know, you're the only person on earth who calls me Ranger."

"You didn't answer my question. How did you know I was back?"

"Word gets around. Are you back for good?"

111

"Just a year. Then it's off again. You know I hate New York. The weather sucks here."

"I still love you."

"You're crazy," I giggled. "Is that why you called?"

"No. I have a job offer for you. I'm the President of a new company and I need an assistance. It still involves video games. You know, we were the best team, Keara. What do you say?"

"I've been a D.J. for the past six years. I haven't been in a real office since I worked for you."

"You'll have your own office. There are two other guys in charge but you'll mainly work for me. You'll know a lot of the old customers. You'll be running the show."

"I'm on my way to Seattle right now for a week. Can I think about it? I'll call you when I get back in town."

"Sure. You're the only one for the job. It's nine to five, Monday to Friday. The salary is up to you, whatever you think is fair. Think about it."

"I will. I'll call you as soon as I get back. Oh, and Ranger."

"What?"

"I missed you."

"Not as much as I missed you."

I slowly placed the phone back in the cradle and started pacing. I punched in Kylie's number.

"Hi, Keara," Greg answered.

"How did you know it's me?"

"I'm psychic."

"More like psycho. Put your mother on, now."

"Hi, Keara. What's wrong?" she asked cautiously.

"Before I tell you, tell me how Greg knows it's me all the time."

"Caller ID."

"Oh God and I might go back out into the working world."

"What are you talking about?"

"Ranger just called me and asked me to work for him. I'm flipping out."

"I don't believe it. How did he know you were here? Are you going to?"

"You know, Ranger. He's not saying who told him. I'm

112

thinking I might say yes. Do you know why?"

"No. I know David won't be happy if you do, though."

"Kylie, think about it. An office. Phones, fax machines. I can call and fax Nick till my heart's content and he can call and fax me. It's perfect."

"What about David?"

"I can handle him. Besides, I'm going crazy in this house day after day."

"I can't believe you'll be working for Dave again."

"Crazy, isn't it? What are you doing home? How come you're not out with Christian?"

"I'm just sneaking out now. Everyone thinks I'm going shopping meanwhile I have a chicken sandwich, cookies and a mini bottle of wine in my purse. I'm meeting Christian on his break. He'll eat in the car and I'll give him a blow job."

"I'm jealous. I'd love to be meeting Nick now and doing the same," I confessed in a whisper, a rush of pain going through my chest.

"Listen, Keara, one more thing I have to tell you. My friend, Tori, she went to Seven Eleven and bought a phone card. You call an eight hundred number and then some code and then his number. It's all paid for and doesn't show up on your bill. No more quarters and you can call from home. Tori buys them by the dozen. Her boyfriend lives in Jersey."

"This is a miracle. I have to have one. You just made my day. A job offer and a phone card. I'm in heaven. Thanks, Kylie. I love you. I'll call you when I get back. Have fun with Christian."

I started nervously pacing again. This called for a cigarette. I would have to go on the porch to smoke. Tabitha was upstairs watching television and she was a human smoke alarm. She went nuts if I smoked in the house.

I stepped over Jack's accident. I'd pick it up later. I had to figure out what to say to David about Ranger. David hated Ranger with a passion. Ranger was behind David's downfall in business. He screwed him to the wall. I should hate him too but I just couldn't be mad at Ranger.

It was Ranger who set me up with David. David walked in one

day and bought a million dollars worth of equipment from Ranger with one condition. That I'd have lunch with him. I refused. Ranger begged. I relented. I went to lunch with David and knew he was the one. I came back from lunch and broke up with Ranger, left my husband, and broke up with all my boyfriends and girlfriends. David was okay with the girls though. He kinda liked that part about me.

I was grinding out my cigarette on the porch when David zipped into the driveway.

"Hey, I thought you quit. No smoking in Seattle, remember?" he scowled, his jaw clenched.

"We're not in fucking Seattle yet."

David stopped as he entered the kitchen. "Keara, look what Jack did. This is every fucking day now," he moaned, his hands on his hips, giving Jack a dirty look.

"It's not his fault. Don't you yell at him," I snapped, running over and hugging Jack. "I'll clean it up."

Taylor was going to have a cow taking care of the house. Between Jack, the pregnant cat, the wild new one, Taylor would be nuts. She didn't share my love of animals but Taylor was easily bought. A shopping trip to the mall would shut her up. Tabitha was the arts and crafts type. For David it was sex, missionary style, nothing fancy.

* * *

I had been too distracted by Ranger's call to enjoy Seattle.

"So, is Seattle our new city?" David asked playfully, stretching out his legs on the plane.

I put down my magazine and forced a smile. "I have to think about it."

I tried to smother my fear. "You're not going to believe it. Ranger called me and he has a new company and wants me to run it. I don't know how he found out we were back."

David's face turned scarlet. "Ranger, that snake, and you didn't hang up."

"I know he screwed us big time but he can't do it again. Maybe if I work for him, I can get something on him now. Besides he'll pay me a lot. He has a big company now. It could mean clients for you."

"You sound like you are taking this job," he said, outraged. "Keara, he wanted to see me fail so he could try and get you."

"But he didn't get me. He knows he could never get me away from you. He knows how much I love you. No one can break us up, David. Our love is too strong."

I could see David's anger fading.

"Do you really want to work in an office again?" he asked, frowning. "Won't you be tempted to drink and do drugs again. Ranger knows how to push your buttons. He'll try and get you to drink."

"You're probably right. But I'm strong now. I've been sober for a year. There is no way I'm gonna blow it now. I worked too hard. Besides, I've been so bored at home. This would keep me so busy. This job will be a challenge. I'll have my own office. Plus it's near Taylor's college. Please, David, don't be mad. I want to work."

"Sometimes, Keara, I think you're acting. Like everything is a joke to you," he smiled crookedly, stroking my arm. "Does anyone know the real you?"

"I love you, David. That's all you need to know," I said, willing my purple eyes to radiate love.

I need a cigarette. Why did I quit? Help me Lord.

The next morning we woke to a light rain. It would be autumn soon in New York. One of the seasons I missed in San Diego. I was going to have to change this blond hair. An autumn red, maybe with some green contacts. I helped David pick out a tie and some socks. He was so color blind that without help everyone in the office made him the joke of the day with one sock black and one maroon. He worked in an office of over three hundred brokers.

I kissed him goodbye and watched him pull out of the driveway. I waited a couple of minutes before I dialed Ranger's private number.

"Hello," he answered, sharply.

"I'm back from Seattle."

"So you're the one who brought this rain," he laughed softly into the phone.

115

"I told David, I want to work for you."

"What did he say?"

"I'm a lady, I can't repeat it."

"I think I have a pretty good idea."

"So, when do I start. I'm rusty, you know. I'm also sober and clean. No more drugs. I've never worked before where I was straight, you know."

"Keara, congratulations. You'll be great. You do everything great. How about starting tomorrow at eight-thirty. I'll bring in some bagels and I'll show you around your new office."

"I'll be there."

I hung up elated. All I could think about was having access to calling Nick and him being able to call me. Nick. It had been so long since I'd heard his voice. The familiar tightening sensation came across my chest with the thought of him. I picked up the phone and punched in 1-800- Collect. I mumbled a quick prayer that he'd answer.

I heard him accept the charges. I glanced up at the clock and counted back three. It was six in the morning for him.

"Guess what?"

"It's too early for me to guess?"

"I got a job. Do you believe it? I'm going to work in a real office with real people."

"Slow down and start from the beginning."

"An old friend of mine called me before I left for Seattle. He's starting this big company and needs an assistance. I get my own office. It's also next to Taylor's college. Not to mention a big fat paycheck. I'm so excited, Nick."

"Congratulations. When do you start?"

"Tomorrow. I'll call you from there with my new number and fax number. You can call or fax me anytime. This will be my first job sober."

"How are you doing with your sobriety?"

"It's hell. I decided not to go to any meetings here. I never really liked sharing and going anyway. I can do this on my own. Besides, I don't ever want to disappoint you by calling you up drunk one day. All the hard work we did. I'm staying sober."

"And how's your painting?"

"Great! That's what I do every spare moment I have."

"I'm so proud of you, Keara. You're an amazing person."

"Thanks."

"I bet you'll call me at the week's end and have everyone eating out of your hand."

"I miss you, Nick. I wish I could hug you before I start tomorrow."

"How about we do a mental hug."

"I'd like that."

Images of Nick floated peacefully in my mind. I felt warm.

I raced up the steps to wake Tabitha.

"Tabitha, Tabitha, wake up." She fluttered her eyelids and gazed up at me.

"What's wrong, Mommy?" she asked, rubbing the sleep out of her eyes.

"Do you feel like the mall? I'm starting a new job tomorrow and I need new clothes. My D.J. outfits are not office material. How about we go to the Gap and then I'll take you to the Arts and Crafts store. While I'm at work you can make something cool. School is in two days, anyway."

"I'm scared to go to a new school, Mom, and a Catholic one too. Are nuns mean?"

"Hey, I got through twelve years with nuns. I turned out okay, didn't I?" I laughed, pulling her out of bed. "Anyway, nuns are not mean. I thought you liked penguins."

We both giggled and started to get ready for our big shopping day. Taylor joined us at the mall for our shopping spree. We spent the day on a high of love, shopping and Sushi.

I woke the next morning feeling anxious. By the time I padded barefoot to the bathroom, a fresh batch of fear surged through me.

"David, did you save me any hot water?" I asked irritably, clutching my black towel.

This broken down cottage only gave three minutes of hot water a shower.

"Yes. I took my shower with low pressure and was in and out. I'm considerate," he grinned.

"This is probably a mistake. I can't believe I'm going back to work. I don't even know how to fax. I'm scared."

"So, don't go. Tell Ranger to go fuck himself."

"I have to pay for all my new clothes."

"I'm starting to make a lot of money, here. The competition in my office is so fierce. You either produce or get swallowed up."

"I'm proud of you, David. The way you were able to jump right in and become one of the boys," I smiled, kissing his cheek. He smelled of Bijan after shave.

"Thanks. I'll take Jack for his walk so you won't have to step in any accidents in your new shoes," he smiled sadly.

"Thanks. I'll call you from my office."

The office. I liked the sound of that. I was going to run an office. La Di Fucking Da.

I quickly scanned through all my new working clothes. I decided on the olive green short sleeve turtleneck and the olive green plaid skirt. The Victoria's Secret push up bra would make the sweater come alive. I blew dried my hair in a wild blonde tangle and slipped into sensible brown suede pumps. I raced down the steps and fixed a quick breakfast for Tabitha.

"Tabitha, wake up, honey." I said softly, carrying in a breakfast tray.

"Mommy, you look so pretty," she smiled dreamily.

"Thanks, baby. I made you all kinds of goodies. Are you going to make me something for my new desk, today?"

"Yes. I'm going to make you something real special."

"Great. I'll be home early. I'll call you when I get settled and give you the number. I love you, Tabitha. Bye."

I walked into the bathroom one more time to check my makeup. Jack came wandering in. He picked up his back leg and started peeing. I screamed and jumped in the tub to avoid getting sprayed.

"Jack, stop, what are you doing?" I yelled in frustration.

He whirled around and strutted into Tabitha's room. There was now a small stream of pee covering the black and white tiles.

Great. I was starting off the day by getting pissed on. Not good, Keara.

After I cleaned Jack's mess up, I sprayed more Fendi on me. I was afraid I'd smell like Lysol.

I felt my mouth go dry as I pulled into the parking lot of the office building. It was strange, I wasn't thinking of a drink but a cigarette. I hadn't had one since I left for Seattle. I moistened my lips, tugged on my skirt and strolled up to the receptionist desk.

"Hello. I'm Keara. I have an appointment with David Forrest," I smiled nervously.

"I'm Talisa," she said in a thick throaty voice, stretching out her hand. "Have a seat. I'll buzz him."

She was petite, about ninety pounds, twenty something, thick raven black hair, big warm brown eyes and an almond cream complexion. She oozed sex appeal. I felt she was bi-sexual too.

I felt a tap on my shoulder and spun around to see Ranger smiling blissfully. He pulled me into his arms.

"You look incredible," he sighed gustily, looking me over from head to toe. "Let's go check out your office."

He grabbed my hand and pulled me down the hall. He fished a key out of his pocket and placed it in the palm of my hand.

"Go ahead and open the door to your new life. You don't know how happy I am to be working with you again," he grinned, rubbing the back of my neck. "It'll be like old times."

OhGod, Keara, what did you get yourself into? Just focus on all those phone lines and that beautiful fax machine.

"The two offices across the hall are my partners, Vincent Fardone and Richard Kaminsky. You'll love Vinny and Rich. They are both wild and crazy just like you," He laughed, clutching my hands. "I love your blonde hair and purple eyes. You always did know how to stand out in a crowd."

I plunked down on the black leather swivel desk chair.

"Ranger, we have to talk. First off, I'm not wild and crazy, anymore. I'm clean and sober. Second, while I was in San Diego, I fell in love with someone."

"Get out," he gasped, shifting uncomfortable. "What about David? Are you still in love with the person in San Diego?"

"Yes, I'm still in love with the San Diego guy. David knows. That's why we moved back to New York. David thinks we'll get back on track here," I sighed, playing with the colorful paper clips in their magnetic clear holder.

"Who is this guy that stole your heart? I'm jealous. I still love you, madly. I have never stopped thinking about you for one minute. When I heard you were back, I went nuts."

I plucked out a picture of Nick from my purse and handed it to Ranger.

"This is who I fell in love with. I never thought I'd cheat on David. Now everything is one big fucking mess."

"He's very good looking. I don't have a prayer. Does he love you?"

"I'm not up to talking about it anymore. It's too depressing. Besides, I'm not here to talk about Nick. I want to work. Show me everything you want done," I smiled sadly, jumping up and hugging him close. My lips brushed his cheek.

"Let's go in my office and start with the mail and then I'll have Amanda show you the computer and how to do the orders."

We spent the morning going over the mountain of mail. We were on the last piece when his partners stuck their head in the door.

"Hey, Dave, you didn't tell me your friend was hot," Vinny smiled, licking his lips. He strutted like a typical Brooklyn guy. He stuck out his hand. "I'm Vinny and I can't wait for you to come in my office and give you a letter," he grinned, gazing at my chest.

I shook his hand firmly. "I'm Keara. With that letter will I be able to buy a vowel or is that only Vanna's job."

"You're fucking cute, you know that."

Ah, New York, it was good to be fucking back. It was refreshing. No more uptight Californians who were afraid to say Fuck as if they might get sued.

"Don't mind my partner, he's really harmless. I'm Rich," he smiled pleasantly.

"Hello, Rich. I love your eyes. They are beautiful."

"Thank you. Yours are pretty wild."

"Yeah but mine are fake. My eyes that is. Everything else is real," I laughed, tossing my head back.

Rich and Vinny looked like Mutt and Jeff together. Rich was tall and stocky with China-blue eyes. Vinny was short and thin like a jockey with black hair and eyes.

Ranger walked me back into my office and showed me boxes of letters that had to be filed. I had a little storeroom in my office filled with Ranger's old files and junk. The office was huge with an L-shaped desk, file cabinets, a computer and fax machine. The walls were empty.

"Ranger, I'm going to have to leave a little early today. Tabitha's home by herself and I have to get her ready for school. She is going to a Catholic school in the neighborhood. She is very nervous."

"Didn't you always say that the nuns were the ones who fucked you up."

"I had to blame somebody," I grinned wickedly, kissing him on the lips.

"Hey, break it up, break it up," Taylor yelled.

"Taylor," I screeched, throwing my arms around her.

"Taylor, you are beautiful. You sure did grow up!"

"You look the same, Ranger. I'm going to school ten minutes from here. So I thought I'd check out the office and what do I find but you all over my mother, Ranger. What's up with that?

You are despicable, Ranger. You have not grown up, I see."

"Taylor, you saw nothing. Come, I want you to meet my partners. They will love you," he grinned, yanking her out the door.

As soon as they left, my hand flew to the phone. I punched in Nick's number.

I could feel my heart fluttering rapidly just from his hello.

"Hi. I'm calling from my office."

"So, how is it?"

"I love it. My office is huge and I can't wait to decorate the walls and put little things on my desk. You have to fax me something to hang up."

"I will. Tell me all about your job."

"There's nothing like working in New York. Everyone is crazy. I met some partners and the receptionist. She is sexy. Everyone says Fuck here every other word. It's just so real here. I miss the beach life but then again everyone is such a burn out there."

"Do you think I'm a burn out beach bum?"

"Of course not. I'm just saying there is more energy here.

121

Anyway, Taylor is here and I already have tons of work. Take down my new numbers. Oh, I had to tell Ranger about you."

"Why?"

"Ranger and I go way back. I had an affair with him before David. I think he's still hung up on me. I had to set him straight."

"Did he come on to you?"

"Yeah, but everything is cool. I gotta go. Take down these numbers and don't lose them."

My heart was still fluttering when I hung up.

"Mommy, Vinny and Rich are the best and Ranger is as sick as ever,"Taylor smiled crookedly, plopping herself down on my lap. "This is a cool place to work."

"Well, I'm glad you approve." I gently pushed Taylor off my lap and shook my numb legs.

"Now get back to school and don't think about playing those video games in the lobby."

I picked up the phone and called David. He answered in a rush.

"Are you busy? I need your help."

"I have two customers on hold. What do you need?'

"Ranger asked me to write a letter. You know I suck at that. Can I give you the details so you can put something together for me and call me back with it soon," I said, panic climbing in my voice. "It's my first day, I have to look like I know what I'm doing."

"I can help you, Keara," he said, laughing hard. "But you'll owe me big time tonight. Deal."

"Deal, you pig. I need this letter, A.S.A.P."

I hung up from David and whirled around in my chair to Talisa, standing in the doorway. She was holding a vase filled with yellow roses.

"Who are these from?" she asked, licking her lips.

I took the vase from her and placed it one the corner of my desk. "Probably, my husband," I shrugged, plucking the card from the plastic fork in the middle. As I started to open the card, the fax machine kicked on and was spitting out a piece of paper. I quickly snatched it from the machine. It was from Nick. I held it to my heart. Talisa gazed at me bewildered.

"I'll be totally honest with you. I have a husband and a

boyfriend. Since you answer the phones, you should know who is who. David is my husband and Nick is the boyfriend. It's a long story but this fax is like getting a tennis bracelet for me. The roses make me feel guilty. Do you hate me?'

"You don't think I have a long story too. You're not in Kansas anymore, Dorothy. I'll take good care of your calls. Don't worry, everyone in this office is having an affair so I get a lot of practice keeping lovers, husbands and wives straight. And besides you are too cute to hate."

"Nick's in California," I sighed, tears stinging my eyes.

Talisa threw her arms around me. "Keara, we'll go to lunch this week and I can tell you all about the married man that I'm dating and my loser boyfriend. I gotta get back to the phone," she yelled over her shoulder.

This was some office I landed in. I would blend in here. I turned my attention back to the fax in my hand. He sent me Nelson Mandela's Ignaural Speech. It was all about the strength inside of us. It was touching. Tears immediately sprang up. I taped it on the center of the wall over my desk. This way I could look at it all day. Of course, I cut the top off where his number was. I made a mental note to tell Talisa that she gave it to me just in case David ever asked. I knew he would want to come in soon and see my office. It was starting.

I called David back. "Thanks for the flowers. I love them. They make my office come alive."

"I'm happy. I have your letter."

As I was scribbling down the last sentence, I felt a pair of eyes on my back. I hung up the phone and spun around.

"Hi. Did I scare you? I'm Michelle but I hate to be called that. Call me Mike, Okay. What's your name?" She asked, looking me over.

"I'm Keara. Sorry I didn't come around and introduce myself but I got bogged down with all this work. Can you help me turn this computer on? I have to type a letter."

She was medium height, a drop overweight, long shiny bright red hair with bangs cut straight across, and cornflower blue eyes. She had a slash of pink lipstick across regular lips. Mike also had a mouth full of crooked teeth.

"Sure, I'd love to help you," she smiled, clicking on my new toy.

Mike was overly friendly but she got me started on the computer. Thanks to Nick's teachings at the restaurant, I was a quick study. I typed the letter, started the filing and checked in on Tabitha. Around three Ranger popped his head in.

"How are you doing on your first day? I hope you love it. Tomorrow, I want you to answer my calls. I get around fifty a day. I'll need you to do purchase orders tomorrow too," he said business like, gazing at my crossed legs.

"I think I'm going to love it here. I feel at home. I have to leave now but here is your letter. You want to sign it and I'll fax it before I go."

"This is brilliant," he said, breaking into a smile. "You haven't lost your touch. I love having you back."

He signed the letter and glided his hand across my leg. "You have incredible legs, Keara. How am I going to work with you? I have a hard on, already."

"Oh God, Ranger, I forgot what a monster dick you have. Get that thing out of here. You could wipe out the whole office with that if you move too quickly. Go, jerk off in your office."

"I think I'll go do that," he said laughing, sliding out the door.

I faxed the letter and closed up my office. I walked up to Talisa's desk on my way out.

"Talisa, do you smoke?" I asked anxiously, raking my fingernails through my hair.

"Of course. Would you like one?"

"Yes. Thank you so much. You know the old story, I just quit but just this once."

"Here. Did you let this place get to you already?"

"No. I think I'll really like it here."

"See you in the morning."

I jumped into my Jeep Cherokee, lit the cigarette and headed down the rain slicked streets for home. I stopped at Seven Eleven for a thirty minute phone card. It was eleven dollars but it meant talking to Nick tonight before David got home. The phone card was more precious to me than diamonds.

The next morning, I streaked out of bed, anxious to get to work. I almost collided with David in the hallway.

"Hey, where's the fire?"

I whipped off his towel around his waist and grabbed his penis. "It's hot right here," I said seductively, licking my lips.

Just as David went to kiss me, we heard a painful animal cry.

"Oh my God, it's Tara. Time for the kittens."

Tabitha came hobbling out of her bedroom. She still limped from the broken leg

"Mommy, where is Tara? I hear her crying. Listen, there she goes again."

Bruce was running up and down the steps. Jack was at the bottom step, making a poop on it.

The door to the linen closet was slightly ajar. I peeked in. Tara was having her kittens on top of the green sheets. The fourth one was just popping out. Tabitha was in awe. David was putting film in the camera.

"Keara, it's your turn to pick up Jack's accident. I stepped in it last night," he said, clicking away at the newborns.

"Mommy, can I stay home with the kittens? I don't want to go to school."

"No you can't stay home. Tara needs a little space right now. Go get her some food and water."

I cleaned up Jack's mess, took my three minute shower and picked out another new outfit. A brown corduroy skirt with matching vest and a striped brown turtleneck. David and Tabitha had already left. I looked in on the newborns before I took off. They were being washed by Tara. Their eyes shut tight, they were meowing softly. Bruce was standing guard outside the closet. Jack was fast asleep on his blanket.

I stopped at Seven Eleven for coffee, cigarettes and another thirty minutes phone card. Last night I used up every minute. This was getting to be an expensive habit.

I paused a minute before getting into the Jeep. It was a pleasant cool day. There was no more jogging on the beach with Jenny. No more lifeguard. I'd never even found out his name or said goodbye.

No more ocean breeze and palm trees swaying. Worse. No more Nick.

My heart started sinking as I started the engine. Nick's face floated in my mind.

I found myself emitting a low guttural animal like sound. I had turned into Chewy from Star Wars. That's it, I'm over the edge. Just call me Chewy. I lit a cigarette. If I didn't see Nick soon, I was going to go insane. I started thinking of all the different positions that he twisted my body into and screamed out another loud Chewy sound. Oh my God, I'm a wookie.

By the time I had pulled up to the company's parking lot, I had smoked three cigarettes.

Great, Keara, now you have to go to smokers's anonymous.

I tossed a handful of Tic Tac's in my mouth and pushed open the glass door. The only one in this early was Amanda.

"Hello. I'm sorry I missed you yesterday. I was swamped with orders. I'm Amanda," she smiled uneasily, pushing her long curly blonde hair back behind her ears. A pair of diamond earrings sparkled on them. She looked like she was fighting emotional overload, like I did in San Diego. She was too thin. The medicine was helping me. I had put on about five pounds.

"I'm Keara. Ranger told me, you would help me get adjusted."

"Yeah, sure. Do you smoke? Why do you call him Ranger?"

"It's a long story. I just started smoking again."

"Want to go have one before we get started," she suggested, rummaging through her desk drawers.

"Sure."

We walked back into the factory where everyone was allowed to smoke.

"Dave is crazy to work for, you know. He is completely disorganized," she said distracted.

"I know. I've worked for him before. I know all his habits. Only this time I'm sober."

"Do you go to AA?" she asked, her features softening.

"Not here. I used to in San Diego. I'm on my own here. I know I can't drink. End of story."

"I just got my three months token," she smiled nervously,

126

crushing out her cigarette.

I immediately embraced her. "I'll give you my home number. You can call me anytime. I'm an old pro."

"Thanks. Okay, let's get started on that office of yours."

We strolled arm and arm into my office. The morning was spent on mail, files, purchase orders, working on the computer and getting acquainted with Ranger's calls. Some of the calls were guys from the old days. It felt good to fall back into the quick wit banter. I put some pictures up on the wall of David, Tabitha, Taylor and Jack. Ranger breezed in and out checking on me. Mike popped in acting all super friendly. She was going out tonight and wanted to use me for an alibi. She hoped that was alright. She got a vibe yesterday that I was cool. This office was too much.

I found myself lingering in Rich's office. I liked him. He was funny, warm and honest. He always took Amanda to lunch every day at noon. No one said a word about it but everyone covered for them. It was a given.

I finally got a chance after lunch to call Nick. I was kinda hoping he would have called me first or faxed.

"Hello," he answered wearily.

"What's wrong?"

"Everything. Working day after day at the plant. Clashing with my Dad. Trying to get back on my feet. I need to move out of my mother's house, we do nothing but fight. It's all getting to me."

"Mmm, sounds to me like you could use an East coast vacation."

"You think that will fix everything?"

"I know it will fix everything. Come East, young man. Please," I begged, sketching the kittens on a yellow legal pad.

"Let me think about it. How will you get out?"

"I'll think of something. I have to get back to work. I love it here. I miss you and come East."

"Maybe I will come East."

I hung up and felt a jolt of electricity go through me. Just the thought of maybe seeing Nick sent me soaring. The conniving wheels were turning in my head. Time to crank out those lies again. I wanted to run down the hall screaming that I might be seeing my baby. Taylor walked in while I was banging my head against the desk.

"Trying to knock some sense into your head, Mommy?"

"I need a cigarette."

"You're smoking again?" she asked in mock horror.

"Yes. Everyone smokes here. It's peer pressure. What's up?"

"I need your computer to type up a quick report for class."

"Be my guest," I shrugged, fishing my cigarettes from my purse.

"Are you okay? You look flushed."

"I just hung up from Nick. That's what the head banging was about. I have to see him Taylor but I need your help."

"No can do. I'm dating half of David's office. I can't chance him hating me."

"At least listen to my plan. I think it is fool proof," I whispered feverishly, shutting my office door and clicking the lock. "Your friend, Brianna, goes to school in Philadelphia. You'll go see her and I'll go with you and say I'm also visiting my friends there for the weekend. Then, I'll have Nick fly to Philadelphia. You know my friends will cover for me. Just think about it. Please?"

A burst of hope surged through me at the possibility of seeing Nick again.

"Let me think about it. I'll call Brianna. I'm not making any promises, though. You're crazy."

I swept her up in my arms. "Give me your report. I'll type it in no time. Why don't you go in the lunch room? Talisa is probably in there. Hang out with her. She's cool."

"Actually, Mommy, do you think you can get me some pot?"

"Of course. George deals. I used to get high with him fifteen years ago. Can you believe he stills works for Ranger? I'll type the report and get you pot. You think about Philadelphia."

"Thanks, Mommy. I'm going to find Talisa."

"By the way, Tara had four kittens this morning. Come over and see them."

"You're not keeping them. You're house already smells like garbage."

"I know but they are so cute. Come back in fifteen minutes.

128

I'll have everything then."

I flew back in the warehouse and connected with George, smoked a cigarette, raced back into my office and typed Taylor's homework. I was on a Nick high. I knew maybe meant yes.

After Taylor left satisfied, I called David.

"How's your day?"

"I'm really busy. I had a great day, though. I made a lot of money, a lot."

"That's nice to know."

"New York really woke me up. In San Diego, I used to go surfing or boogie boarding when I could have been making all this money. What was I thinking?"

"I'm staying late. I have to catch up on my filing. It's been crazy here all day. I'm thinking next month we should take a long weekend somewhere. What do you think?" I asked in a throaty voice.

"Good Idea. How about San Francisco? We can check out if we want to live there."

"Sounds perfect."

"I have to go, Keara. It's your turn to bring home take out. Let's do Chinese, okay?"

As usual he played right into my hands. This time there was no guilt nipping at me just the longing for Nick exploding through my veins. My next call was Tabitha and the kittens.

"Hi, Sweetie. How are your furry friends?"

"Oh, Mommy, can we keep them? Tara lets me pick them up."

"We'll find them good homes and you can visit. How was your first day at school?"

"I love Sister Mary and I made lots of friends. I already have tons of homework, though."

"I'll be running late, Tabitha. I'm bringing home Chinese and I'll bring you an extra special dessert."

"Thanks, Mommy. Want to hear the kittens names?"

"Yeah, lay them on me."

"Scruffy, Tuffy, Buffy and Fluffy. I'm doing a report on them for school, already. Can you type it for me at work?"

"Sure, no problem. I'll see you later Tabitha. Love you."

As I replaced the receiver in the cradle, Ranger strutted in smiling.

"What are you doing here so late?" he asked grinning, sprawling across the black chair by my desk.

"I wanted to catch up on your files. Somebody has to take care of you," I said in a silky voice, rising from my chair.

He pulled me on his lap and kissed me. I kissed him back passionately.

"I like it when you work late," he murmured, reaching for my breasts.

I slapped his hand off them. "Ranger, you know we can't start this," I protested mildly, getting up from his lap.

"Why not? You feel so good, Keara."

"I'm still fucked up from the Nick thing. Ranger, I might need to take some vacation days next month. Is that okay? Paid vacation days, that is."

"Anything you want, Keara. Anything."

I'm worse sober than drunk. I know I'm bad but I can't stop.

The week flew by. I met another interesting character in the office. She came in on Friday from the Far East. Her name was Tina and she was the overseas sales person. Tina had long silky jet black hair and big black eyes. She was Japanese and Italian and gorgeous.

She gracefully strutted in my office. "I heard all about you from David. He told me I would love you," she said in a sly tone, stretching out her hand to shake mine.

"What exactly did Ranger tell you?"

"Ranger, I like that name. Is that your pet name for him?"

"Whatever."

"He told me you're fucking nuts. Is this true?"

"I was fucking nuts now I'm just fucking normal," I grinned, taking my yellow roses out of the vase and holding them upside down.

"What are you doing with the roses?" she asked, arching a carefully waxed brow.

"I'm going to save them and dry them out."

I twisted a rubber band around the stems and pinned them

130

upside down on the wall.

"That looks like some kind of Voodoo ritual. I think maybe Ranger is right, you are fucking nuts," she said with a grin as she exited my office.

She came back in five minutes.

"Keara, David told me about the letters you have been writing for him. Do you think you could help me out with this letter? I wrote down some things, you just need to put them in order.

He also told me only you can call him Ranger. Is there something I should know?"

"Uh, I'm special," I laughed, winking at her. "When do you need this letter?"

"By the end of the day. Oh, Keara, do you know, you have the only computer that has a CD player in it. I guess you really are special."

"I didn't know about the player."

"I'll be right back with a CD and show you how to work it."

She came back in clutching "Phantom of the Opera" CD , her sleek black hair streaming behind her. She had on a navy blue Chanel suit and on her slim wrist was a gold Rolex with diamonds.

"Have you seen Phantom?" she asked, clicking my mouse and setting up the player.

"Not yet, but I do have tickets to see it next month."

"You are all set. Just click here and enjoy, special lady."

As the music started to fill the room, Talisa buzzed me.

"Keara, line two is David and on line three is Nick. What do you want to do?"

"I'll take Nick. Please tell David I'm on long distance and I'll call him back. Oh and Talisa, please hold all my calls while I'm on with Nick. Thanks."

A ripple of pleasure went through me as I picked up line three.

"Hi. Can I help you?" I asked in a velvety smooth voice.

"Do you always answer your phone so sexy?"

"I knew it was you," I giggled. "Guess what?"

"You've become president of the company?"

"No, better. I have a CD player in my computer. I'm listening to opera right now."

"Cool. So how is everything going?"

"I love the job, the people, my office. I miss you terribly. Move to New York and everything will be perfect."

"I can't move to New York but maybe a visit. How about the first weekend in November?"

"That's perfect," I shrieked, bouncing up and down in my chair.

"Take it easy, Keara. Are you sure it will be safe?"

"Yes. Don't worry. We'll have the best weekend in Philadelphia. We'll do the Liberty Bell and South Street. I can't wait to touch you."

"Me too."

I hung up feeling like I had floated up to the ceiling. Someone was going to have to scrape me down. Most people needed air and water to survive. I just needed Nick.

Rich glanced in my office. "Hey, why do you look like you just ate the canary?" he asked playfully, gazing at the pictures on my wall.

"That was Nick on the phone. He is coming in for a visit," I said excitedly.

"Did his mommy give him permission?" he asked teasingly

"Very funny. I don't know, I cover for you all the time with Amanda and you do nothing but tease me."

"That's because I care about you," he chuckled, hugging me tight. "Next week, we'll have to work on getting you away for your weekend."

"Thanks, Rich. I appreciate the help from a pro."

"No problem," he winked, as he strolled out into the hall.

Talisa buzzed me again. "Keara, I have David again on one and calls for Ranger on four, five and six."

"Okay, I'll take David. Tell everyone else to hold on. I'll get to them all."

I was still flying high from Nick's call as I pressed one.

"David, sorry I didn't get back to you. I'm totally busy with calls."

"That's alright. I just wanted to know if you want to do anything tonight?"

"Let's do Sushi and a movie with Tabitha. I'll call you later."

I hung up and began the process of soothing Ranger's customers. Taylor breezed in at the end of the day.

"Mommy, do you have any cigarettes?" she asked in a tense voice.

"Sure. Top drawer. What is wrong, Taylor?"

Her face clouded as she sank down into the chair by my desk. "I have a date with Michael tonight, Adam's harassing me twenty four, seven, telling me he's going to kill me and school sucks."

"Why are you going out with Michael? He's engaged. He's using you."

"He's rich."

"But he doesn't spend it on you. Get a tennis bracelet, at least."

"I don't know how to ask for stuff like that."

"Oh my God, I almost forgot, I need David to do a letter for me."

I grabbed the phone and frantically dialed David's number.

"David, I need you help with another letter. Can I fax you over the info and you'll put it together for me right now. Please."

"Mm, same deal as before."

"Of course. Oh, and please call Adam, he's threatening to kill Taylor."

"Don't worry, I'll take care of my girls."

I hung up and drew a deep breath. "Taylor, David will take care of Adam. Oh by the way, Nick gave me a date. The first week in November. Could you call Brianna and set it up?"

"How are you going to pull this off, Mommy?"

"I'm going to call my old friend, Gina, in Philadelphia. She is always having affairs. I'll have her write me a letter, inviting me to Philadelphia for an all girl party for that weekend."

"You're crazy. Can I borrow your black velvet Betsey Johnson's dress for my date?"

"Yes. Just take it off when you have sex. The last time you borrowed something, it came back gross."

"Oh Mother, puhleese."

"Get out and go check on Tabitha and the kittens. I have to get back to work."

David called back with another brilliant letter. Tina was

impressed. She confided in me.

She was a single mom. Her three boyfriends were all married. One was a singer, one a politician and one was a rich playboy. All from different countries. A girl after my own heart.

* * *

The month flew by quickly. Tabitha didn't limp anymore. The kittens were creating havoc in the house. Jack was chewing on a new red and yellow blanket. His hind legs had started collapsing on him. Taylor was getting serious about Michael but he was still engaged. David was making lots of money and I was counting down the days to see Nick.

We were getting ready for our long weekend in San Francisco. Taylor drove us to the airport Thursday night.

"I don't understand, why you guys can't stay in New York," she grumbled, her hands gripping the wheel tight.

"Taylor, you know we said one year in New York. Why don't you think about coming to California and living with us this time," I said in a motherly tone.

"I love New York."

"Me too," Tabitha chimed in. "I want to stay in New York."

"David, explain to them why we have to move," I muttered, pushing my hair back behind my ears. I had given up cigarettes again and was dying for one.

"Girls, we have discussed this. I have been given the opportunity to open my own branch office on the West coast. San Francisco seems like the best choice," he said in his Mister Rogers voice.

Why did he have to be so nice? Gag me. In less than twenty days, I would be wrapped in Nick's arms, happy as a kitten sucking on Tara's nipples. All the king's horses and all the king's men could not put my marriage back together again.

Taylor pulled up to the curb at the airport.

"Bye Babes. Be careful with my Jeep. Take good care of Jack and the cats. I'll bring you back something expensive. See you Monday night, don't forget us."

"Bye, Guys. Have fun," she half smiled, giving us all air kisses.

"Do you think we'll get the Jeep back in one piece?" David

134

asked, as Taylor peeled out into traffic.

"Forget about the Jeep. What about the house? With all those animals and accidents. We are talking nightmare."

* * *

We came back rested and tanned. San Francisco was warm and sunny. New York had turned cold. It was time for me to get rid of the summer blonde.

I strolled into work tanned with dark auburn hair and green eyes.

"You look fucking great," Talisa shrieked, scrambling over her desk and running her long red manicured nails through my hair.

"Do you have a cigarette? In a couple of days. I'll be face to face with Nick," I sighed, biting my lip.

"Keara, I'm so glad you're back," Mike exclaimed, running toward me.

Talisa handed me a Marlboro Light and matches.

"You look so different," Mike smiled, pulling me toward the warehouse. "Let's have a smoke together. I have to talk to you."

I whirled around and rolled my eyes to Talisa.

"Calm down, Mike. What's wrong? Let me take a wild guess. Gary, right?"

"Yeah, that fucking bastard hasn't returned any of my calls after we were together," she groaned, pain filling her eyes. "I don't know what I'm doing with an asshole like him when my husband is the best."

I threw down my cigarette and crushed it with the heel of my black suede shoe.

"Mike. All guys are assholes. Hang in there. Everything always works out. Stop calling him. Go out with your husband tonight for a nice dinner. I have to get to my office and catch up. Stop getting yourself crazy, he'll call."

I was just through my mail when Tina came in clutching a file to her chest.

"Wow, nice look."

"Thanks."

"I have Antonio coming in tonight and he's taking me out tomorrow to buy me a new BMW. I can't have these anywhere near

135

my house," she said, dropping her voice to a whisper, waving the file at me. "These are all the songs and poems, Philippe wrote for me. Keep them under lock and key for me."

"Give them to me. I'll lock them up with the love letters from Marco. Don't worry, my lips and box are sealed. You kill me, Tina."

She spun around and was gone.

This office has Melrose Place beat for sure.

Talisa buzzed in. "Welcome back, Keara. See all those lines lit. They are all for Ranger and they all want to talk to you."

"Thanks, Talisa, I'll take them all." I slipped in a Tina Turner CD and picked up line one.

Ranger rolled in before noon. He had spent the morning at our New Jersey office.

"You look incredible. Want to fuck?" he smiled suggestively, yanking me to my feet and whirling me around.

"No," I said firmly, breaking loose of his grip. "Ranger, listen up, we have a million calls to go over, the mail and the purchase orders. Pay attention or I'll stab you. You have a meeting in an hour with Paul Kingston to go over the plans for the new store."

He slumped down into the seat and rubbed his hands over his face. "Oh, Keara, it's so hard to work with you. I'm always turned on."

"Maybe, I should quit," I grinned wickedly.

"Keara, how about lunch?" Talisa asked, sticking her head in my office.

Ranger's face turned crimson.

"Did I interrupt something?"

"No. Ranger was just whining to me how he can't get along without my great skills."

"I'll be in the warehouse," he muttered, flying out of the room.

"What was that all about?" Talisa asked, gazing at me with her coffee brown eyes.

"Nothing, he just missed me. I don't want to talk about him. I'm going to see Nick in a couple of days. I feel like I'm gonna die."

"I got you a special present for your special weekend. I'll give it to you later."

"Aw, thanks, Talisa. I'm sorry I can't make lunch. I have to work through it because I'm behind from being away."

"Okay, but plan on it tomorrow," she smiled, reaching over and kissing me on the lips.

I found myself kissing her back. Why is it that everyone wanted to kiss me but Nick? I had been applying Blistex daily to my lips. If Nick wouldn't kiss me this trip, it's over. My heart started to soar thinking of what it would be like to kiss Nick. By the time I turned my attention back to the mail, silent tears were streaming down my cheeks. It had been six long months since I had felt his touch.

Talisa buzzed in. "Keara, your David on line two."

"Thank you," I sighed, my voice cracking under the sudden emotion.

I wiped the hot tears off my cheek with the back of my hand and picked up line two.

"Hi, I was just getting wet thinking about you," I said in my silkiest voice.

"Wow, big tonight."

"I can't wait."

I had switched over to my happy hooker wife mode. This was how I used to be before Nick.

I was going to have to fuck his brains out this weekend. The letter from Gina inviting me to Philadelphia would be here tonight. I gave myself until Sunday to tell him. After all, it was next weekend. Guilt started nagging at me. I couldn't bear to give anymore pain. Operation Philadelphia had to go smooth.

As I was picking up the phone to call Nick, I heard Rich's door slam shut. Uh oh, another fight with Amanda. I put the phone down and tiptoed over to his door. I gently tapped on it.

"Come in," he barked, on the other side.

I slowly opened the door and eased inside. His face betrayed all his emotions.

"Hey you, it's my big weekend. I have to tell David my story. What do you think?"

He blew out a breath. "If you were my wife, I'd insist on going

137

with you."

"But it's a girl weekend."

"I'd stay in the hotel and keep busy and see you at night."

"You're making me nervous," I said cringing, pacing back and forth in front of his desk.

"I'm just playing Devil's advocate."

"I know. Do you want to talk about anything?"

"Amanda's fucked up. There's nothing to talk about," he growled, twisting a paper clip.

"I'm just down the hall."

I opened the door and was face to face with Amanda. "Just leaving," I muttered, strolling down the hall to gossip with Talisa.

God, I love this place. Lies, deception, the language, off the wall people, affairs. I have really found my home.

During the weekend, the three of us painted the kitchen white. Then David painted big black cow spots on the white walls. He also tiled the kitchen floor while I hung curtains with cows on them. Tabitha was enjoying the kittens. They were big now and it was time to find them homes. The weather had turned nasty and cold. Jack was always shivering. I knew he would not be moving with us to San Francisco. The thought filled me with an overwhelming sense of sadness. I couldn't imagine ever being without Jack. The ringing of the phone jolted me out of my gloomy thoughts.

"Hello," I answered anxiously.

"Oh you poor thing, you sound awful. You didn't tell him yet,"Kylie murmured on the other end.

"No."

"Please don't get caught."

"No kidding. What's up with you and Christian?"

"I caught him again with Jana last night. I went to surprise him and I got the surprise," she sobbed into the phone.

"Oh, Kylie, I am so sorry. Want me to come over?"

"No. I'm on my way to Spencer's."

"Take care, Kylie. You'll get through this. I love you," I sighed heavily, placing down the receiver.

I gazed into David's friendly hazel eyes suppressing my fear. It was Sunday morning and I just made him cry out in ecstasy. My cries of course were fraudulent.

"Keara, what are you thinking?" David asked, brushing the hair out of my eyes.

"Oh, I was just thinking about Gina's letter. She's having a pajama party and a Psychic at dinner for all us girls," I said, in a calm voice. "So, I'm thinking about going. I'd love to see everybody, you know."

"You already have your mind made up."

"Well, I kinda ran it by Taylor, she would drive up with me. It would be perfect because I could drop her off at Brianna's."

"What about me and Tabitha?" he asked, clearing his throat.

"I'm sure you two can have fun without me. How about next weekend we all go away?"

"This is beginning to feel like San Diego," he said, choking on his words.

"This is just a girl's weekend. You are reading too much into this."

"Fine. When are you leaving?" he asked, sighing.

"I'll probably leave Friday after lunch and be back Sunday afternoon. Let's not beat this thing to death. I love you, David," I said firmly, rolling over on top of him.

The week passed quickly. David was cold and distant. Ranger was exhibiting signs of jealousy. Nick was excited about coming East. The office was all counting down with me. I was in a constant adrenaline rush.

Friday morning, I was completely numb like a dentist just shot up my whole body with novocain. I found myself babbling incoherently to clients. Anxiety was shooting wildly through me. At noon, everyone gathered around me, wishing me luck. Talisa gave me a candy necklace to wear around my neck. Rich put his arm around me and walked me to my Jeep.

"Well, kid, good luck," he smiled affectionately, kissing my cheek.

"Thanks for being there for me, Rich." I hugged him tight.

I settled into the Jeep, turned on a Sinatra tape and headed for Taylor's house. My eyes started to burn and threatened to tear. Complicated emotions twisted in my heart. If David caught me, he'd be devastated but in a few hours, I would be pouring myself into Nick's strong Hercules arms. Pain and excitement simultaneously washed over me.

I pulled up outside of Taylor's house and honked. She scooted out the door carrying a backpack and an overnight bag. What would I do without Taylor?

"Hi, Babes. Ready for our trip? Hopefully it won't be the trip from hell."

"I have my period and I feel sick," she groaned, rubbing her temples.

"I'm sorry. Do you want to stop and get something for it?"

"No. I'm already medicated. Do we have to listen to Sinatra the whole trip?"

"Put on whatever you like. I'm flying. My mind has left the building."

"Mommy, you can't get caught. David will kill us both," she said anxiously, biting her nails.

"Everything will be fine. How's your love life?"

"Sucks. Adam is still saying he is going to kill me. Michael is still engaged to that pig. I hate guys. Mommy, I have to sleep. Brianna wants to go out when I get there. Do you mind?"

"Of course not."

I drove the three hours to Philadelphia in a complete state of panic. My heart was doing tumblesaults while guilt was ripping through me. Dear God and guardian angels, I implored silently, please make this weekend perfect.

"Taylor, wake up, we are almost at the college," I said softly, shaking her arm gently.

"Uh, where are we? Did I sleep the whole time?"

"We're at Brianna's dorm and it's cold outside. Let's make a run for it."

We raced up the steps of the dorm fighting the cold blustery winds. Our noses were cherry red when we stepped inside Brianna's room.

"This weather is insane," I growled, rubbing my hands together.

"You'll get used to it," Taylor and Brianna said in unison, laughing.

140

"Brianna, can you drive to the airport? I don't know where it is."

"Sure, Keara. Want to freshen up in the bathroom?"

"Thanks. Taylor come with me."

I touched up my makeup and fluffed up my red hair. I had on a short light purple velvet dress that flared around the bottom. Since I last saw Nick six months ago, I had gained ten pounds. There was no more jogging or gym. Would he notice? My breasts were fuller but so was my butt. Over my dress, I was wearing my black and white spotted fake fur coat. I placed the candy necklace around my neck.

"Brianna, Taylor, do I look alright? I'm getting hysterical, help me," I said, quivering with fear.

"Mommy you look great and you know it."

"Keara, you look adorable. He'll flip when he sees you. Let's go. It's time."

I followed behind Brianna and Taylor in a trance like state. Brianna's long honey blonde hair was swaying back and forth like a pendulum. She was my height, thin, pale complexion and icy blue eyes. Before I knew it, we were standing at United Gate 17. I sat with my eyes glued on the door.

"Girls, if he doesn't show up, let's make a pact. I go off the wagon just for tonight and it's shots of tequila all night."

"Okay, Mommy."

"Okay, Keara."

"Oh, Mommy, looks like you are staying on the wagon."

I spun around to see Nick walking through the doors. I raced up to him and flung myself in his arms. All my fears dissolved. An aura of pure love surrounded us.

"Nick, you look and feel incredible," I smiled blissfully, burying my head in his chest.

"I missed you, Keara," he whispered, kissing my head.

"Alright, you two, break it up. Brianna and I have to go drinking yet," Taylor grinned.

I snuggled up against him in the car and felt like purring. We rode in silence just hugging one another. Brianna pulled up next to my Jeep.

"Okay, you two lovebirds, we are here. Get out."

"Here, Nick, take my keys and put your bag in the Jeep. Start it up too, it's freezing out there. I want to say goodbye to Taylor and Brianna."

He grabbed his black nylon bag and shut the door.

"Listen up, girls, I still need you both. I have to call David, yet. Let's go to the Diner for some tea. Then, Brianna, I'll need you to come and call David with me. This way he'll be really convinced I'm with you two. He knows I don't see my friends till tomorrow. Please," I begged, digging my nails into the leather seat.

They both rolled their eyes at once.

"I have to go to the bathroom. You're going to have to let me out, Brianna."

"I guess I just have to go with you," she said slyly.

We sprinted to the bathroom where there were two phones out of sight from Nick.

"Thanks, Brianna, for helping me. This means a lot to me," I said sincerely, pushing in our eight hundred number with trembling hands.

"Don't mention it."

"Hello," David mumbled into the phone.

"Hi. Are you sleeping?"

"Just about," he said flatly.

"Me, Taylor and Brianna are having coffee at a Diner. Tomorrow, I'll see Gina. Tonight, I'm sleeping at the dorm with the girls."

"What's the number there?"

"I'll put Brianna on, she can give it to you."

She gave David the number and acted cool. I quickly said goodbye.

"Brianna, please keep your phone off the hook or don't answer."

"No problem. I have a machine."

We scurried back to the table. The girls said their goodbyes. Brianna gave us directions to a hotel nearby. Nick was finishing up his chicken noodle soup.

"So, how do I look? I'm up ten pounds since I saw you last,"

I said, battling an urge to hurl myself across the table and kiss him.

"You look healthy. You were too skinny in San Diego. How's your stomach?"

"Much better. I'm gaining weight from being in the office. Everyone eats there all day. I'm hooked on Jell-o and whipped cream. I eat it all day."

"Your office sounds crazy."

"Is it ever, but I love it. I fit in perfectly. Like my necklace?" I giggled, with excitement.

"It looks delicious," he grinned, a twinkle in his eye.

"Let's get out of here," I whispered anxiously, popping out of the booth.

I felt utterly shameless as we entered the dark motel room.

"Nick, I have to take a hot bubble bath. I have no hot water at home and the tub is rusted. So, I need a couple of minutes to soak."

"Take your time. It's been a long flight. I just want to stretch out on the bed."

I went into the bathroom with all my cosmetics, lotions and a scented candle. Hoping to emerge a siren. My legs started to tremble. My heart was beginning to thud in my chest. I poured some blue bubble bath foam into the steamy hot water. Hopefully, this would relax me, as I eased into the tub. Would he kiss me this time? It was a question I was obsessed with.

After practically burning off my skin in the bath, I glided out of the bathroom wearing my silk paisley short robe in a cloud of Bijan and a touch of makeup. I put the candy necklace back on. Nick was stretched out on the bed watching Letterman. I stood by the side of the bed and felt a couple of tears straying down my cheek.

"What's wrong, Keara," he said in a hushed voice, his eyebrows arched.

I cleared my throat. "It's been such a long time. Six months long. I'm scared, nervous. I feel funny."

He pulled me gently into his arms and started nibbling on the candy.

"You smell delicious," he said soothingly, running his hands over my body.

My robe came undone and he playfully licked my nipples. I felt

143

a river was flowing between my legs. With David, I was dry as a desert. Tonight Nick took me to Niagara Falls. The deafening roar of the falls was pounding in my ears. Just as I was crashing over in the barrel, I let out a sizzling scream.

"You're going to get us kicked out of here," he chuckled, cradling me in his arms.

I couldn't speak. How could I go back to New York after having this outer body experience? Nick brought me to places that no one had ever come close to. I knew this visit would leave me in excruciating pain. I would want him more than ever.

The next morning, I slipped quietly from the covers and took another bubble bath. Hot water. Bubble baths. Nick. Was this heaven or what?

I slid back under the covers. Climbed on top of him and visited another wonder of the world. Twice before breakfast.

Taylor and Brianna met us for breakfast at the Diner. We spent the morning with the girls shopping on Market street in the city. I tried to call David a couple of times but there was no answer or machine on. My stomach had it's old familiar flip flop feeling. Had he figured it out? Was he on his way here? Was my life about to be over?

I bought myself a black knit dress for work. A black fake fur for Taylor. A Philadelphia t-shirt and hair clips for Tabitha. A green t-shirt with a black star on it for David. Nick picked out two thermal shirts. After the girls left mid-afternoon to nap, we headed for the Liberty Bell and museums, strolling down South street chatting happily like newlyweds. Nick loved Philadelphia.

Monday, we are talking suicide.

I called Gina, to make sure David hadn't called her. He hadn't. She was meeting me tomorrow for breakfast, to check out Nick. I gave her the name of the hotel, in case of a problem.

It was starting to drizzle. We ducked inside an amber-lit Italian restaurant in an old bank building that was converted. The hostess led us downstairs into the vault which had a couple of small tables set up. We were the first to be seated down there.

"Today was fun," I sighed happily, reaching for his hand. "When I lived here, I hated it. Today you made it interesting. It

144

was perfect except for the fucking rain."

"What's with the fuck all the time. Ever since you moved back that's all you say."

"It's a New York thing. My whole office says it every other word. So, it has become a habit now, I guess. Does it bother you?" I asked, tilting my head to the side.

"Sometimes. No one at my office says it."

"Tell me what you are doing with your life?'

The waitress at that moment came over and took our order. I knew my stomach wouldn't be able to handle anything more than soup. Nick ordered the shrimp scampi and a bottle of Pelegrino.

"So, before we were interrupted, what are you doing? Are you staying with your Dad? Are you staying with your Mom? Are you seeing anyone?" I asked all in one breath.

The petite young waitress bought us the bottled water with two glasses. I asked for lemon slices and some wine glasses to drink the water out of.

"Okay, let's try this again. What's up with you? Tell me everything."

"I'm making good money at the factory with my Dad. I have started to dabble in the market. I trade for myself without a broker on the computer. I have my own system. I'm doing okay. I want to save a lot more before I move out and to answer the last question, I haven't dated at all. I want to get my life in order before I can concentrate on seeing anyone."

Wrong answer. I wanted him to say, Keara, come back with me and we will live happily ever after.

"What about you? How are things with David?"

"Well, you know I love my job. I'm alive again and I love making my own money. As far as David goes we are not really getting along but he'll never let me leave. I guess, I'm not ready to either."

We checked into the Hilton, the hotel where I'd met my first husband. I had also stayed there plenty of times with other boyfriends. Of course, I didn't tell Nick any of this.

I walked through the door chewing the inside of my cheek. I still felt fear that David would find us. My mind was in a state of panic that I would have to call soon.

"Maybe, I should take a hot bubble bath," I said, plopping down on the bed.

"Let me help you get undress," Nick said in a soft velvety voice, sliding off my brown turtleneck sweater.

He gently eased us down on the bed and the games began. I went for the gold. After our marathon love making session, I slipped out of his arms. I started looking for my underwear.

"What are you doing?" he asked, yawning.

"I need to go downstairs and call David."

"I have to call my Mom. I didn't tell her where I was going," he frowned, rising out of bed.

"What are you going to say?"

"I don't know. I think she knows I'm with you though. She suspects we are still in touch."

I can't believe he has to check in with his mother!

I dressed quickly and took off for the lobby feeling a nervous wreck.

"Hello," David barked into the phone.

"Hi. You don't sound happy."

"It's a zoo here. The cats knocked over the potpourri basket and Jack had a couple of accidents. I'm cleaning the mess now. Give me the number and I'll call you back."

"I'm in a pay phone."

"Just give me the number."

I gave him the number and hung up shaking. By giving him that number, I knew I had just signed my death certificate. I pinched the bridge of my nose and tried to compose myself. The phone rang.

"Hello," I said, trying to be calm.

"Now I can talk. It's crazy here. The kittens leave tomorrow and Tabitha is upset."

"David, I really can't talk now. Dinner is over and we are all on our way to some bar. I tried to call you today but no one was home."

"I took Tabitha to a movie. What did you do?"

"Shopping, of course. I brought presents for you and Tabitha.

146

I have to go, David. I'll call you tomorrow when I'm leaving. Goodnight. I love you."

"Bye, Keara. I love you, too."

I was fucked. I felt it. I rode the elevator up, trembling. I had visions of David tracking me down and killing me. Should I tell Nick, he might get shot tonight? Why the hell doesn't he kiss me?

I moistened my lips as I stuck the key in the door. Nick was in the shower. I quickly reviewed the situation in my head. David has a phone number to a pay phone. So what. I clicked my heels together three times and said I was safe. I slipped out of my clothes and into the king sized bed. I drifted off to sleep before Nick finished in the shower.

I woke up around six and said a grateful prayer that David didn't find us. Nick was sleeping peacefully. I went under the covers and decided to disturb him.

Before I jumped into the shower with Nick, I called Gina and arranged to meet her for breakfast at our hotel. She hadn't heard from David. Everything was cool. I then called Brianna and asked her to drop Taylor off at ten-thirty. Nick had a noon flight.

Gina knocked on the door as I was finishing brushing out my hair. I opened the door to see my old friend smiling brightly.

"Gina," I yelled joyfully, hugging her. "You look great."

"So do you, so do you," she exclaimed, her pale blue eyes sparkling.

"This is Nick."

"Hello, Nick," she smiled, extending her hand out.

Just then the phone rang and scared us all.

"It's Taylor with a problem, I'm sure," I said uneasy, my mind and heart started to race.

I picked up the beige phone. "Hello," I answered, turning my back to Gina and Nick.

"I can't believe you answered," David said, his voice filled with pain.

I hung up the phone shaking and lightheaded. I knew there was no color left in my face.

"Who was that?" Nick asked, concerned.

"Wrong room number. Let's go to breakfast," I said, fear

evident in my voice.

Gina gave me a look of alarm.

As Nick opened the door, the phone started ringing again.

"Let's get out of here," I said, nervously.

We walked to the elevator in an uneasy silence. My heart, brain and stomach were exploding all at once. The elevator door opened and a hotel clerk stepped out.

"Are you Keara?" she inquired, holding a piece of paper in her hand.

"Yes," I said, cringing.

"There is an emergency with your daughter, your husband is on the phone. You can use that house phone over there," she said flatly, pointing over to the phone on the wall.

I looked over at the bewildered expressions on Gina and Nick's faces.

"You two, go down. I'll be right there."

The elevator door shut. I slowly picked up the phone.

"Hello," I snapped.

"Keara, what the fuck is going on? I call the hotel and ask for Nick Bartoli's room and you answer. Imagine my surprise when I discovered Nick really had a room there!"

"Nick is my best friend, for God's sake. I didn't meet him to have sex. I missed him and wanted to hang out. Let's just get a divorce, David, and get it over with," I hissed.

"Hey, I'm the one who is supposed to be angry here. Why are you so mad?"

"I'm tired of playing games. I want out."

"Keara, come home."

"I'll come home when I'm ready. Just leave me the fuck alone," I yelled into the phone and slammed it back on the hook.

As I went to press the elevator button, the doors opened and Gina popped out.

"Keara, what the hell happened? I'm trying to keep Nick calm down there."

"What a hell of a reunion, Gina. I'm never going to change, obviously. Anyway, as you probably already know I've been caught. David is freaking out. I'm fucked."

"How did he catch you?"

"He had the number to the pay phone downstairs. Don't ask? He connected it to the hotel. But the real question is, do you think Nick is cute or what?"

We both shook with laughter and walked arm and arm into the restaurant. I slid into the booth next to Nick.

"What's going on?" he asked, his eyebrows arched in wonder.

"Let's talk about it on the way to the airport. Right now I need a cup of coffee," I sighed, signaling the waitress.

Gina and Nick already had omelettes in front of them. I ordered an English muffin. The mixture of pain and fear subsided. I was working, making money. David was making a small fortune. If he divorced me, I'd survive, financially. Plus, I could be with Nick. If I could only pry him away from his mother.

"We have to meet Taylor in the lobby. She should be here, now. Wait till you see her, Gina," I smiled, draining my coffee cup. I threw a twenty on the table and sprang to my feet. "I'll pay for breakfast. This way when I'm broke, you guys will owe me some food," I chuckled, grabbing both their arms and steering them towards the exit.

Taylor and Brianna were sitting in the lobby when we entered. Taylor strolled over when she spotted us and hugged Gina. We all said our goodbyes to Gina and Brianna.

We braced ourselves for the cold and ran for the Jeep. It had started to snow. Nick threw our luggage in the back and I started up the Jeep. I turned the heat full blast.

"Wow, it's cold here," Nick exclaimed, slamming the door.

"This is nothing, it's not even below zero," I said casually. I didn't want to get off the weather subject. "The roads get icy too."

"So, Keara, tell me about the phone call. I assume it was David," he frowned, rubbing his hand together.

"What, David called? Mother, did you fucking get caught?" Taylor yelled, from the back.

"We're fucking dead. I knew I shouldn't have helped you."

"Relax, everyone. Yes, David called but everything is cool. Don't worry, Nick, I covered for you. He doesn't want to kill you."

"You're really bad, aren't you, Keara?" he asked, gazing into my eyes.

"Yes, I'm the evil temptress."

"Mommy, this might not be so bad. You can get a cool apartment and I can hang out there," she shrugged, lighting up a cigarette.

I pulled up to the curb at the airport.

"Taylor, sit in the front seat, while I go in with Nick."

"Don't take all day, Mommy. The cops will probably give me a hard time, parked here."

"I think you can handle it."

She gave Nick a big kiss on the lips. I knew she did that on purpose. Nick grabbed his bag and I linked my arm in his. We walked slowly through the terminal to his gate.

"I don't know when I'll see you again," I mumbled, hugging him and nuzzling his neck.

"I had a great time. Thanks, Keara," he said softly, kissing me on the head. "I hope you find the happiness you deserve."

"I hope you do too," I said my voice trembling.

Tears blurred my vision as I ran towards the exit. I didn't look back.

Taylor had already shifted positions. She was lighting me up a cigarette when I climbed in.

"Here, I bet you need this."

"Yes. Thank you. It seems there is always a crisis and I can't give these up. At least, I don't want to drink."

You're such a liar, Keara. You wanted to get wasted at that airport bar.

"Mommy, I hate to do this to you but I need to sleep. Brianna had me out the whole time. I have a lot of homework when I get home too."

"Go ahead. I have a lot of thinking to do," I frowned, inhaling deeply on the cigarette.

"Everything will work out for you. But, David, will probably kill me," she grumbled, curling up in the seat.

"No he won't. He's Mister Rogers. Mister Rogers doesn't ever get angry. It'll blow over by the time we get home, you'll see."

Taylor nodded off to sleep. I lit another cigarette and put on a

Sinatra tape. Silent tears streamed down my face as I drove towards home. Home. It wasn't where my heart was.

"Taylor, wake up, we are almost at your house."

"Mommy, are you okay?" she asked, rubbing her sleepy eyes.

"Yeah. Do you think I can hang out with you? I don't feel like going home yet."

We trotted in her bedroom and collapsed on her unmade bed. Her phone started ringing. God only knew what it was under.

"Uh, oh, I bet it's David. He can sniff me out wherever I am," I groaned, rolling over, burying my face in the pillow.

"It can't be," she said, her lips pressed together seriously.

"Hello," she answered, fearfully.

"Yes, yes, I know. I'm sorry."

Oh my God, it was David. Here we go again. I was back on the merry-go-round.

Taylor handed me the phone rolling her eyes at me.

"Hello," I grumbled.

"Keara, come home," he said in an anguished voice. "Let's talk. Pick me up and we'll go for coffee. Just honk, I'll come out."

"Alright, I'm leaving Taylor's now."

I pressed the off button and threw the phone down on the rumpled black sheets.

"Alrighty then, I'm dead," I exhaled loudly.

"Mommy, I told you he'd be mad at me. I feel awful," she scolded me, her hands on her hips.

"Pick one, you can't have both."

"I know, I know."

I sprinted to the car, trying to cover my face from the icy wind. Nick had probably landed and had warm sun shining in his face. I still couldn't accept the fact he didn't kiss me. Why was I risking everything for him? My parents were most likely getting a good laugh at this in heaven. Pay back for all the years I tortured them.

Oh God, I'm home. I honked the horn and rubbed my dad's dog tags together for luck.

David leaped out of the kitchen door and ran towards the Jeep. He entered the passenger's side looking deathly white.

"Hello," he sighed, under his breath.

151

"Hi. Where to?"

"Drive down to the marina and park there," he mumbled.

I parked overlooking the bay. I left the Jeep running so we wouldn't freeze to death.

"Why, Keara ? I thought we were finally getting back on track," he said in an icy voice.

"I don't know what to say. I had to see him one more time to be sure."

"Be sure about what?"

"I had to be sure, I wanted to be with you," I said, my voice shaking. I started chewing a big hole on the inside of my cheek.

"This is killing me, Keara," he cried, wiping his tears away with the back of his hand.

I stretched out my arms. "I'm sorry, David. Please forgive me."

"I want us to go to a marriage counselor. I really want us to work out, Keara."

"Okay, I'll go. Anything you want."

"I want us to go home now and make love."

"Okay, David," I said, forcing a smile.

As I drove home through the icy streets, being careful not to crash into anything, I made a silent vow. I would never get caught again.

Tabitha was in the kitchen making hot chocolate when we entered.

"Hi, Mom. Did you hear about the kittens?"she asked, in a sad voice.

"No. Tell me."

"Before you start, Tabitha. I'm going upstairs to lay down. I'm exhausted. Goodnight, everyone."

David hugged and kissed her goodnight. I plopped down on the floor next to Jack. His tail was thumping against the tile. It was music to my ears. I affectionately rubbed his ears and kissed his face.

"So, Tabitha, tell me all about the kittens," I said, studying her face.

"Daddy's secretary came over and took them. She works for a

shelter and promises to get them the best homes. Tara's real sad now but Bruce is fine."

"You know, we couldn't have kept them. We have to move soon. No one will rent to us with six cats."

Tara and Bruce were now fixed so there would be no more kittens.

"I'm just sad," Tabitha said, sipping her hot chocolate.

"Tabitha, I know you know what happened this weekend. How do you feel about all this?" I asked nervously, making the hole in my cheek worse.

"Mom. I saw "Bridges of Madison County" with you this summer. I saw your pain then. I feel sad for you. I know what's going on with you."

I bounced up from the floor and squeezed her tight. She was remarkably deep for a child.

"I love you, Tabitha. You are so smart."

"Taylor called me too, Mommy. I'm not a baby, anymore. I know more than you guys think I do."

"Okay," I smiled, kissing her face all up. "Thanks for understanding. I better go upstairs."

"I have to stay up. I still have tons more homework," she whined, putting her mug in the sink.

"I'm really proud of all your A's. I know this school is hard."

"Krista is having a sleep over next weekend. Can I go?"

"Of course, Babes," I replied, as I started slowly creeping up the steps.

I had experienced the most incredible sex with Nick all weekend. The last thing in the world, I wanted to do was have sex with David. I stood outside the bedroom door. Let's see. I could fill up the tub and get a fresh razor. I could go in there and pretend my husband can take me to the moon. I hadn't even have a chance to linger over all the wonderful moments I had with Nick. I could throw myself down these steps and hope for brain damage. I could go in there and take it like a man. What the fuck, I could do this. I took a deep breath and turned the knob. Oh God, maybe I should have taken the brain dead.

The next morning, I woke up still entwined in David's arms.

153

"Hey, what are you doing still sleeping?" I asked, shaking him gently.

"I guess, I really needed to sleep," he mumbled, rubbing his eyes.

"You're going to be late and we're not going to have enough hot water unless we shower together."

"That's okay with me," he grinned, biting my neck.

"You, animal," I said in a sexy growl.

Along the way to the bathroom, I yelled at Tabitha to get ready for school. Tara was curled up on her chest. Bruce was stretched out on her desk. Tabitha's homework was lying underneath him.

I jumped out of the shower with my body shaking and teeth chattering. "This is crazy, David. I can't wait to move. This house is a nightmare."

"How about if we go away a lot? Thanksgiving is next weekend. How about a nice long romantic weekend?"

"Sounds nice," I said, offering him a loving smile.

"I'm also going to make an appointment with the marriage counselor."

"Okay, whenever. Let me know," I said sincerely, blow drying my whole body.

I couldn't get warm. I knew it was more than the cold shower. All the emotions were whirling around inside me, ravaging my heart and soul. I found myself pushing back sudden tears as I was holding the black knit dress in my hand. Nick's smile when I came prancing out of the dressing room wearing it, floated in my mind. Desire for him came flooding back. I had to be such an actress for David otherwise I felt he would fly in and kill Nick. Was the Oscar worth it?

Tabitha and David had already raced off by the time I climbed into the Jeep. I felt sick with despair as I started the engine. I stopped for cigarettes, coffee and a phone card. Some things never change.

Mike and Talisa were sipping coffee at the front desk.

"Keara, we are all dying to hear what happened," Mike screamed, her eyes wide.

"I got caught," I said nonchalant.

"What?" they all yelled at once.

"Yes, David caught me in Philadelphia with Nick. It's a long story but the bottom line is David has forgiven me. I just have to go to a marriage counselor with him and do some sucking up."

They were all looking at me intently. Amanda had come out of her office and was leaning against the doorway.

A messenger came briskly down the hall carrying orange and yellow roses. "These are for a Keara," he called out.

"Right here," I said, waving my right hand.

He placed the arrangement in my arms. I plucked the card out of the plastic holder and read it aloud. "I love you, Keara. Now and Forever, David."

There was a round of wow from my amazed co-workers. I started trotting towards my office with the roses.

"Keara, how do you do it?" Talisa asked, shouting out from her desk.

"I swallow," I laughed wickedly, over my shoulder.

I walked swiftly into my office and sank in my chair clutching the flowers. Instantly, I fought back tears as I swiveled back and forth.

I need to be locked away until I come to my senses. Somebody, please lock me up.

Talisa buzzed by intercom. "Keara, Ranger is on one. You know, you should be teaching a class, like Cheating 101. I would sign up in a minute."

We both burst into a giggling frenzy as we hung up. I picked up Ranger on one.

"What's so funny?" he asked.

"I was just thinking about the size of your cock," I replied, still laughing.

"I heard David caught you. That must not have been funny."

"God, Talisa has a big mouth."

"Are you okay?"

"Yeah, of course. David will never divorce me."

"I wouldn't let you go either."

"Ranger, are you coming in? Where are you?"

"I'm in Jersey. I won't be in. Can you take care of everything?"

"No problem. I'll beep you if anything important comes up."

"Oh, Keara, if you need to talk, beep me too. I'm here."

"Thanks."

I stood up on my tippy toes and stretched my arms to the ceiling. Time to dive into this mound of paper work.

The intercom buzzed. "Keara, you have Nick on one, Taylor on four and a Mary Duffy on six. Do you want them all?"

"Talisa, please get rid of Taylor and Mary for me. I just want Nick. Tell Taylor, everything is cool and I got roses. I'll talk to her later. Thanks, Talisa."

My heart was in my throat as I picked up line one.

"Hi, stranger," I said in a sexy drawl.

"Just checking to see if you're still alive."

"Everything is cool. I told you, I covered for you. David is not mad at all."

"You don't have to move out?" he asked, amazed.

"No. Nick, listen, I had the best time this weekend. Do you love me, Nick?" I asked, my voice filled with the fear of anticipation.

"Keara, would I have flown three thousand miles if I didn't."

The tears were spilling down my cheeks and splashing on Ranger's mail.

"Keara, are you okay? Please don't cry. Come on, we had such a nice time. Don't spoil it."

"I have to go," I cried into the phone. "I'll call you later." I hung up the phone, locked my office door and crawled under my desk. I hugged my knees to my chest and rocked back and forth.

What the fuck was wrong with me?

The sky was ink black as I headed toward David's office. He'd made an emergency appointment with a marriage counselor.

David was standing outside his glass office building talking to Kelly, his secretary. She was a young, pretty blonde. She was holding a bag of Cat Chow. Kelly took care of all the stray cats around the building. I gave her a quick smile and waved. David hopped into the Jeep.

"You look tired. Want me to drive?"

"No. I'm fine."

156

"I made reservations for Thanksgiving weekend. You'll need to take off a couple of days."

"I can arrange that. Where are we going?"

"Woodstock. Keara, why you are so sad?"

"David, I had a tough day at work. Ranger didn't come in and I was swamped," I said, forcing a smile.

Michael Rizzo opened his office door and ushered us in. He extended his hand to us.

"I'm Michael," he said, warmly.

He was of average height, early forties, thin with thick black hair and vivid green eyes.

His eyes are what made him attractive otherwise he looked like your average Joe.

We sat down on a brown leather couch. There was a dark wood end table next to me with a Kleenex box and a small digital clock on it. Michael sat across from us on a brown leather swivel chair. It was a cross between an office and an easy chair.

I slid off my cow coat and laid it across my lap. I was wearing a black ribbed turtleneck, a short black velvet skirt, black tights and black boots. Ninja Adulteress.

"So, who would like to start? Why are you two here?" he asked, rubbing his chin as if he had a beard.

"Keara had an affair and I thought it was over. Then this weekend, she went off with him again. Keara, doesn't like to talk about things. I'd like to know what goes on in her head. I love her and want our marriage to work."

"Keara, would you like to say something?" Michael asked, studying me intensely.

I shook my head.

Just give me a fucking A to wear on my chest and let me go home.

"See it's hard for me to get her to talk about her feelings or to have a conversation," David said, frustrated. "We had a great marriage. Then Keara, sobered up and started having an affair with my partner. I know deep down she loves me. I think she is just confused right now."

I threw David a reassuring smile.

157

"I do love you, David. That is why I'm here," I said in a low tone, stroking my fake fur coat.

The rest of the session went along the lines of me looking remorseful and David explaining how I was just different. I spent the session daydreaming of Nick and hoping I wouldn't get called on to repeat anything.

Later, we trudged out into the frosty air and drove home in cold silence.

* * *

David and I slowly started to repair the damage from my affair. We were seeing Michael twice a week and I had them both convinced that I'd stopped calling Nick.

The blinking phone lines brought me back to earth. I started gnawing on an acrylic nail as I decided to pick up Sal first. Sal was twenty-seven years old, lean and muscular Italian hunk. He had dark chocolate hair and eyes. Sal also asked me out constantly.

He was good for the ego.

"Sal," I said in a silky murmur. "Sorry, to have kept you waiting. I was on long distance."

"Yeah, it was probably your boyfriend. Right?"

"Yes."

"I can make you forget him. I have a cabin in Vermont. I'd love to take you there."

"Sal, you should be asking Taylor there, not me."

"I find you exciting, Keara. Your daughter is nice but I want you."

"Silly boy," I laughed.

"Keara, where is Dave, he owes me money, I can't wait any longer."

"He's not in today, Sal," I said in a business like tone, holding up my index finger to my lips as Ranger came bursting through my door. "I don't expect to hear from him till later but I promise you, I'll work on him ."

"Think about working for me. I'll double whatever he's paying you."

"Thanks, I will. I have two other lines. I have to go."

I slammed down the phone and spun around to face Ranger.

"Ranger, I have two other calls, but you must give me a check for Sal. I can't keep stalling him."

"He likes you. Did he ask you out?" Ranger asked, jealousy creeping into his voice.

"Why? Do you think if I fuck him, he'll forget the bill?"

"You're bad, Keara," he yelled, over his shoulder, sprinting out the door.

"Ranger, you better get back in here with a check," I screamed after him.

The other two lines wanted money too. This job was no longer fun. It was making me stressed I popped in a Kenny G CD and swallowed two extra strength Excedrin.

Too bad I couldn't drink my lunch.

On my way home, I stopped at the jewelry store and ordered a Tiffany silver key chain for Nick's birthday. I had it engraved, "Best friends 4 ever Keara."

Thick wet flakes were coming down in a fury. At least it would be a white Christmas. We were going to Florida after Christmas. David had a rich client who had a forty-room mansion there on the beach, where we'd be staying. I was going to have to take off from work again. I made a mental note to butter up Ranger.

By the time I pulled up in front of our run down cottage there was about two inches of snow on the ground. It was hard to imagine that just a couple of months ago, I was digging my toes into the warm sand. Now my toes felt like they were going to snap off from the cold.

Taylor and Tabitha were sitting on the floor watching a family sitcom show. Jack was curled up beside them. Bruce was giving Tara a tongue bath on her head.

"Who wants to go sledding at the park?" I asked, brushing off giant flakes from my coat.

"Mom, can I bring the surf board?" Tabitha asked, jumping up and down.

"Of course."

"Mom, you know Adam will probably be there,"Taylor said crankily.

"Good. This way David can confront him in person. I'll call

David now and have him meet us there. It will be fun."

The park was a white mass of giggling happy children playing in the white powder. David met us there and we joined in on the child's play. I was hoping the combination of wet snow and the cold would numb my brain not just my body parts. No such luck. As I was lying in the snow making angels with David, my thoughts were of Nick.

The next morning, the roads were icy and treacherous. Tabitha was excited to have no school. Snow days didn't happen in San Diego. I was sitting in bumper to bumper traffic, smoking cigarette after cigarette. Thoughts of Nick kissing someone on New Year's Eve were again spinning in my head. By the time I strode into the office, I felt like I was going to throw up.

"Keara, are you okay? You look so pale," Talisa asked concerned.

"Yeah, just getting used to the snow instead of sand," I sighed, darting into my office.

I peeled off my coat and sweater. Ranger loved heat. He kept the office like an inferno. There was no happy medium here. Too cold outside. Too hot inside. I wanted San Diego back. I punched in Nick's number on my phone consol.

"Hi, sorry to wake you," I said in a scratchy voice.

"It's okay. Do you have a cold? You sound funny."

"I could be getting one. It's so fucking cold here."

"Are you sure you weren't smoking a lot?"

"Nick, I miss you, terribly."

"Uh oh, I know that voice. What's wrong Keara?"

"I want to be with you. I want to spend New Year's with you. I want to move back there and live with you," I said, fighting tears.

"Keara, come on, don't cry. Let's get through the holidays first and talk about us after. How about I fax you something?"

"Okay," I muttered, sketching the Empire State Building with me jumping off it. " Sorry I got crazy. I have to get back to work. It must be all that white stuff outside getting to me."

"Don't be sorry. I'm always here if you get depressed. I loved the wolf book you sent me."

"I got you something special for your birthday too."

160

"I can't wait. No more smoking, Keara."

My body was rigid with pain as I hung up the phone.

"Keara, I hate you," Talisa said, in a giddy voice, standing in my doorway. She was holding an arrangement of wild flowers in her arms. "I can't believe all the flowers your husband sends you. You are so lucky."

"I know," I laughed painfully, taking them out of her hands.

"What's wrong, Keara, you look so sad today?"

"It's probably just the holiday blues. You know stressing out over Christmas."

"Tell me about it," she frowned, strolling out the door.

I opened the envelope and slid out the card. It read: Dear Snow Bunny, Last night was the best. I'll sled with you anywhere. Love, David.

The fax machine came to life as I read the last line. Nick had sent me a page full of office jokes. Time to smoke. As I was fishing my cigarette out of my purse, Taylor came in and pelted me with a snowball.

"You fucking bitch, " I giggled, brushing the snow off my desk. "You're dead meat. I'll get you and your little dog too."

"Come on, Mommy. I only have fifteen minutes in between classes. Let's go get some coffee."

"Sure. I don't feel like working, anyway."

"I see David is still sucking up to you," she grinned, fingering the card. "Obviously he is one fucked up dude."

We sprinted out of the office and ran into Rich and Vinny in the parking lot.

"Where do you two think you are going?" Rich asked.

"We need coffee. Want anything?" I asked, in a sexy drawl.

"Yeah, for you to stop moaning over that loser in California."

I scooped off a pile of snow from the back of Rich's Mercedes and smacked him with a snowball. Taylor was pelting Vinny. It turned into a snow war. The girls naturally won.

I turned the heat up on full blast driving to the deli.

"Mommy, you work for insane people, you know that."

"I know, I really blend in. Taylor, I need to make Nick jealous. Help me invent a lover."

"A rich and handsome one, of course. He has to have a ponytail and a black Porsche," she said with a mischievous gleam in her eyes.

We decided his name would be Jason Stevens. I picked the Stevens after Bewitched, that was Samantha's last name. Jason would be in his late thirties and a corporate lawyer. I would meet him this weekend at a Christmas party at the place where Taylor worked. After we ironed out all the details, Taylor left for class and I went back to the office. I ran by my plan to Mike, Tina and Talisa. Everyone would help.

It snowed on and off all weekend. At least the snow made the cottage more appealing. The trees and bushes glistened with snow and icicles. The snow covered the brown grass and weeds making it a carpet of white powder.

We spent the weekend painting the hallways, downstairs, and upstairs. I painted all the walls a midnight blue color. David sprayed gold and silver stars over my midnight blue walls. Tabitha decorated the house for Christmas. The weekend was spent in total harmony. Tra la la la.

Monday, mid-morning, I was at my desk sipping a cup of black coffee when Talisa buzzed me.

"Nick's on four. What do you want me to do?" she asked, pumped up with the task of deceiving a male.

"Give me ten minutes with him. Then rush into my office screaming that I have to see what just what was delivered for me. See if you can get Mike to do it with you. Thanks."

I punched in line four. "Hi, Nick," I said casually, doodling on a pad.

"Keara, I just got my birthday present. It's beautiful."

"I'm glad you like it. What are you doing for your birthday?"

"Just having dinner with my family. Nothing exciting. What did you do this weekend?"

"Oh, I just went to a party with Taylor," I said, mischievously.

"Why does your voice sound like that's not all that happened?"

"It was just a Christmas party," I giggled.

"Did you have fun?"

"Look, Nick, I'm not going to lie to you. I met someone this

162

weekend."

"How do you mean that?" he asked in a frosty voice.

"Oh God, I don't know. I wasn't looking to meet anyone and this guy ...

"Keara, Keara," Talisa and Mike screamed bursting into my office. "Come out to the front desk and see what you just got delivered, now."

"Uh, sorry Nick for the interruption but you know I work with crazies."

"Keara, come on now," Mike exclaimed.

"Nick, let me call you back."

"Okay, I'll be here."

I hung up and jumped off my chair to hug my friends. "Thanks, guys. That was great acting. I'm impressed."

"No problemo," They both said, trotting out of my office.

Talisa came back in and kissed me. "I wasn't acting that time," she smiled slyly, strutting out of my office.

I pinched myself to see if I was dreaming half this stuff. No, I was really here.

Ranger popped his head in. "Keara, we need to go over the check book and I want to take you Christmas shopping."

"Ranger, I don't need anything."

"How about something from Victoria's Secret?" he asked, his face flushing.

Talisa buzzed in. "Keara, I think it might have worked. Nick is back and on seven."

"Thanks, Talisa, I'll take him." I spun around to Ranger. "Get out," I ordered, pointing my index finger to the door. "I want to talk to Nick in private."

"Okay, okay, just tell me who does Vinny have in his office. His door is locked."

"I think Mike might have wandered in there, you gossip monger," I said, winking at him. "Now, get out."

I pressed in seven. "Hi Nick, sorry I didn't get to call you back. It's a zoo here."

"So, what was all the commotion?"

"Oh, nothing really. I was telling you I met this guy. He's a

163

lawyer. He was really nice to me at the party."

"Of course, Keara, you are great. You still haven't told me anything yet."

"Oh, so when I went out to the reception area, there was a huge stuffed bear with Godiva chocolates."

"Do you like him?"

"He's nice. It's like I just met him though but he's crazy about me. I guess I know what you must feel like with me acting like that. I don't know if I like it."

Talisa buzzed in.

"Nick, hold on a minute. I'm getting beeped."

I pressed the intercom. "Thanks, Talisa. Perfect timing."

"You really have other calls. Do you want them? You have Sal on three and Donna on one."

"Yes. I'll take them both."

I pressed in seven again. "Nick, I have to go."

"I'll call you tomorrow."

"Sure. Bye, Nick," I said in a dark whisper.

Was it working? Did he actually buy my story? Was he jealous now? A tiny jolt of hope rippled through me.

Grow up, Keara. Nick is never riding up on that white horse and taking you back with him.

The rest of the week I spend weaving in details of Jason Stevens to Nick in our conversations. Tina, Mike and Talisa all helped by sticking their heads in when I was on with Nick and making things up about Jason. Nick was more attentive but I really couldn't tell if he was really jealous. My scheming this time was not paying off.

Everyone was in the Christmas spirit but me. I wanted to throw Santa down in the street and stores when I saw him and beat his chest with my fists. I wanted Nick. A simple request. Why the fuck couldn't he deliver? Maybe if I put a gun to Rudolph's head...

The office party sucked. Everyone was festive and drinking. I sneaked out and called Nick from my office.

"Hello, Merry fucking Christmas."

"Why the Scrooge?"

"Everyone is drinking. I just don't want to be around it."

"I'm sorry, Keara, you're not having fun. How's the

164

boyfriend?"

"I don't want him Nick. I want you."

"Keara," he sighed heavily. "Do we have to go through this again?"

"Let's just end it, then. It's way too painful for me."

"Keara, please, we have been through so much together. Let's not end it like this."

"I never want to hear your voice again," I snapped, slamming down the phone. My whole body was shaking uncontrollably. I ran to the bathroom and threw up.

* * *

Florida was hot and sticky. A welcome relief from the cold and ice. We stayed at David's client's mansion on the beach. I was in awe of the lavish furnishings, house, cars and servants. We met for breakfast each morning in the huge dining room with Frank and Inga, an attractive, older couple who acted quite down to earth despite their wealth.

On the outside, I was having a marvelous time, on the inside, I was dead. My heart ached every day. By New Year's Eve, I was hoping to have a heart attack to stop the misery.

New Year's Eve, we went to the opening of our friend's restaurant. He had a successful restaurant in New York and was now hoping for one down here. David had invited three clients who lived in Florida to join us. Frank and Inga came too.

I wore an old DJ outfit that Nick loved, a sleeveless denim vest with flower rhinestone buttons and a scoop back. The skirt was white chiffon over a puffed out satin slip. Tabitha was dressed in a long blue floral dress. David wore his dark gray Ralph Lauren suit with a blue Polo dress shirt and a funky Nicole Miller tie.

"So, Keara, how are you feeling on this vacation?" David asked, in a low tone.

We were slow dancing to the song, "Somewhere out There." I had requested it. I had dedicated it in my mind to Nick.

"I'm having the best time, David. This was a fun New Years," I smiled awkwardly. " I think we are making great progress in therapy." I kissed his cheek.

"I thought so. I really feel like you mean it this time."

I smiled weakly. "David, stop worrying, everything is cool."

Keara, Keara, do you think, maybe, your New Year's resolution should have been no more lies.

We flew back to New York, rested, a little color, and happy. Well, my happy and their happy were not the same. I was happy to get back to work and hope Nick would call. They were happy thinking I was happy being together again. Oh God, I was never going to be happy.

The weeks went by tortuously slow. Nick didn't call. It was getting close to my birthday.

One day, Mike came running in my office. She was noticeably pale and her eyes were red.

"What's wrong Mike? You look like hell."

"I got caught. I was sloppy. My husband heard me on the phone, put two and two together and blew up," she said in a tense voice.

"You couldn't deny it?" I asked quietly, a chill going through me, remembering that fatal phone call in Philadelphia.

"So, what's the proper waiting period before I see my boyfriend again," she smiled nervously. "I thought I would ask a pro. What should I do, Keara? I'm scared, I don't want to lose my husband."

"Mmm, first thing, you have to swear that it is over. Beg his forgiveness. Then, agree to go to a marriage counselor and get back on track. Of course, a black teddy, wouldn't hurt."

"But he is so mad."

"If he truly loves you, he'll get over it. He's not going to want a divorce. You have kids."

"So, how long? What do you think? A month maybe."

"I guess, a month sounds about right."

"Want to have a cigarette with me?"

"No. I gave it up. Quit cold turkey on New Years. I kicked drinking, I can do this."

"Good for you but I need one bad," she grimaced, trudging out the door.

* * *

My big birthday finally arrived. Forty years old. I was no longer as young as I felt. Time to shop for a good plastic surgeon.

166

David sent yellow roses, of course. The office had a cake for me. Ranger took me out to lunch and whined how much he wanted me. Nick still hadn't called. I had tried to call him but Lou had answered and barked at me never to call Nick again.

These past few weeks I had been able to split myself into two, the loving mother and wife. I had the therapist eating out of my hand. David was convinced I was all his. The other half walked around in pain, confusion and misery. I spent the day pretending to be happy. The famous Keara giggle. The big toothy smile. I'd perfected my act so well that I even fooled myself sometimes.

I was just leaving the office early to get my eyebrows waxed, when Talisa buzzed me.

"Hey, birthday girl, Nick is on two. I take it, you want him."

My heart started beating wildly. I immediately became dizzy and my mouth went dry. I cleared my throat and punched in line two with a trembling hand.

"Hello," I said, trying to sound casual.

"Happy Birthday, Keara. I hope all your wishes came true."

They did now. "I thought you wouldn't call."

"I didn't think you ever wanted to hear from me again," he whispered. " I was afraid you'd hang up on me. I want us to be friends."

"Me too, Nick. My days are so empty without hearing your voice."

"I've been miserable too. Friends forever?"

"Yes. Friends forever. You made an old woman very happy."

"You'll never be old, Keara. You have the youngest spirit of anyone I know."

Waves of love, warmth and happiness washed over me. I shed my zombie skin. I could feel my emotions rising, my face getting flushed. I felt like a puppy getting rescued from the pound.

"What are you doing for your birthday?"

"Taylor and the girls from the office are taking me out to a disco. We are dancing the night away."

"I'll call you next week and you can tell me all about it."

"Promise," I grinned gleefully.

"Promise."

I hung up feeling ecstatic. The adrenaline was pumping through my veins again, like old times.

My birthday turned out to be expensive for David. He gave me several gifts over the course of the weekend. On Sunday afternoon, he threw a surprise party at my favorite restaurant. He hired a DJ and a stripper. The whole office was there plus all my friends. Later that night he handed me a box wrapped in cow paper with black and white ribbons tied around it.

"What's this?" I asked, arching my waxed eyebrows.

"A special gift for a special person," he smiled lovingly, brushing back my copper hair.

"David, you are crazy. You already have spent a fortune."

"Just open it, Keara."

I slowly unwrapped the paper to find a green box with Rolex stamped on it. With trembling fingers, I opened the lid. Inside was the most gorgeous gold and silver Rolex with a navy blue face. It was magnificent.

"David, oh David, I love it, I love you. Oh my God, I love it," I cried, jumping up and down.

"Put it on me, hurry."

He clasped it on my wrist and kissed me on the lips."Happy Birthday, Keara."

"I love you, David," I said brightly, admiring my new watch.

* * *

The weather in New York was disgusting. A blizzard had already paralyzed the city. Work shut down along with the roads. With the wind chill factor, it was below zero every day. The freezing cold was getting to me. I suggested Puerto Rico for the Valentine weekend. We all needed sun desperately. David was working fifteen hour days. Tabitha was still keeping those A's and despite medication still had a rash from nerves. Taylor's love life was in a shambles. I knew if I didn't steal her away on Valentine Day, she would be a candidate for suicide. My office had whispers of lay offs. Nick and I were slowly rebuilding our friendship. Jack was dying.

David and I started discussing seriously our moving to San Francisco now. Our lease was up here July first. David was given the go ahead to start a West coast branch of his office since he was totally convinced Nick was out of our lives, he was comfortable with the move. I was making incredible progress in therapy. All an act, of course, but Michael and David were sold. I started to hint to Ranger that I would be moving on soon.

We decided that David would go out for a week in the middle of March to look for a place. I would join him on Thursday for a long weekend. This could be my chance to see Nick. Only this time I couldn't get caught. My heart stood still. The old familiar feelings and longings for Nick came rushing back.

Keara, you have been on this merry-go-round long enough, get off, girl. Now.

I walked briskly into the office on a cold windy March day. It looked like rain any minute.

"Hey, Keara,"Talisa smiled, breaking a chocolate chip cookie in two on her desk. "Why do you look like the cat that ate the canary lately?"

"I'm planning on seeing Nick this month. I don't know how yet, but I know I am."

"Keara, I have something to tell you," she whispered, gesturing for me to come closer.

"Oh no, what, what?" I asked, clutching my heart.

"I'm giving my two weeks, today."

"No, anything but that. Please, no."

"Don't make me feel bad. I know you're leaving in June."

"Do you have another job?"I asked, scooping up a piece of cookie.

"Yeah. Lots more money too. You know I'm broke."

"I'm sorry that you are leaving but happy that you'll do better," I smiled, hugging my friend.

Nuts, I don't have the strength to train another receptionist about Nick and David.

"Keara," Amanda called out, from her office. "Can you come in here for a minute?"

"What next," I muttered, strolling over to her door. "What's up, Amanda?"

"You know I broke up with Rich, don't you?"

"Yes. I heard, " I mumbled, chewing my cheek.

"I'm still with my husband but I've started going out with one of our clients. Tyler, the filthy rich, cute one," she giggled. "Anyway, I need your help, please." She pressed her hands together like she was praying.

"Boy, Amanda, I need a scorecard with you," I said teasingly, rolling my eyes.

"I told my husband I am going to Atlantic City with you. Please cover for me. Like screening your calls before you answer. I really need this, Keara," she pleaded, tapping a cigarette on her desk.

"Okay, okay, but you'll owe me, of course, big time."

"No problem, thank you. Oh, one more thing, don't mention this to Rich."

This office certainly blows Melrose, Peyton Place and any other soap away. Who were these bizarre people? Was this the Twilight Zone or what?

I was slipping out of my black leather jacket when Talisa buzzed me.

"Rich on three."

I pressed in three. "Hello, stuck in traffic?" I asked?

"Yes. Keara, I need a friend. Can you have lunch with me today? Around one?"

"Sure, Rich, but no more mommy jokes," I said firmly.

"Okay, you win," he laughed heartily, into the phone.

Talisa buzzed in. "You have your husband on two and Kylie on three."

"I'll take both. I'm going to miss you so much, Talisa."

I pressed in three first. "Kylie, tell me something good."

"How's this? I just met this cute Jewish guy at my mother's house and I really like him."

"No more Christian?" I asked mockingly, writing Nick's name all over my yellow pad.

"Christian gave me nineteen nervous breakdowns this year, I had enough."

"Are you going to see this guy again?"

"Yes, he is flying in to see me," she said happily.

"You can use me the weekend of the twentieth, I'll be in San

Francisco. I'm sure everyone in my office will be using me too."

"That might work, Keara. I love you. I'll keep you posted. Bye."

I pressed in two, feeling a little jealous that Kylie was over her obsession with Christian.

"I called to tell you, I got the tickets for San Francisco. I'm leaving Monday night and meeting Paul there. He's going to help me look for a place. He needs to talk to me too. His marriage is on the rocks but don't breathe a word. Our other friends don't know."

"I have enough with my own friends, don't worry, lips are sealed."

"Oh, I almost forgot, the reason for the call. I have a problem with your ticket for Thursday. I'm using our free ticket for you to get there and there is no direct flight. You have a lay over in Los Angeles for an hour and have to switch planes. Are you okay with that?"

"That's fine, don't worry. All I'll have is an overnight bag to carry. It's not a big thing the lay over or changing planes."

"Great. See you tonight. It's your turn to bring the food home. I'd like Chinese."

"No problem. Love you, bye."

I hung up the phone and blessed myself. Thank you, God. The answer to how I could see Nick just fell from the sky. The layover. It was only an hour but I knew I could make it work. I was going to see Nick. I scrambled out of my chair and sprinted out the door to scream my unbelievable news to everyone. I smashed right into Ranger as I raced into the hall.

"Wow, what's with you? I bet it has to do with Nick," he snarled, arching a brow.

"Yes, I'm going to California for a weekend and I might see him on a layover," I said breathlessly, jumping up and down.

"What? You are taking off again. We have to talk, Keara."

"I don't think so. I've got everyone of your clients eating out of my hand. Your files are in perfect order. Your office has never ran better and you know it, Mister," I said proudly.

"How long this time?" he sighed, in irritation.

"I'll have to leave around noon on Thursday so I need Friday.

Then I'm taking the red eye back so I'll come straight to work on Monday."

"Have fun," he shrugged, walking into his office.

After I shared my lucky news with all my partners in crime, I called Taylor.

"Hello," she answered wearily.

"Taylor, why do you sound so exhausted? Don't you have to be in school soon?"

"I only had two hours of sleep. I'm trying to finish this report and I have cramps."

"Next weekend I need you to stay with Tabitha at the house."

"Why, Mommy? I hate your fucking house, between Jack and the cats, it's a mess."

"You'll have the Jeep and a place to hang out with what's his name?"

"His name is Matt, Mother. Why don't you like him?"

"I just don't. He is not good enough for you and he looks like Magilla Gorilla."

"Oh, and excuse me with Nick. Nick, who lives with his mommy still and going on what?"

"That's different. Besides, David is successful. Anyway, I need you for the weekend."

"Okay, what are you up to? I can tell it in your voice, evil woman. You have something cooking. I know you all too well."

"I have a lay over in L.A. and you know what that means."

"I don't want to know anything. You're on your own this time. Get caught and I'll kill you."

"Get some rest and get to school."

Next call was to Nick. I was feverish with excitement. Just the thought of seeing him again sent liquid heat all through my body. My skin became hot as I dialed his number. My throat went dry.

"I have to fly to San Francisco next Thursday and my plane has a layover in L.A. for an hour. Do you think you can meet me at the airport for some coffee talk."

"I guess so. What time?"

"I'll find out everything and fax you."

"Why are you going to San Francisco?"

"David has business there."

"So, I only get an hour of your time."

"Yeah, but we will hug the whole hour. I miss you so much. Can you bring Barney? I wish you could bring Zeus too."

I hung up and was intoxicated by the moment. This was the best high. Funny, I didn't think about reaching for that drink anymore. I hadn't even had a cigarette since New Years.

Ranger breezed in and tossed down a thick contract on my desk.

"I need you to retype this. I made a lot of corrections. I need it by five."

"Oh, Ranger, you just work my fingers to the bone. My manicure will probably cost extra tonight with all this wear and tear," I smiled devilishly, licking my lips.

"How much is your manicure?"

"Thirty-five. I have the best."

"Here, it's on me tonight," he grinned boyishly, reaching into his pocket.

"Thanks, Ranger," I said appreciately, jumping up and giving him a friendly peck on the cheek.

"Get typing," he ordered, his face flushed.

David left on Monday. I spent the rest of the week shopping for the perfect outfit to wear on my flight.

I pranced in the office Thursday in a frenzied state. It felt like burning hot lava was flowing through my veins. My stomach was churning and a hippo was sitting on my chest.

Mitchell was handing Amanda a Styrofoam cup of coffee and a scone. He looked firmly in my eyes as I approached the front desk.

"Hello, Keara, how was Atlantic City? I heard you two had a blast," he growled, watching me intently.

"It was fun, but nothing beats Vegas," I said calmly, trotting past the two of them.

Talisa was snickering sitting at her desk breaking apart a blueberry muffin.

I flung off my jacket , threw down my purse and buzzed Talisa.

"Talisa, can you come in here, please."

She came strolling in giggling uncontrollably.

"I'm glad you see the humor in this," I half smiled, taking the lid off my hot coffee.

"Do you fucking believe him?"

"No, was I convincing enough?"

"Yeah, but what the fuck do you care. Amanda's a bitch. You know, I hate her. So, today's your big day."

"I know, I'm so nervous, I could die. What do you think about the outfit?"

I was wearing a long black cotton skirt with light purple flowers on it that went down to my ankles. On my feet, were black leather lace up boots. On top, I had a short sleeve light purple sweater.

"You're just dressed normal," she said her voice laced with surprise.

"Okay, now look." I hiked up my skirt to reveal black silk stockings hooked up to a black lacy garter belt and lacy black underwear. I dropped the skirt down and pulled up my sweater to show her a matching black lacy underwire bra.

"Sexy Mama," she whistled, licking her lips. "You are delish, Keara."

Amanda stomped into the room.

"Gotta go," Talisa said, scooting out the door.

"Thank you so much, Keara. I know, Mitchell, can be a prick. Sorry that happened. He's been driving me crazy. I have been going to extra meetings too. I think I'm going to have a breakdown."

I embraced her in a bear hug. "Don't break down over Mitchell. You two don't have kids, so why do you stay with him? You don't love him. No one likes him."

"He is so rich, Keara. I grew up poor, the youngest of eight."

"It won't be worth it if you go back to drinking and drugging, though."

"Are you seeing Nick, tonight?" she asked, changing the subject and avoiding my eyes.

"Yes, so if you'll excuse me, I have to get this office in shape so I can leave."

"Sure. Thanks again. I owe you."

I flopped down in my chair and took a sip of my coffee. It was cold. Just as well, I was so hyper anyway, the coffee would have just made me worse.

"What's with the nun's outfit?" Tina asked, strolling in wearing a crisp beige Ann Taylor pantsuit.

"Is this what nun's wear?" I asked seductively, slowly pulling up my skirt.

"Oh, Keara, I love it. You are too much. Is this all for your boy, Nick?"

"Who else? So, what am I hiding for you today in my secret box?"

She gracefully slid into the chair beside my desk. "I'm getting rid of everybody. It's only Nikko now," she smiled crookedly, inspecting her bright red nails.

"Who the hell is Nikko?"

"I met him on my last trip to Japan. He's setting me up in my own business and my own condo too," she said smugly, tapping her nails against my desk.

"Wow, Tina, I am so happy for you. I really am. You are my idol."

"Would you consider working for me?"

"Thanks but no. I'm leaving here in July for the West coast. I just hate the weather here."

"Keara, it's me you're talking to. It's not the fucking weather. It's Nick."

"Whatever," I shrugged, picking up a piece of mail.

"I have to go. I am going to miss you, Keara. You're the best."

"So are you, Tina, so are you." We hugged tight.

Talisa buzzed in. "Dave, our beloved boss is on three for you."

"Thanks, Talisa."

I picked up Ranger. "Hey, where are you?"

"I'm on my way to Jersey. Not coming in today," he said, sounding hurt.

"Ranger, are you upset that I am seeing Nick?"

"Yes, I guess so. I guess you could say I'm a little jealous. I've been stuck on you, Keara, for over fifteen years. It's just hard to see you head over heels in love with someone else."

"I'm sorry, Ranger. I'll quit, okay."

175

"Don't you dare. I'm so dependent on you."

"Ranger, I told you it was only for a year, though."

"I don't want to talk about it. Have a safe flight and enjoy yourself."

"Thanks, Ranger. See you Monday."

Rich sauntered in as I hung up the phone. He started instantly massaging my shoulders.

"You look tense. Who was that on the phone? The momma's boy."

"It was Ranger. Go on, keep teasing me, I won't tell you the latest Amanda gossip."

"I don't give a fuck about Amanda."

"Sure, sure."

"I don't. She is fucking nuts."

"Of course, she has to be to break up with you." I twirled around and leaped up to hug him.

"I love you, Rich," I smiled affectionately. "Amanda's fucked up."

"You know, Ranger, is in love with you."

"I know, I know. Hey, let's stop talking about fucked up people, check this out," I exclaimed, yanking up my skirt.

"That Nick is one lucky guy, one lucky guy," he muttered, walking out.

I heard Taylor childish giggle outside my door. It was time. She was taking me to the airport. Taylor drifted into my office looking tired.

"Ready, Mommy?"

"Do you have ringing in your ears?" I asked, swallowing hard.

"No, but then I'm not cheating on my husband," she said smart alecky, cracking her gum.

"I'm gonna throw up," I said, putting my hand on my forehead.

"Let's go, Mom. I have to get back for Tabitha and your fucked up animals," she said rolling her eyes and pulling me down the hall.

I staggered on the plane as if I was forced to walk the plank. What if David hired someone to see if I was meeting Nick? What if David surprised me in L.A.? Fear, Anxiety and excitement rippled through me the whole plane ride. When the captain

176

announced we had landed in L.A., I couldn't breathe. I fished through my purse for my inhaler. I did a quick squirt and unbuckled my seat belt.

God, Keara, your life is over if David is out there.

I floated out with the rush of the crowd. I was trembling inside and out. I spotted his handsome face in a flash. My eyes quickly darted around making sure the coast was clear.

"Give me a hug, you," he said softly, yanking the bag out of my hand and squeezing me tight. "I've missed you so much," he whispered, caressing my hair. "Where do you want to go?"

"Just for a ride. I only have an hour."

He opened the passenger's door and I slid in. Flashbacks went through my mind of the old days in San Diego in his car. The tears. The love. It was all whirling around in my head.

"Here's Barney," he smiled lovingly, handing me my old pink stuffed dog.

Around Barney's neck was Nick's red tuxedo bow tie.

"Oh, Nick, how cute," I exclaimed, my eyes brimming with tears.

"And since I couldn't bring Zeus, I made you a package of his hair," he grinned boyishly, handing me a ziplock bag of black brown dog hair.

"Oh, Nick, I love it. Thanks," I cried, tears now streaming down my face.

"Why are you crying?"

"You made me so happy. I just feel so good when I'm around you. I can't explain it."

"I really missed you, Keara," he said softly, keeping his baby blue eyes on the road.

"Well, I have something for you and Zeus," I said in a silky murmur, hiking up my skirt to my waist and sliding off my bikini underwear. "This is for you to remember me by and Zeus can sniff them and remember all the times I scratched his belly."

"Now you don't have any underwear on,"

"That's okay. I wanted you to have them just in case one day you want to jerk off in them."

"Keara, must you talk like that."

"Yes. I am from the streets of Philadelphia. I can't change who I am."

"I won't be jerking off in them. I'll keep them in the box that I have everything you send me."

"Whatever," I shrugged, stroking his thigh. "Pull over, Nick, so we can talk. Look there is a parking lot."

Nick pulled into the lot and cut the engine. It was a cool breezy night.

"Keara, I thought we were going to have coffee somewhere."

"There's not enough time, Nick, besides if I don't suck your cock right now, I will surely explode," I said in my most tantalizing voice, unzipping his black slacks and pulling up his white turtleneck.

"I see you are still the evil temptress."

"Can't help it around you. You set me on fire. Oh, I have an added attraction," I smiled wickedly, pulling out a small round vibrator from my overnight bag.

"What's that?"

"You'll see."

I turned on the vibrator. Placed it against my cheek and went down on him. In a matter of minutes, I was slurping hot liquid protein. Not only did it satisfy my thirst for him, it put out the fire between my thighs. I was reborn. Amen.

"Let's sit outside for a moment," he said in a low tone.

"Okay."

I reached into my Kipling back pack. I noticed the monkey had fallen off. I pulled out a miniature Scope bottle. I sloshed some around in my mouth and spat it out the window.

"I see you come fully prepared," he chuckled, pulling up his pants, outside the car.

"Guess I was a boy scout in another life."

He strolled over and flopped down on the brick wall surrounding the parking lot. I hopped on his lap.

"What will you be doing in San Francisco?" he asked, stroking my arm.

"Shopping."

"You're a bi-coastal shopper, now?"

I laughed, glancing at my Rolex. "Nick, I have to go. It's late."

I kissed Barney goodbye and leaped from the car. We raced toward the terminal hand in hand. It was last call for boarding. I dropped my bags by my feet and gazed firmly in his eyes, willing him to kiss me.

"I don't know when I'll see you again." Raw emotions hung thick in the air between us.

"Take care, Keara." he sighed heavily, hugging me close.

"Time to go," the stewardess yelled out.

"Bye, Nick," I mumbled, spinning around and walking swiftly to the gate.

I glanced back to see him standing there with tears streaming down his face. I quickly turned my head and raced down into the plane. No kiss. Tears. But no kiss.

I buckled my seat belt and started changing over to the loving wife. The character I would portray when the plane landed. Within the hour, I landed in San Francisco airport. This time I strolled off the plane without fear and anxiety.

"Keara, Keara," David was shouting.

He kissed my cheek and swung his arm from behind his back. He was holding a yellow rose.

David was checked in at a regular hotel room in the city. As he was putting the key in door, I felt numb. What just happened? Was I just with Nick a couple of hours ago? All the emotions, I successfully held back on the plane were surfacing now. Nick held the key to my heart. My heart had changed the locks on David. I fought off the dizziness as I entered the room.

"Oh, David, this is so nice," I exclaimed, glancing around the room. He had three bouquets of flowers brightening the ordinary room. They were in cranberry juice glass containers. On the table was a spread of cheese, crackers, French bread, fruit and a bottle of sparkling apple cider. He also had a variety of candles in different sizes and colors around the room, in navy blue heart shaped clay trays. A box of Ghirardelli chocolates laid on the flowered bedspread.

"You are too good to me," I cried, throwing my arms around his neck.

The next morning we headed across the Golden Gate to look for our new house. A hot searing pain shot through my chest. I clenched my eyes shut tight. Nick's face flashed before me.

"Are you alright, Keara?" David asked, his hazel eyes looking alarmed.

"I'm fine. Just a little jet lag and a slight headache. Don't worry."

"This house I haven't seen yet. The broker called me late yesterday and told me I would love it."

As the rented white convertible Mustang climbed the hills, the view became more breathtaking.

"David, we are not going to be able to afford this place. It's spectacular up here. These houses are a couple of million dollars."

"Keara, I don't think you realize how much money I have been making. New York was the best thing we did. To go back there and start over. I got right back into my old work habits."

"From beach bum to Wall Street tycoon. I like it," I giggled, as he turned into the driveway.

Both our mouths dropped open and we both cried out in unison. "This is it."

It was a simple ranch house on a hill overlooking the bay, surrounded by about an acre of woods. Huge pots of overflowing brightly colored flowers were everywhere. A Japanese garden was on the side of the house complete with a small cement pool. A waterfall tumbled over the rocks and into the dark water of the pool and a wooden deck wrapped around the house with a variety of plants and flowers on it. Everything blended to make it a picture of peace and tranquility. If this wasn't enough, there was a small stream gurgling softly in the woods. It came completely furnished too. A mixture of wicker, glass and Oriental furnishings created an ambience of elegance. I knew I had to live here.

The landlord strolled over to meet us as we emerged from the car.

"Hello, you must be David and Keara. I'm Steven," he said, with a slightest suggestion of a lisp, extending his hand.

I shook his hand firmly and gazed into his dove gray eyes. He was sixty something, rail thin with black hair streaked with gray, pulled back into a ponytail. His skin was white as chalk. He had an aura of peace around him. I wanted that.

"I just love your house. It's incredible. Are they yours?" I asked, pointing excitedly to three beautiful white fluffy cats with squashed in faces.

"Yes, you are looking at Pasta, Noodles and Linguine," he said softly.

"I love them," I cried, dropping to my knees to pet them. I picked them up one by one and kissed them.

"I see you're an animal lover. Do you smoke," he asked, tucking a stray strand of hair behind his ear.

"We don't smoke or drink. I have always believed your best friend is someone who can give you their paw."

"Keara, likes animals more than people," David chimed in, bending down to pet Noodles.

"Do you have any children?"

"A twelve year old daughter who is a straight A student and loves animals just as much as her mother," David said proudly.

"You sound like the perfect family to rent to. I go by auras not credit applications. If you want the place, it is yours."

"Draw up the lease and we will sign it," David smiled happily.

I was restless on the red eye home. David was sleeping soundly on my shoulder. I was wrestling too many demons to sleep. David was giving me a house and life that most people only get to dream about. I should be kissing his feet not sucking Nick's cock. What the hell was wrong with me? Should I check myself into a hospital for psychiatric evaluation?

If you did that, Keara, you would never see the light of day.

* * *

Work was no longer fun. Talisa and Tina were gone. Rich, Vinny and Ranger fought constantly among themselves. Some workers were laid off. Everyone was nervous about who would be next. Amanda was away at a rehab place. Talisa had been replaced with Sonia, a petite Spanish girl who barely spoke English. I didn't want her to know about Nick. She was confused enough about the job. I told Nick to use a different name each time he called.

I nervously crept into Ranger's office. He was signing a letter

I had just typed. Ranger looked up and smiled.

"Keara, another great letter."

"Thanks. Ranger, it's time."

"For what? Do I have an appointment with someone?"

"I'm giving my notice. I'll be leaving in two months."

"No, no, I won't accept it. You can't leave," he pleaded, rising from his desk.

"I told you from the start that this was temporary," I sighed, biting the inside of my cheek.

"You are going back to Nick."

"No. I'm really not. I'm going to work things out with David. I really mean it."

"Sure. Just exactly how far is San Francisco from San Diego?"

"That's not the point. We are renting a two million dollar house. David doesn't want me to work. I can work on my inner child. Paint. I'd be stupid to blow it."

"I don't want to talk about it right now, okay?"

"Sure." I tiptoed out and shut the door behind me.

The weather was still freezing in New York. There was still traces of dirty snow on the ground. I didn't know what to pack for Washington, D.C.. We were going there for Easter weekend. I bought a new spring dress but didn't think it would be warm enough. Taylor was once again watching the house and animals. She couldn't come because she wanted to work. She was making good money on the weekend as a shot girl. Matt worked at the same bar as a D.J..

David was sleeping as I slipped under the covers. We were planning on leaving at five in the morning to beat the traffic. Jack's barking at three woke me up. I heard the banging on the door. I knew it would be Taylor with a problem. What did she do all those years I was in San Diego? I raced down the steps and opened the door to a very drunk Taylor.

"What's going on?" I asked, suspiciously glancing behind her, to see if she was alone.

"I had a little accident at work and I just need to lay down."

"Taylor, I don't believe you drove here this drunk. Are you nuts?" I yelled, yanking her in the house. "What kind of accident?

Where is Matt?"

"He is still working and thinks I got sick," she said, slurring all her words.

My senses started to fill up with the bar smells on her. I felt nauseous.

"Tell me about this accident," I demanded, hands on my hips.

She pulled down her pantyhose and underwear. "Look," she said, pointing at her vagina.

"Oh my God," I screamed, feeling like I was going to pass out.

Her vagina was swelled up to the size of about a baseball. I'd never seen anything like it in my life.

"What the hell happened? We have got to get you to a hospital," I shrieked, running up the steps to wake David.

"Wake up David, Taylor is hurt," I cried hysterically. "We have to get her to a hospital."

"What's wrong?" he asked, slowly rising out of bed and rubbing his eyes.

"I don't know but it's ugly. Get dressed, now."

We taped a note for Tabitha on her bedroom door and raced Taylor to the hospital. We found out on the ride there that Taylor had fallen off the roof of the bar. She was wasted and had to go to the bathroom. Instead of waiting in line like a normal person, she decided to go to the one next door in storage. For some insane reason she decided to use a ladder to climb up to the roof. From there she walked along the ledge and into the window of the bathroom, slipped and fell. She landed straddling a trash can in the alley. Taylor was lucky to be alive and in one piece.

The Emergency room immediately shot her up with pain killers and put a catheter in. She didn't stop screaming Mommy, the whole time. I threw up and passed out. David had to call her father.

We spent Easter weekend by Taylor's side in the hospital. They didn't have to operate but she had to be watched carefully. She would be bedridden for at least two weeks. The big black baseball between her legs would take months to go down. At least she quit her job.

* * *

It was getting close to my leaving the office. Ranger was

becoming depressed and so was Rich. Rich and I had become close friends. We would go to lunch and bitch about Amanda and Nick.

I was balancing the checkbook when Sonia buzzed me.

"Keara, David on Four."

"Hello," I said, cheerfully into the phone.

"Keara, do you feel like going to Boston this weekend?"

"What for?"

"I have an important client that I have to wine and dine. I thought we could make a weekend of it."

"I don't think so. Taylor is still recovering and hangs out with us on weekends. Plus, I don't like just sitting there while you guys talk business. I hate it. You are better off without me. You can have a cocktail then. You know what they say about people that don't drink in the business world."

"You're right. I'll be back on Sunday. Are you okay with that?"

"Sure. I have the kids. I'm really busy now. It's your turn tonight. I'll take Sushi, please."

"No problem, bye."

I quickly hung up the phone and called Nick.

"What are you doing?"I asked, biting the inside of my cheek.

"Just doing my stock market charts. You are up to something. What is it?"

"I was just wondering what you are doing on Saturday night?"

"Why?"

"David is going out of town. I thought we could have a phone date," I said, in a romantic voice, twirling my hair around my fingers.

"What is a phone date?"

"You call me up at a set time and we pretend to go on a real date. We'll dress up and have fun. Use our imaginations. What do you think?"

"I think you are crazy but it sounds like fun."

"Alrighty then. How about Saturday night, your time nine, mine will be midnight."

"Fine with me."

Midnight was perfect. I would take Tabitha and Taylor to

dinner early. Tabitha would be in bed and Taylor would go off with her friends. David will have checked in by eleven. By midnight, I will have turned into the evil temptress once again.

By the time Saturday rolled around, I was tense and jittery.

"Keara, are you okay?" David asked, packing his Polo sweater in his overnight bag. "You seem stressed."

"It's the move and I'm leaving work this week. Then we have to put Jack to sleep. It's all too much for me."

"I hate leaving you like this," he frowned, putting his arms around me.

"Don't be silly. You go and dazzle Jay and his friends."

"Are you sure?"

"Yes. Now get the hell out of town," I laughed.

The night dragged on. Taylor and Tabitha bickered all through dinner. I took Jack for a short walk and tucked Tabitha in early. Taylor took off with some friends. David called at eleven a little drunk. By eleven-thirty, I was dressed in my new sheer Victoria Secret black short night gown with matching black underwear. I lit five scented vanilla candles on the bureau. By the bed, I had Penthouse Forum with erotic stories in it. Finally, it was midnight.

"Hello," I answered, in a velvety voice.

"Hello, Keara, where do you want to go tonight?"

"I want to play on Jupiter and Mars."

"That sounds like a song. How about humming a few bars. I don't know the old songs like you do, only the new ones. How about your favorite? I can sing that."

"Oh, yes, please do."

Nick crooned Stray Cat Strut in my ear. He knew how much that song drove me wild.

"Oh, Nick, you are making me crazy," I groaned, sprawled out on the bed. My hand gently massaging my clitoris.

By the time he got to the last verse, I was moaning his name softly into the phone.

"Now, it's your turn," I whispered seductively, picking up the Forum.

I started to read one of the kinky letters pretending I was making it up. By the time I got to the bottom of the page, he had come.

"I never had phone sex before. Have you?" I asked, crossing my fingers.

"No, never."

"That was fun, should we now pretend to smoke cigarettes."

"Gross. You haven't slipped up and smoked again?"

"No. Not once and I'll be two years sober soon and I don't even crave it anymore."

"I'm so proud of you, Keara," he said, sniffing.

"Nick, are you crying?"

Silence. More sniffing.

"Nick, why are you crying?"

"I really miss you, Keara."

"I love you, Nick. Let's do our mental hug, okay? On the count of three. One, two, three."

A warm silence for a minute.

"That felt good. Thanks for the silk boxers with Marvin the Martian on them. I love them."

"Nick, let's do breakfast, tomorrow. No phone sex. Just coffee talk. I have an hour phone card. I can call you at nine your time."

"Sounds like a date."

Monday morning, I sprayed Fendi perfume all over my nightgown and underwear. Tossed them in a Priority Mail bag and sent them to Nick. His new secretary would definetly wonder what was going on.

My last week sped by quickly. There was a goodbye party at the office with cake and presents. The best present was from Rich. He gave me one hundred dollars worth of phone cards. I was really going to miss him. Ranger was so depressed that it made me uneasy. Mike and Amanda cried. It was certainly one hell of a year and office. I was going to miss their craziness.

I spent my first week off packing and putting things in storage. The new house had everything so I just had to bring clothes. I still hadn't told Nick I was moving.

One of the conditions of the house, was that we had to take it in June, even though our N.Y. lease was up in July. It was decided that Tabitha and I would move there the last week of June and

David would come fourth of July weekend. We would fly in with Bruce and Tara. Jack would be put to sleep. He could barely walk and couldn't control his bladder or bowels. Jack wasn't a dog to me. He was my best friend, confidante and soul mate. A piece of me would die with him. I called Kylie the night before.

"Hi, I need you to come over this week and take all the furniture and plants."

"Sure. Do you need me tomorrow with Jack?"

"No. David will be there. I rather not talk about it."

"It's for the best. He is suffering."

"I know," I said sobbing into the phone. "I have to go."

I hung up the phone and flung myself on the floor next to Jack. He was sleeping on his blanket. I sobbed into his fur, my arms thrown around his neck. I kissed his face and told him over and over again how much I loved him. David and Tabitha entered the room and immediately started crying too. Tomorrow would be hell.

Jack died at two in the afternoon the next day. Taylor came by and took Tabitha out for the day. David and I were by his side to the end. We drove home in painful silence. That night we cried ourselves to sleep.

Kylie came over the next night and dragged me out of bed. I was still crying.

"Keara, get up. I brought my neighbor here. He's with David. They are packing the van with all your stuff. I told him I would buy him dinner for the use of his van and help. Wait till you see him, he is really cute."

"Kylie, nothing matters anymore. Jack is dead. I feel like I died too," I said, hot tears running down my face. "I can't believe he is gone. I'm really freaking out."

"Keara, get it together. He was in pain. Come on, let's go to Seven Eleven. We'll get coffee, have a cigarette and buy you a phone card. You will feel better."

"Nothing will make me feel better. Besides I don't smoke anymore."

"You can have one tonight," she said firmly, yanking me to my feet.

"I must look a mess."

"Here, put a hat on and your sunglasses," she said, scooping them up from the bureau and handing them to me.

She slipped her hand into her jacket pocket and pulled out a brown velvet box.

"Here, this is for you. Open it."

"What is it?"

"Your going away present."

I opened the box to find a beautiful gold pussycat bracelet. Each gold cat was linked together in a sleeping position.

"Kylie, I love it. It's beautiful. You are crazy."

"You're crazy giving me all your stuff. Besides you talked me into Europe with my new sweetie and changing my life. You helped me through all my breakdowns. Stick with cats. No more dogs."

Downstairs, David and the neighbor were packing the van with the wicker furniture.

I had a cigarette at the store and bought a phone card and drank a black coffee. Kylie was right. I started to feel better. By the time we drove back, her neighbor was gone. Taylor and Tabitha pulled up behind us.

"I better get going, Keara," Kylie sighed, her eyes glistened with tears.

"I love you, Kylie," I cried, squeezing her tight. "Have the best time in Europe."

"I love you, Keara," she exhaled loudly, as I exited her car.

"Why is Kylie crying Mom," Tabitha asked, strolling up besides me.

"She is sad that I am leaving. How was the movie?"

"It was intense."

"Tabitha, go finish up your packing, please."

I spun around to see Taylor and David hugging.

"Taylor, want to have a cigarette?"

"Hey, when did you start again?" David asked in a surprise voice.

"It's just for tonight," I mumbled, slipping my hand in Taylor's and walking toward the porch.

"I'm going to help Tabitha pack," David announced.

We stood on the porch and lit our Marlboro Lights.

"Do you believe how hot it is, not to mention muggy?" I asked, casually.

"Yeah, this weather sucks,"Taylor grumbled, blowing a cloud of smoke into the sticky air.

"Taylor, you know, I would love for you to live with me in San Francisco. It would be good for you. You need a change from this lifestyle. S.F. has a great college, too."

"I'm not ready to move. I'm not like you. I like one place. You had four different houses in San Diego," she growled, lighting another cigarette from her old one.

"Sorry if I like experiencing everything. That is what life is all about. Do you want the words "what if" on your tombstone? I sure don't. My father died so unhappy because he didn't get to do anything he really wanted to do. You are a waitress, failing in college and Matt controls you. Come with me, Taylor. Try something new. Try a new school. New friends. New life."

"No, Mommy," she said, bursting into tears and throwing herself into my arms. "You stay here, Mommy. This year was so perfect with you here."

"I can't stand it here, Taylor. New York is not for me," I said soothingly, rubbing her back. "I can't stand the brutal winters here or the suffocating heat of summer. I love California."

"You are going because of Nick."

"No, I'm not. I really am going to start a new life for myself. Tap into my creativity. Will you at least think about coming to S.F.?"

"I don't know Mommy, you are good with change. I'm not."

"I love you, Taylor. I am only a phone call away."

"I'm gonna miss you so much, Mommy," she sobbed.

"Why don't you sleep over." We'll put blankets on the floor and have a Mommy and me sleep over."

She just nodded her head.

The trip to the airport was miserable. Taylor came along and sobbed the whole way.

David was anxious to get to work. Tabitha hated leaving friends again. Bruce and Tara were meowing loudly in their cages.

I was wishing Jack was in his cage, ready to fly with me. Goodbye New York. Goodbye Jack.

* * *

Part Three

San Francisco

The car rental didn't have my Mustang that I ordered. Instead they stuck me with a gold four door Oldsmobile. This after waiting two hours in line.

"Mom, I can't ride in this ugly car," Tabitha groaned loudly, standing by the trunk.

"Tabitha, it's all they had. We don't know anyone yet. It's cool."

As we drove up to the house, a huge smile had spread across Tabitha's mouth.

"Mom, this is just beautiful. I love it. Wow, from a shack to a palace. You're the best."

"There is also a heated pool. We can swim as soon as we unpack."

"Do you think Tara and Bruce will be okay living outside? They are house cats."

"I promised Steven, no cats in the house. So we have to stick to that. They will be fine."

Steven and his trio of fluffly cats were waiting on the deck.

"Welcome home," he smiled.

"Thanks. We are so happy to be here. Steven, this is Tabitha."

"Hello Tabitha," Steven said softly, extending his hand.

"Hi. I love your cats. Can I play with them?"

"Of course. They love to be the center of attention. There is a path on the side of the house that leads down to a studio. I am living there right now. Then I'm off to Japan for six weeks. If you have any questions, please come down. I left a list on instructions in the kitchen."

"Thanks."

"Come on Tabitha, check out the inside and your room. I know you'll love it."

She scrambled to her feet, full of white fur and ran inside. "Which room is mine?"

"This one right here. You can see the garden from your

191

window and hear the waterfall. Look at these gorgeous paintings of angels on your walls. Don't you love this cute little desk and chair? You can do your homework there. There is another bed under the sofa that pulls out."

"Mom. All my friends have these. I always wanted one. This is so cool. I love it so much."

"I'm glad. Now let's see how much Bruce and Tara will love it."

We carried the cat cages to the porch and opened their doors. They were both scrunched up in their cages meowing softly. Noodles, Pasta and Linguine were waiting patiently for their new friends to come out and play.

"Let's go for a swim Tabitha and leave them alone. They will come out soon."

Tabitha dipped her hand into the pool. "Oh, Mom, the water is heaven. It's like ninety."

As I changed into my bathing suit, I fought the urge to call Nick. I glanced around the beautifully furnished room. Too good to be true. I couldn't blow this. I could be happy here and content. If I chanted this every day, I knew I would be alright.

By the third day I gave into my urges. I had already cut my hair short with a layered look and dyed it blonde. I kept the green contacts. Tabitha was swimming happily in the pool when I called.

"Hello. How are you?"

"Hi, stranger, where have you been?"

"Would you believe, I'm around the corner?"

"Get out. You're in San Diego," he said in an excited voice.

"No. San Francisco," I laughed, raking my pink nails through my short hair.

"What are you doing there?"

"I live here, now."

"What," he shouted into the phone.

"Yes, I live in Tiburon. It's a small town near San Francisco."

"When did this come about?" he asked in a shocked voice.

"I don't remember. I didn't want to tell you because I wanted to surprise you. Surprise!"

"I can't believe you left New York, Keara."

"The weather made me crazy there. Anyway, I want to see you. David will be here soon. So if you can fly in tomorrow, it would be perfect. I have Tabitha here with me but she goes to bed early. I can sneak out then."

"Just like that, you want me to fly in and you seem to have it all planned out."

"Yeah, there is a hotel in town. I checked it out. We'll do breakfast. Come on, it will be fun. Be spontaneous. Be daring. Be wild. Come to San Francisco."

"Call me tomorrow and let me think about it. I don't know. I'm still in shock."

"We have the same time now. This is so exciting. Talk to you tomorrow. Sleep on it. "

I hung up the phone with shaking hands. My whole body started to tremble. It felt like a fever was breaking out all over my body. My toes even tingled.

Keara, don't do it. Don't ruin this paradise. Don't take the bite of the apple..

I wrestled with my emotions all day as I lounged by the pool. This was supposed to be my fresh start. No more Nick. My big chance to be normal. No more lies, and already I was being sneaky. I went to bed thinking what I would wear when I saw Nick.

The next morning, Tabitha and I went for our daily swim. I had already made arrangements with Nick to meet me at a hotel in town at midnight. My nerves were frazzled as I doggy paddled in the heated pool. I needed to tire Tabitha out so she would sleep soundly tonight.

"Tabitha, let's dive for pennies."

"I just like floating on the raft, Mom. I'm tired from racing you across the pool a thousand times."

"Okay, rest now and then we are diving."

"Why are you so hyper today?"

"Must have been the donut at breakfast, too much sugar, I guess," I said nervously.

After soaking in the sun, we ate a hearty meal of pasta. Tabitha couldn't stop yawning all through dinner. She was sleeping soundly by eleven.

I freshened my makeup and settled on my blue jeans and a lime green t-shirt with matching cotton sweater. It brought out my hair and eyes. I checked in on Tabitha again. Closed my bedroom door and climbed out the guest bedroom window. I was afraid to use the front door. I padded barefoot across the deck to the car. I glanced over at Stephen's cottage. His lights were out. I cruised down the hill my heart thumping loudly in my chest. Chills were going through me and my teeth started chattering.

Don't worry Keara, your drug is down the hill.

He was pacing back and forth in front of the hotel. I parked the car and walked slowly toward him.

"Keara, where are your shoes?" he asked laughing softly, embracing me.

"Didn't feel like wearing them. Let's go inside, I'm freezing."

I tossed my car keys on the table and withdrew a small candle from my pocket. I placed it in the ashtray and lit it. I spun around and gazed directly in his baby blues, peeling off my sweater.

"Nick, I need to feel you deep inside me, now."

He injected me with the drug I needed. His supply was endless. I screamed, moaned and floated into the dawn.

"I'll be right back," I said, bolting out of bed, still trembling from the orgasms.

"Where are you going?"

"I have to check on Tabitha. Let me have the key so I can let myself back in."

"It's on the table."

I scooped up the key and raced out of the room. I flew home. Chaka Khan was singing on the radio, Through the Fire. A sign. I sneaked back in the window and checked on Tabitha. She was sleeping peacefully. I left a note on her bathroom door saying I went for a walk and would be back with donuts. I changed into gray shorts, gray sweatshirt and laced up my Nike sneakers. This time I went out the front door.

I cruised down the hill this time a drop calmer. He was leaving soon and I didn't get caught. My emotions were raw as I entered the hotel room. My stomach was queasy. He was sitting on the edge of the bed glancing through the paper.

194

"Want to go for a walk?" he asked warmly, putting the paper down on the bed.

We drove in an uneasy silence to a trail by the bay.

"This is a beautiful place. You really are lucky to live here," Nick said lovingly, strolling along beside me.

"Yes. Do you believe this? The boats, bridge and the mountains. It's special," I said, massaging the throbbing pain in my temples.

"Are you okay?"

"You know you make me crazy, Nick. I love you but I am here with David. I've decided to make a go of my marriage here."

"Can't we still be friends?" he asked, cocking his head to the side.

"I don't know, Nick. My heart breaks when I hear your voice or see you."

"Whatever is best for you, Keara."

"Oh, Nick, I am so fucked up. I don't know what to do."

We drove back to my car in a silence as thick as the fog hanging over the Golden Gate Bridge. Here I go again, wondering if he would kiss me this time. He might not ever see me again. This would be the perfect time.

I crawled out of his car and over to my gold monster. He was right behind me. I quickly licked my lips.

"What are you planning to do here, Keara?"

"Concentrate on painting."

I threw my arms around him and buried my face in his chest. He kissed the top of my head.

"Your hair is going to fall out if you keep dying it like this."

"Then I'll have fun shopping for wigs."

He laughed and glanced at his watch. "Wow, I better get a move on or I'll miss my flight."

"Bye, Nick, I love you," I said, swallowing hard, blinking back tears.

He squeezed me tight and whirled around. I watched him get in his car. I was emotionally crippled as I started the engine. I turned off the music. I knew I would snap if I heard any kind of love song.

I pulled into the driveway with a box of chocolate covered donuts. Tabitha came sprinting up to the car.

"Mom, Tara killed a bird, a baby bird."

"Where is it?" I asked, handing her the donuts.

"By the front door," she said, already checking out the box.

"It's your cat, Tabitha. Don't you think you should remove it."

"Please, Mom, I can't."

"Alright, I will, even though I have been sick. I threw up last night. I think all that food was too much for my stomach. I didn't sleep at all. Do you mind if I take a nap?"

"No. I can play with that clay set you bought me. I'll make you a picture frame."

"Thanks. I'd love that."

What a difference between Tabitha and Taylor. Tabitha at twelve was still a sweet innocent little girl. Taylor at twelve already had lost her virginity, was getting high, drinking and smoking. Taylor was just like me.

As I was crawling under the covers, Tabitha came in the bedroom with the portable phone.

"It's Daddy," she said sweetly, handing me the phone. A trace of chocolate lingered on her upper lip.

"What's wrong? Tabitha said you are sick."

"It's nothing. Too much Italian food last night and you know my stomach. Nothing a swig of Mylanta won't fix."

"Oh and I thought you were sick because I'm not there."

"That too."

"Get better. I'll be there tomorrow."

"Uh, about tomorrow."

"Oh no, what's up?"

"Heather will be coming in too. She is having problems with her sobriety. I couldn't refuse her. It's also my two years next week so we can celebrate early."

"Company, already," he said, sounding disappointed.

"I'll make it up to you. Promise."

"That sounds good. I love you, Keara. Bye."

I hung up knowing he couldn't be bought with a box of chocolate donuts. Maybe this ache in my head, heart and between

196

my thighs would go away by tomorrow.

"Tabitha," I yelled out. "Take the phone back and bring me two Excedrins, please."

Heather kept me so busy wrapped up in her problems that I didn't have time to think about Nick. David was busy the whole time hooking up computers, fax machine, printer and phones in the spare bedroom. Steven removed the futon so he could bring in a desk. He was going to work out of the house and then look to open an office in town later.

"Keara, are you listening?" Heather asked, stretched out on a raft, floating in the pool.

I was sitting on the edge of the pool, dangling my feet in the warm water, while sketching the view across the bay. Tabitha and David were soaking up the rays.

"Yes, every word. You know my answer, don't drink. Look, what did you hand me when you got off the plane.?"

"Your two year token," she sighed.

"Yes and it wasn't easy for me to get here. But I did learn along the way that drinking does not solve a thing or make it better."

"But I am so uptight when it comes to sex being so sober and he's high."

"Don't compromise your sobriety for an orgasm or else you will be sorry."

"You're right."

Heather left confident in her sobriety. David was happy in his new one-man office. Tabitha was content playing with the cats and designing clothes for her Barbie dolls. Everything seemed to be working out except I was still restless and missing Nick. I started putting more and more energy into my drawings.

David was keeping New York hours. He rose every morning at four and fell asleep by nine at night.

I ducked into his office carrying a Power Bar. "Here eat this. You need to keep up your strength with your crazy hours."

"Thanks, Keara."

"I was thinking. I'm going to get up early too. I'll get up at seven and go for a nice long walk and that way I'll be tired when you are. Besides, I gained about five pounds with these donuts I've been eating."

"That's a good idea," he smiled gleefully, chewing on the bar.

Of course, I wasn't doing this out of the goodness of my heart. I knew seven in the morning was the perfect time to call Nick. I needed to talk to him again. I was getting cabin fever. I spent the day gathering up quarters. The sight of the change was getting me excited.

The next morning, I drove to the shopping center where there were a lot of phones to pick from. I pulled out my velvet pouch that I kept the change in and dumped it in my hand. The operator on the other end told me the call would be one dollar and forty cents. I plunked it in and listened.

"Hi, Nick," I said flustered, rubbing the quarters together.

"Keara, are you okay? You don't sound so good."

"Yes," I exhaled loudly. " I can't stay away from you. You are too deep in my soul."

"I missed you, Keara."

"Tell me what's new. Are you painting?"

"Well, Heather came to visit.....

That's how it started. Our coffee talk in the morning. We gossiped, laughed, shared dreams, told jokes and sang songs. I was spending thirty dollars a week on phone cards. The only one who knew about my coffee talk was Taylor. I had promised everyone else that Nick was history.

Taylor came for a visit in mid-August. San Francisco was too cold and foggy for her. The summer meant beach to her. Taylor was also preoccupied by Matt. He told her if she stayed too long he would cheat on her.

"Mommy, I changed my ticket. I have to go home early," she grumbled, pulling on her sweats. "It's way too cold here. I liked it better in San Diego."

"If Matt is threatening you, don't go out with him. He is so immature, anyway. You are young and gorgeous and can have anyone, Taylor. Use your power while you have it. Don't waste it on Matt. I am so baffled you like a guy like him in the first place."

"I love him. I can't explain it. You should not be giving me a hard time. Need I say more."

"Go and run back little slave girl."

"Oh, I like that coming from someone who would kill for a quarter."

"Promise me that your Christmas visit will not be like this."

"Okay, Mommy, I promise."

The next morning she was in a frantic rush to get on the plane. I wish she wasn't so much like me. Her father was totally straight. Why couldn't she have a drop of him?

Tabitha started school in September and made new friends easily. We had a great summer together. Now she was anxious to hang out with her age group. When I wasn't sketching, I spent my days reading spiritual books and meditating. This house for some reason made me feel closer to something, deep inside myself. I was in constant awe of the surroundings. It was a magical retreat. The deer grazing daily, the skunks scampering about. At night, I started feeding a raccoon, who came by the deck, waiting patiently for food. I'd creep out on the deck and place the food in the middle of us. I'd then wait at the door and even though he kept a careful eye on me, he'd run for the food. He'd scoop it up and eat it in front of me. This would make me laugh. I was convinced it was Jack. Steven was too. He told me it was odd behavior for a raccoon. They usually traveled in groups, were deathly afraid of humans and they attacked cats. Rocky, that's what I named him, loved the cats. I became obsessed with him. He would sit with them on the deck. I started taking pictures of him and making an album. I blew one picture up and placed it next to Jack's. They had the same eyes. Jack was back.

Once again I started obsessing about Nick and needed a way to see him again. I hadn't made any friends here but Steven, who was always going away. I couldn't tell him. So I had no one to cover for me or to use. He had just came back from Japan and was already packing for Canada. I loved taking care of his cats. They loved to be brushed and hugged. They also loved Melrose Place. I would let them sneak in on Monday nights to watch it with me. Bruce and Tara were happy being wild. I had no one I could confide in except the animals.

It came to me one night as I was sitting on the deck under a blanket of glittering stars and a full moon. Rocky was eating Oreos cookies, his favorite. I would spring it on David at breakfast. I stood up and blew a kiss to Rocky and trotted happily off to bed. Visions of Nick were dancing in my head.

Why can't I be normal and have sugar plums dancing or chocolate donuts.

I started my day as usual, coffee talk with Nick. He constantly pushed me to do something with my life. He believed I had all these creative juices locked up inside me. Nick would yell at me when he found out I slept the afternoon away. I found myself battling depression daily. David didn't even notice. Tabitha was always with the new friends.

I pulled up in the driveway to an audience of half a dozen cats. A black cat from the neighborhood had now joined the tribe. They knew I'd be carrying treats. I hopped out of the Jeep and shook the Pounce container. They came scurrying over by my feet. I shook out the treats in the driveway and the feasting began.

David was taking a coffee break by the pool.

"Hey, shouldn't you be working?" I scolded him playfully.

"I just needed a break from that room. Join me for a cup of coffee."

I returned with a big mug of steaming black coffee and settled down next to him.

"Are you happy, Keara?" he asked, putting down the Journal.

"Yes. You know, I love this house, the view, and the animals. Don't forget, Jack is back, too."

"I just thought maybe you should do something. You seem bored. That could be dangerous for us. I'll wake up one day and you'll be off in the jungle or something because you went nuts."

"Alright. What about this for a start. On Wednesdays, cause there is never anything good on television, we go out. I'll take the ferry to the city during the day. Get my nails done, a little shopping, maybe a museum. Then I'll hop back on the ferry and meet you for a dinner date at a restaurant on the water. Sound good?"

"One correction."

"What?"

"How about we make every other Wednesday that I come into

the city. I'll meet you wherever and we'll have dinner at a new restaurant each time. Sound good?"

"Perfect," I smiled, sipping my coffee.

The groundwork was laid. Now all I had to do was mark my calendar which Wednesdays would be the city and which would be here. Tiburon Wednesdays would be safe to meet Nick in the city. I'd be able to spend the whole day with him till I had to catch the ferry that night. He could sleep over and instead of coffee talk on the phone we could meet in person. That old familiar rush of adrenaline went pumping through my veins. I was back in business.

I was fidgeting the whole ride to the phone in the morning. I used my inhaler before I called Nick.

"Nick, how are you?" I asked breathlessly, into the phone.

"Why are you so out of breath?"

"Oh, just having trouble breathing this morning. Thinking about you naked, I guess."

"You forget, I know you. Want to tell me what you are up to?"

"I want you to think about coming to S.F. in three weeks on a Wednesday."

"Why? You told me last time we were together that you couldn't see me anymore."

"I can't stay away from you, you are my addiction, you know that, anyway."

"You can get away?"

"Yes, I worked it out."

"I bet you have."

"Oh, Nick, don't say it like that."

"You're not planning on leaving David, are you?"

"Do you want to be with me?"

"What does that have to do with leaving David?"

"I don't know, I'm insecure."

"You know you might just stand on your own two feet and decide not to ever see me again. Once you get to make your own choices you might feel different about everything."

"That's crazy. I love you too much."

"Oh well, when do you want me to come in?" he sighed.

"The third Wednesday of this month."

Nothing mattered to me but seeing Nick. I wasn't even going to dwell on whether he would kiss me or not, this time. The important thing was that he was coming to S.F.. I had something to look forward to.

The first Wednesday I ventured into the city, I had a weird experience. I was eating a vegetable sandwich sitting on the steps of the Embarcadero Center. It was a sunny, crisp day. A gypsy type old woman approached me while I ate.

"Excuse me, but I would like to do a reading for you," she said, her crinkly blue eyes sparkling with delight. "You have an incredible aura."

Mmm, that is what Steven told me. He told me it was purple.

"I'm sorry, I'm not interested," I said politely, wiping my mouth with a napkin.

"Please, just five dollars for ten minutes."

"Okay," I shrugged, digging into my purse for the money.

The ten minutes turned into an interesting forty minutes. She saw that in two years, I would come into my own. That I'd be successful with the career I would chose. She saw something in the arts. She told me that I have a very strong bond with a friend that can't be broken. She also saw my alcohol problem. That issue we talked about at a great length. She had been sober for thirty years. She gave me her card and I promised to stay in touch.

As the ferry drifted into the dock, I could see David waiting for me. He was holding in his hands a gold wrapped box. Great, he bought me a present for our first date.

* * *

I purchased acrylics, an easel and some canvases. I had excelled in art through high school. My parents hadn't encourage me to do anything with my life. They believed girls got married and didn't have careers. They would not send me to college.

I started painting Rocky and his night time friends. Word had spread through the forest I was an easy touch. Besides Rocky, there was now Pepe the skunk. He traveled with his two kids. There was also Pauly the possum and a family of deer. I was becoming one of those Disney characters that were always surrounded by the animals. While David and Tabitha slept, I was pouring my heart out to my furry friends. At least I wasn't singing. I was not crazy or Snow White for that matter.

A sudden burst of adrenaline whizzed through me as I was finishing up painting Rocky. Nick was coming in tomorrow. I drew a deep breath. I needed to meditate. I was split in two. Heart and mind. Personality and soul.

The next morning, I slipped on my favorite black dress with silver stars and moons decorating it. I tried to empty my mind of Nick thoughts and concentrate on acting normal.

Keara, don't sweat it. You're a pro at this. You should have been a Kennedy.

"David, I'm ready for you to drive me to the ferry," I said, clearing my throat. A nervous tickle had developed in my throat. I dug in my purse for some mints.

"Don't worry, you have plenty of time."

David chatted happily on the drive into town. I kept a smile frozen on my face and nodded at the appropriate times. My body was numb. He pulled up to the curb just as the ferry was drifting in.

I swallowed hard. "I'll see you tonight," I said, averting his eyes.

"Okay, we'll eat here at the ferry landing, tonight. Have a great day."

"You too," I cracked a smile, grabbed my sketch book and took off for the ferry.

I strolled down Van Ness street telling myself this is the last time. I ducked into the Midnight Cafe, where we were supposed to meet. He wasn't there. I smiled with relief. Something probably came up last minute and he couldn't make it. I'm going to march out of here and buy a present for David. I pushed open the glass doors, flipped on my sunglasses and walked straight into Nick.

"Nick, I, uh, didn't think you were coming," I stammered, licking my dry lips.

"Give me a hug, Keara," he said, his mouth curling into a sexy smile.

"You feel so good, Nick," I whispered, my voice shaking slightly.

"Are you taking me on a tour of the city?" he asked, smiling with his eyes.

"Yes, let's do Fisherman's Wharf. I've been there a dozen times but never with my best friend. Oh, Nick, I am so happy that you are here," I said breathlessly, twirling around him.

We did the whole tourist thing. Fisherman's wharf. Clam soup in a bread bowl. Wax Museum. Cable Car. I sketched him the entire day, everywhere we went.

When we went back to his hotel room, he checked his halo at the door. I entered the flames of hell.

On the ferry ride back home, I sketched the weary faces of the commuters. I tried searching for someone who perhaps had a deep dark secret too, thinking I could capture it in their eyes. All I really needed to do was take out a mirror.

"Keara, Keara," David shouted, waving happily at the ferry landing.

"Hi, David," I smiled thinly, brushing my lips across his cheek.

He looked handsome standing there in gray wool slacks and a navy blue long sleeve Polo shirt and Polo loafers. His thick salt and pepper hair had turned silver. My aging preppie.

"How was your day?" he asked. "I got us a table for seven. Let's have Virgin Marys first."

"Sounds great. My day was perfect. San Francisco is the best city. I love these Wednesdays."

"I'm happy that you are so happy," he smiled, steering me towards the bar.

Thank God, I had no desire to drink, just to be with Nick. Which was worse for my health?

The next morning I dropped Tabitha off at school and raced to Sausalito. I was supposed to meet Nick at Starbucks. My chest had the familiar heart attack feeling streaking across it. I had to squash the urge to pull over and scream at the top of my lungs the whole ride. I pulled up outside the coffee shop right on time. I dug in my purse for some quarters for the meter. All I needed would be a ticket from Sausalito. I hated using my precious quarters. I plunked in the three quarters.

Nick was sitting outside Starbucks sipping hot coffee.

"I love seeing your face in the morning," I squealed, in childish delight. "How was your night?"

"I watched a movie on HBO and went to sleep."

"You didn't explore S.F. or bring anybody back to your hotel room?" I asked, giggling.

"Oh, are you talking about the seven midget hookers, I had last night?"

"You're a male Snow White. I knew it." I grinned, punching his arm.

"Speaking of Snow White, how are your animal friends?"

"They are great. I'm sketching them all and I am taking an art class next weekend."

"I am so happy. You're sober, creative, talented, nothing can stop you, girl," he laughed.

Yes, there is. I can't get you to kiss me.

"I'm chasing my dreams. What about you?"

"Oh, working the plant. I took a couple of classes in the market, too," he sighed, breaking off a piece of blueberry scone.

"Nick, move out. Unless you try, you'll never know what it's like to chase your dreams. Your dreams Nick. Not Lou's."

"I will, Keara. You know I like to take things slow," he said, slowly rising from the chair and brushing off the cake crumbs from his jeans. "I have to go, now. I have an early flight."

"Oh, Nick," I cried, jumping up and hurling myself into his arms. "It was the best."

I bit my lower lip, hard.

"Paint me a picture of Rocky."

I could only nod my head as he turned and walked toward his rental car.

I drove home thinking of getting collagen shots in my lips. Would he kiss me if I had big lush lips? He still wasn't dating anyone. I knew he loved me. He just couldn't admit it because I was married. He knew I was not leaving David. That is why there would never be a kiss. I was stuck in affair Hell.

I breezed into David's office. He was taking an order on the phone. He looked up and smiled lovingly as I crossed the room. I rubbed his back, kissed the top of his head and reached for one of the portable phones. I ducked into the hallway and pressed Taylor's number in frantically. Her stupid answer machine picked up.

I decided to go for a swim. The pool was heated to a delicious ninety-two degrees. I flipped the switch by the rocks and the soothing waterfall came trickling on. I could completely zone out for the afternoon.

I was basking in the warm sun on my silver float, when Taylor called back. I paddled over to the steps and plucked the phone out of David's hand.

"Thanks, David. Want to swim later?" I asked sweetly, standing on the second step in the pool.

"Sure. I just have to straighten out the office and I'll be out."

I put the phone to my wet ear. "Hi, Babes."

"Okay, Mommy, what is the crisis? I can't believe you are swimming when it is freezing here."

"You know what the crisis is. See, if you move here, you'd be warm right now."

"Why don't you just launch the loser. He still lives at home. Hello, Mommy, wake up."

"Why don't you break up with Matt?"

"I did. I met someone else, his name is Alex, and he has been sober for a year now but it's too soon to talk about him. So, come on, tell me about your date," she said in a sarcastic tone.

"I don't feel like it now. You are making me depressed. Does Alex go to AA?"

"Oh, Mommy, hold on, there is my beep. It is probably Adam, who still harasses me."

I wrapped myself in a big fluffy pink beach towel and flopped down on the lounge chair.

"I have to go, Mommy. I got rid of Adam on the phone and now Matt is at the door. Hang in there. I'm sorry I can't talk now. You know David is the best thing for you and you have to think of Tabitha. We have been through this Mother Dearest. You cannot survive on your own. I'll call you later tonight. Oh, and Alex goes to AA."

I trudged across the deck into house. David was closing down the office.

"David, I am so sorry, all of a sudden I got a headache. Must be too much sun. I have to go lie down," I said wearily, pressing the tips of my fingers on my temples.

"Do you need anything?"

"Could you please pick up Tabitha for me? I just want to go to sleep," I groaned, throwing myself across the bed.

When I woke up, David gave me a candle in the shape of a Great Dane. There was no end to this man's kindness.

* * *

When David and Tabitha went to bed, I would set up shop on the deck. I worked by candlelight and the soft glow of the moon. I painted to the music of Louis Armstrong, Kenny G and Fiona Apple. Steven had given me his boom box CD player. After my last stroke, I'd flop down by the candles and meditate for thirty minutes. My furry friends sleeping peacefully around the deck. Painting seemed to soothe my soul. I was able to paint my pain in the eyes of the creatures. The canvas was definitely my therapy.

Steven was the only friend I had made in San Francisco. For some reason though, I didn't trust him. He was too Zen. Always leaving me little Zen notes and preaching kindness. He drove a brand new BMW convertible and wore expensive clothes and shoes. David on the other hand, made lots of friends, they were all rich and successful.

One weekend he coaxed me into going to a party at one of his friend's house. I hated parties now. Watching people sip wine and listening to the tinkle of ice in their cocktail glasses made me anxious. I felt I couldn't hold a decent conversation. Sometimes I did miss my old friend, the bottle.

"David, let's not stay long." I said miserably, running my hand over my black tights. I had on a plain black velvet dress. My short hair was now shoulder length and a dark auburn. My eyes were blue.

"I know, Keara, but this is important for business. Richard is a good client and has lots of rich friends," he smiled, reaching over to squeeze my hand. "I made Richard a lot of money so tonight I'm hoping he will brag a little about me."

"Alright, just don't leave my side and we are out of there in an hour," I shrugged, biting the inside of my lip.

207

We pulled up to a large white sprawling ranch house in Mill Valley. I slowly stepped out of the Jeep and wrapped my arms around myself. I glanced around the twinkle lit yard where most of the guests had spilled out. A heavy scent of gardenia was in the air. A wall with water streaming down it, flowed into a small square pool. A hot tub on the upper deck was surrounded by huge clay pots of brightly colored flowers. A rectangular table was set with candles and flowers, filled with all kinds of fruits, cheese, crackers and caviar. I surveyed all the wine bottles scattered around the deck.

The sound of light laughter in the cool night air rang in my ears. I needed two Excedrin washed down with Mylanta. David gave me a comfortable squeeze and we emerged into the party.

Richard motioned for us to come over. He was standing by the hot tub with a glass of red wine in his hand. By his side was a striking older woman, around late seventies, with lively blue eyes.

"David, Keara, I am glad you could make it," he said heartily, shaking our hands. "This is my beautiful friend, Isabel Spencer."

"Hello, Isabel," I smiled shyly, reaching out to shake her hand.

There was a warmth in her hand that sent tingles to my heart. I knew instantly she had something to do with my future.

"Keara, what a beautiful Irish name," she said with a gentle smile. "I have a bottle of Perrier at my table. Would you like to share it with me."

"Yes, thank you," I nodded numbly.

We threaded our way through the well-dressed crowd. I shot a glance back at David and saw him drinking a Corona. He knew he was safe with beer. I hated beer and didn't mind the smell on him. He knew better than to have a glass of wine.

Isabel walked over to the table and picked up the bottled water and two wine glasses.

"Let's go inside by the fire. I feel chilled," she said, handing me the glasses.

We sank down on the white couch by the fire. I put the glasses on the wooden cocktail table. The room had a Southwestern look. Isabel poured the sparkling water into the glasses.

"Cheers," I smiled, clinking her glass.

"Cheers, Keara, it was a pleasure meeting you. I sensed that you could use a friend."

"I've been sober for two years now so I'm a little nervous at these social gatherings."

"Good for you," she said with delight. "You must be very strong."

"When I want to be," I said, with a sad smile, tugging at the hem of my dress.

"Is David your husband?"

"Yes. We have been married for thirteen years."

"Happily," she asked, sipping her water.

"Yes and no. It's a complicated issue. We had a crazy lifestyle and marriage that worked for us till I sobered up. Now I am so confused with finding out who I am and what I want out of life."

She patted my hand. "It's okay, darling, we all need that. Do you love him?"

"Oh, God, I don't know. He is the greatest man alive. He's kind, generous, and loving, everything any woman would want in a man. But I'll be honest, I've had an affair and fell in love," I whispered, my eyes darting around the party looking for David. I spotted him by the sliding screen door, talking to a group of men. He caught my eye and winked. I winked back.

"Is the affair over?" she asked, gazing into my eyes.

I blinked back tears. "No, I still love Nick."

"You're eyes starting dancing when you mentioned his name," she grinned. "Does Nick love you?"

"Yes but like a friend. He is a boy, twenty years younger than David, just starting his life. I have been there, done that. I have a twenty year old and a twelve year old. My tubes are tied, I can't give Nick children. I wouldn't want them now even if I wasn't fixed."

David was maneuvering his way through the crowd. He had a look of concern as he approached me.

"Sorry to interrupt you two but I just called Tabitha and she's not feeling well. I told her we would leave now," David said worried. "It was nice to meet you, Isabel."

"Same here, David. I hope your daughter is alright."

"Sounds like she just ate too much junk food."

209

"Keara, please call me. I'd love to finish our little chat. Let's have lunch next week," she said happily, gripping both my hands.

"I'd love too," I smiled, leaning over and brushing my lips across her porcelain cheek. She hardly had a wrinkle and there were no signs of surgery. I left the party with a warm feeling. Isabel could be the perfect friend. A new ear to bend about Nick.

I called Isabel Monday morning after my coffee talk with Nick. We made arrangements to have lunch the following week. I was taking an art workshop in Monterrey on the weekend so I was doubling up on my painting. Paul, David's friend, lived there. So, David and Tabitha would stay at his place while I stayed at the inn where it was being held.

The workshop was a smashing success. The teachers were impressed with my paintings. When it came time to unveil the painting we worked on in class, I received a standing ovation. This was my new high. Everyone hugged and congratulated me. I was totally stunned. I hadn't expected this kind of a reaction. I excused myself saying that I had to go to the bathroom. With shaking hands, I fished out my phone card from my purse. I punched in the code and called Nick. He answered on the first ring.

"Nick, I'm a success. Everyone loved me. The weekend was just too much. The teachers just kept praising me. Oh, Nick, I am so happy," I said excitedly.

"I never had any doubt. You're a natural artist, Keara. You were the best D.J., it's all part of your creative spirit."

"I can't talk now. I just wanted you to be the first to know." I hung up and ran straight for the bathroom.

David and Tabitha picked me up outside the hotel. I couldn't sit still the whole car ride home. They both shared my excitement. We called Taylor from the car phone. This was my family, where I belonged. I pinched the bridge of my nose and closed my eyes.

"Mom, how about Sushi to celebrate?" Tabitha asked, grinning from ear to ear.

"Sure, why not," I smiled, willing Nick out of my head.

"Do you think Picasso ate Sushi?" David asked laughing.

We all burst into giggles. One happy family.

One sick puppy. Help me, God, angels, anybody up there.

210

I awoke the next morning feeling confident. I always had a crazy reputation. No one ever took me seriously, but now, I felt I would be seen in a different light, being sober and an artist.

* * *

I met Isabel at the Estee Lauder counter at Macy's. She bought an orange shade of lipstick and I bought more skin cream. We wondered through the store chatting happily. I found her fascinating. She had been married to a politician, a gambler, and a wealthy playboy. She had been on her way to be a professional ballerina when she was mugged in New York and injured her knees. She had lived all over Europe and had friends all over the world. She even was at Sinatra's sixty's birthday bash.

At lunch, we celebrated my standing ovation with iced tea. Isabel seemed genuinely happy for me and interested. We made a date later in the week for her to come over and see my paintings.

I bounced into the house calling out David's name. There was a yellow note taped to his office door. He was jogging. I grabbed the portable phone and rooted through my purse for the phone card. I bet every cheater in America had one of these. I flopped down on the deck to keep an eye out for David. I punched in the code and Nick's number. Pasta and Tara strutted by and curled up by my feet.

"Hello, this is Nick," he answered business like.

"Hello, this is Keara," I said in a silky murmur, my eyes locked on the driveway.

"What is going on?" he asked delighted.

"Just had a lunch date with Isabel. I have a feeling she could be my lucky star."

"What did she say?"

"She is coming over to look at my work. I guess all my letters to the angels has paid off."

"I have good news too."

"Let me guess. You won the lottery and want to pick me up on your way around the world."

"Sorry, but that's not it."

"I wrote to Gary Majors and he just called me and wants to meet me."

211

"Who is that?"

"So you really don't listen to me in the morning," he laughed affectionately.

"Yes, I do. I can't think now," I whined, stroking Pasta's head.

"He has his own radio show and is a big shot in the market. I'm meeting him in two weeks, for a possible job."

"Oh, Nick. I'm so excited for you," I exclaimed, jumping to my feet. I caught a glimpse of David turning the corner. "I have to go, Nick. I'm late for Tabitha. Congratulations. Bye."

I pressed the off button and scrambled all the buttons just in case David were to press redial.

"Keara, how was lunch," he asked, arching an eyebrow.

"Great," I smiled, I could feel my face flushing. "David, I think Isabel can help me. I really like her."

"Just remember how you met her. You owe me," he chuckled.

"Forget it. All I can think about is painting. In fact, I'm going to go buy more paint."

I grabbed my purse and keys off the wicker table in the hall and ran. As I turned to wave goodbye, I could see David's mouth curved in disappointment.

The sound of Nick's voice was still fresh in my mind. A smile spread across my lips as I thought of hugging him. Goose bumps immediately sprang up across my arms.

"I love you, Nick," I sighed, blowing my words into the wind.

"Keara, wait a minute," Steven yelled out.

I spun around and hoped that he didn't see me talking to myself.

Hey, wait a minute, I am an artist now. There is an excuse for my behavior now.

"What's up, Steven?" I asked, leaning against my Jeep.

"I need to talk to you and David about the house," he said in a serious tone.

"Is anything wrong?"

"I got an offer on the house for much more rent than you are paying."

"So, we have a lease."

"That is why I want to talk to you both."

"Look, Steven, I can't concentrate on anything right now but painting. Talk to David," I hissed, getting into the Jeep.

I felt like telling him his aura was green. What happened to all his kindness speeches now. He was just like everyone else. Money ruled him, even though he tried faking it. Maybe this was a sign. Maybe we were required to move so I could tell David I wanted my own place. I just had to take a chance. My vet had asked to buy some of my paintings and a couple of David's clients had bought some for their country houses. Everything happened for a reason. Fantasies of my own studio and seeing Nick floated in my head. No more double life. David was fuming when I arrived back home. Obviously, Steven had been by.

"David, calm down. Tell me what happened."

"That fucking phony bastard. He got offered a lot of money and wants us either to pay more or move now. We have a contract. He has some balls. We are not moving or paying higher. See, I warned you about him, and all his monk's stories."

"But David," I interrupted. "We will be uncomfortable living here now seeing him all the time. It might effect our work."

"What do you suggest?"

I took a deep breath. "Maybe this happened for a reason. Maybe we should get separate places," I said in a voice, a little more than a whisper.

"What?" he screamed. "Where did this come from?"

"I just thought since we had to move maybe we should have separate places."

"That's good, Keara. Our lease is up so let's get a divorce," he said sarcastically. "Are you totally out of your mind?"

"It was just a thought," I laughed uneasily, raking my nails through my hair.

"Oh, you have a hobby now so it's goodbye and good luck, huh?"

"David, shut up. It's not just a hobby. I want to be a painter. Come on, we never really communicate. You know, it's only Tabitha that keeps us together now. We have grown apart and you know it."

"As far as I'm concerned, we've been getting along better than ever, all the therapy and everything." he mumbled, throwing himself down on the bed.

Uh oh, I could see two tears surfacing over his lashes. Time for emotional blackmail.

"I'm sorry, David." I murmured, flopping down beside him and rubbing his back. "I'm not going anywhere without you."

Tabitha peeked her head in the room. "Everything okay, you two?" she asked.

"Yes, of course, but we might have to move again. Are you okay with that?" I asked in a motherly tone, motioning for her to sit next to me on the bed.

"Why what happened?"

"Steven has people who are willing to pay a lot more money for this place. Even though we don't have to move because we have a lease, it might be uncomfortable to live so close to Steven here."

"Will I still go to the same school?"

"Of course."

"I don't mind, if I don't. Some of the kids at this school are so snobby. I really don't like the school all that much."

"Tabitha, why didn't you say anything to me before?"

"It's not a big deal, Mom. I like my friends from there but they get teased a lot too."

"Do you get teased?"

"Sometimes. Some of the kids say I sound like Mickey Mouse."

I reached out and gave her a big hug. "Tabitha Fisher, you have a beautiful voice. Those are just spoiled rich kids talking. They're just jealous that you are so brilliant and beautiful. Next time they say anything tell them to go fuck themselves."

"Oh, Mom, I can't say that."

"Maybe we should talk to your teacher?" David asked concerned.

"No, don't you dare. Oh, God, I shouldn't have said anything to you two."

"Hey, let's drop everything and have Sushi," I smiled, hugging them both. "Then we can take a swim under the stars. Our next place might not have a pool, you know?"

"Do you guys know that this will be our eighth house," she said with a slight irritation in her voice. "Will we ever settle down?"

"Tabitha," I smiled gently. "Look at all the experiences you had, all the new friends. This gives you character and strength all this moving around."

"I just want my own room so that I can put up a poster without worrying about a landlord," she said pouting, slowly walking towards her room.

Sadness descended on me as I rifled through my makeup bag. I was trapped by David and Tabitha's needs.

"What are you thinking about?" David asked softly, coming up behind me.

"I was thinking if I wanted a spider roll or my usual California roll." I gave him a thin smile.

I crept out onto the deck after midnight. Our moonlight swim had exhausted them. I lit the vanilla candles. I would miss this deck and view. I didn't even want to think about life without Rocky. Luckily, I was able to take all my feelings and transform them onto the canvas. I was on the brink of tears as I stepped back and surveyed the results. It was my best. I made a mental note to call Isabel and get her here on the double. I folded my arms across my chest and tipped my head back to gaze at the twinkling stars. I closed my eyes tight and wished on one. Tears leaked slowly over my lashes as I cleaned my brush.

Tabitha was quiet the next morning as I drove her to school. I didn't press her. I raced to my favorite phone booth to call. As usual I'd gotten to know all the locals at the center. They'd pass by and tip their hats or give a friendly wave. No one ever asked why I talked endlessly every morning, clutching my phone card, day after day.

"Hello, this is Keara," I giggled, running my hand over the silver metal cord attached to the phone.

"You sound strange. What is wrong"

"Oh, I'm okay. Same old, same old. You know, I confronted David about leaving."

"What happened?"

"I'd rather not talk about it right now. It wasn't good, let's put it that way. But Nick, listen, I painted last night like I never painted before. I know I can go somewhere with this."

"What can I do to help?"

"I'm going to call Isabel now and see if she can help me. When I am ready to talk about David, I just need you to be there."

"No problem. I wish I could hug you now."

"In my dream last night you did more than that."

"What did you dream?" he asked, sighing.

"Oh, just that I spread peanut butter all over your thing and sucked it all off," I said, shaking with laughter.

"I hope you had milk in that dream, too."

"I don't know about milk but I did have cream. Lots of cream."

"Keara, you are getting gross," he laughed affectionately.

"I have to go Nick."

"Let me know what happens."

"I will. Bye. Oh, Nick, one more thing. It was chunky peanut butter."

"Goodbye," he shouted, laughing.

I flew home and called Isabel. She would be over at noon. As I was putting a plate of fruit and cheese together, David came up behind me and threw his arms around my waist.

"David, please, I am a nervous wreck now. I need space. This is like my first showing," I said tensely, pulling his arms off me.

"I understand. If you need me, I'll be in my office," he smiled warmly.

How was he a New Yorker? He's a born Californian with that permanent sunny disposition. He is so fucking nice I could spit.

Isabel Spencer arrived at the stroke of noon. Even her name sounded regal. I shifted nervously as she gazed from one painting to another. I wrestled with the thought of diving into the pool and staying on the bottom. I speared a chunk of cheese with a toothpick and nibbled on it's corner. She spun around with a radiant smile on her face.

"I love them, Keara," she exclaimed, reaching out to hug me. " I really love your paintings." I held back my tears as I returned the hug.

Thank you, God. Thank you, angels. I prayed fervently in my

216

head.

"My best friend, Ian Dieth, has a successful gallery in Los Angeles. I'll call him today and tell him about you. You must send him off some slides of each piece by the end of the week."

"Oh, Isabel, thank you, thank you," I cried, tears of joy sliding down my cheeks.

"Keara, my dear, this is why I was drawn to you at that party. There are no coincidences in life. There is a reason for everything. I can sniff out talent. It will bring me much joy to help you."

"I don't know what to say."

"How about yes to lunch. I'm starved."

The rest of the week was a blur. Getting the slides out. Prayers. Waiting for the phone to ring. I craved a drink or a Valium but I was coming up to three years so there was no way I was going to blow it. I just gritted my teeth and waited by the phone like a lovesick teenager. The tension between us and Steven had become unbearable. He found a reason to complain about every little thing even about my feeding Rocky. David searched every available minute for a new rental. Knowing David, he didn't forget my threat to leave so I knew the next house would be even more spectacular.

The phone call came the same week as we were preparing to move. I was packing a box of candles when David yelled to me that Ian was on the phone. I dug my short nails deep into my palms as I grabbed for the phone.

"Hello, Mr. Dieth," I answered, mustering up a confident air.

"Please call me, Ian. Isabel was right about you. You have talent. Will you be coming down here in the near future ?"

I moistened my dry lips with a quick flip of my tongue. "Yes, I can come anytime."

"Great, how is Friday? Say one?"

"Perfect. I'll see you then. Thank you."

I hung up the phone shaking all over. My bra felt soaking wet. David sprung to his feet and hugged me. I sucked in my breath.

"David, I'm going to L.A. on Friday to meet him," I said, my voice trembling.

"What do you mean, you? We are a team, remember?" he asked, dripping sarcasm.

"I'm going alone," I said in a deadly whisper.

"Fine."

"David, we need more masking tape for the boxes. I'm just going to run out for some more."

"At a time like this? I'll get it."

"No. I need this simple task to calm me down."

"Okay, I'll finish up in my office and we'll do something special."

"Great," I said, flying out the door.

Still trembling, I drove to my lucky phone booth. My head was spinning as I punched in the card's numbers. I felt faint.

"Nick," I screamed. "Ian Deith called, and wants to meet me."

"Fantastic! Is David going too?" he asked, disappointment evident in his voice.

"No."

"Will you try and call me afterwards?"

"You'll be my first call. I'm sorry, Nick, I can't see you while I'm in L.A."

"Don't be. Sounds like you're beginning to live your dreams."

"You met with Gary, he told you to move to Chicago? Move, Nick. Get out of that house."

"I'm not ready yet. Let's just concentrate on you, first."

"Okay. Goodbye."

"Bye, Ms. Picasso."

I pinched the bridge of my nose and closed my eyes. What the hell did I come out for besides Nick? Oh my God, tape, we are moving. Moving and the holidays are almost here. Which means Taylor and shopping for presents. Another Christmas and I knew Nick wouldn't be under my tree. I dabbed at a tear that sprung up in the corner of my eye and scurried across the shopping center to buy tape.

By Friday, we were all packed and ready to move into another furnished house. David always did have a knack for getting the best deals. He'd out done himself on this one, another million dollar house. This time at the very top of the hill. The view was even better. The house was all glass and from every window you could see the Golden Gate Bridge. The house was so high up, it was like looking down from a cloud. It was on an acre, so Bruce and Tara had plenty of land to roam. I imagined there would be some new Rockys. But I only loved the one back at Steven's. I was leaving Jack again.

Tabitha was a little trooper. She knew we liked to travel light and went through all her stuff and threw out a lot. I treated her to a new sleek bob haircut and a new outfit.

As I was applying blush to my cheeks, I noticed I could use a touch up on my hair. Silver was threading it way through my dark auburn hair which now tumbled down my back. My acrylic nails had long fallen off . I'd been so preoccupied with painting, I'd neglected myself.

"Keara, let's go or you will miss your flight," David yelled out, from across the hall.

"I'm ready," I screamed back, my voice tight with tension.

I swirled around once more in front of the mirror. I was wearing a plain simple black knit dress. I did have about fifteen grand of jewelry tastefully glittering on me.

"Keara, you look beautiful. But if you don't get away from this mirror you will miss the appointment."

"I feel fat."

David rolled his eyes. "You are not fat. You never looked better. But I'll give you a fat lip if you don't leave right now."

"Alright," I chuckled weakly, grabbing my black leather Coach bag and heading out the door to my destiny.

I gritted my teeth the whole fifty minute plane ride. My brain whirled with thoughts of meeting Ian. What did he want to tell me about my work? Could he make me a success?

My heart was beating wildly as I glided into Ian's office. I pulled up every strength from within to appear cool, calm, and confident.

Ian was over six feet tall, tight curly brown hair and a long beak of a nose. He was British and gay.

Ian gestured for me to sit down.

"Would you like some tea or coffee, Ms. Fitzgerald?"

"No thank you and please call me Keara."

"I was impressed with your work, Keara. Tell me a little about

219

yourself."

"Well, I recently moved to San Francisco from New York. I've been sketching on and off all my life. This fall things started really pouring out. I tried acrylics. I read every book on painting I could get my hands on and took some classes for some formal training. My veterinarian has bought two of my paintings and the animal shelter has asked me to paint a mural on the wall in their cat section. I also have some private clients."

"I'm putting together a showing with different artists who paint animals also. It will be a charity event for the Wild Life Preservation. Would you be interested?"

"Yes," I said a little too loud.

"The other artists all live here in Los Angeles. I'd like for you to meet them."

"I'd love to."

He stood up and stretched out his hand. I clasped it firmly.

"It was a pleasure to meet you. I have a friend who teaches painting in the Haight. I'd like for you to call him and discuss taking a class with him. I'll give him a call and tell him to expect you."

"Thank you Mr. Dieth."

"Ian. I'll be in touch, Keara."

I walked out of his office in a state of shock. All I could think of was to go home and paint. For the first time, I had no desire to call Nick. It looked like I had a new addiction.

Saturday was spent moving. I was going to call my friends to share my good news but decided against it. Kylie, Stella, Jane, Heather. I now felt I moved in another world than them. Yoga, mediating, painting. I was starting to feel good about myself. I looked around for Bruce and Tara. It was time to bring them to our new house. New beginnings once again.

I spent the month painting my heart out. As Taylor would say 24,7 (twenty-four hours a day, seven days a week). I had even cut my phone calls to Nick in half.

I was driving to my yoga class when a phone booth caught my eye. I had about ten minutes left on a phone card. I swung the Jeep around and pulled up beside the booth.

He answered on the third ring.

"Hi, Nick, sorry I haven't called lately."

"I know you're busy."

I noticed a hint of sadness in his voice.

"So what are you up to? Have you thought anymore of moving to Chicago like Gary suggested?"

He cleared his throat.

"I can't."

"Why?"

"Lou had a major stroke. I can't turn my back on him now. He's out of the hospital so I'm over there day and night. You know since he divorced my mom he has no one but me. I've even given up the shelter. I have no time at all between working the plant and nursing him back to health."

"How about a nurse?"

"I can only afford one part time."

"I'm so sorry, Nick."

"It's okay, but enough of my sad story, tell me something good."

"Well. I'm going to L.A. at the end of this week to meet the other artists. I sent Ian more slides and he's pleased. I love the teacher he hooked me up with. I feel I've already improved one hundred percent. The shelter loved my mural and I'm now doing one down at the Marine Center. Oh and guess what?"

"There's more?"

"Yes, it's about Taylor. This new guy she met has been real positive for her. She's now thirty days sober and drug free."

"Wow, I'm impressed. But, Keara, I'm really impressed with you. You even sound different."

"I am different, Nick. It's you I have to thank, though. You let me love you when I needed to do that. You always believed in me and pushed me . Plus, one of the reasons I stayed sober was because I would have hated to call you and tell you I slipped up. So, whatever it's worth, you got me there. I really feel all grown up for once."

"So you're all ready to fly from the nest."

"Maybe more like Dorothy, you know, went to Oz in search of

221

something and all along she really had all the answers. Anyway, I have to run. I have a class in two minutes."

"Bye, Keara, I really miss you."

I hung up and blinked back my tears. Funny how things changed around me constantly.

What a world, What a world.

* * *

Taylor arrived for the holidays. Since the show was right after New Years, I was painting and taking classes day and night. There was no decking the halls this year. I did manage to toss a string of stars and two ornaments on a few long branches that were in a glass vase. I bought four pointsettas and placed them in a large round wicker basket and replaced all the candles with red ones.

Taylor threw down her bag and raced over to the window.

"Oh, Mommy, this is breathtaking. I love it here. This house is so cool. How long do you have it for?"

"Another month. David is looking in the city for a new place. You know me, always moving and changing."

"Mommy, let's go see your paintings. I'm dying to see them."

"First, tell me your news and I want to see your token. I'm so proud of you, Taylor, so proud."

We hugged and kissed. Taylor slipped her thirty day token into my palm.

"That one is yours. I have the original one. I go to three different meetings, so I took a token at each meeting."

"This is great. So, tell me before David and Tabitha get back, what is your great news?"

"Well, I have improved my grades one hundred percent and this semester I'll be going to school in Paris as an exchange student. Do you believe it?"

I burst into tears. "Oh, Taylor, I'm so happy for you. I always wanted you to discover the world while you were young. I never got the chance, I partied instead. This is the best news."

The door swung open and David and Tabitha exploded into the house.

"Taylor," David shouted. "You look fantastic."

"Hi, Sissy," Tabitha said excitedly, hugging Taylor. "How do you like those dead sticks Mom calls a tree."

Taylor glanced over at them. "Mom, do you think you've taken this creative thing a bit too far?"

"Who, me?" I laughed, embracing everybody in a group hug. "Oh, David, where is Isabel?"

"Who's Isabel, again?" Taylor asked her brows arched with interest.

"Isabel introduced me to Ian and got the ball rolling. She also has become like a grandmother to Tabitha. They are inseparable."

"She's in the garage, Mom, looking at your new paintings. I'll go get her,"Tabitha volunteered happily.

"No, we will all go. Taylor hasn't seen any paintings yet. Then we have to get dressed and celebrate."

* * *

Before I knew it, it was time for the big event. The holidays were over. Taylor flew back to New York and was getting ready to go to Paris. David had found a house in the city, this time to buy. Isabel was planning a trip to Hawaii with Tabitha for her spring break. Nick was depressed he couldn't be at my showing.

We flew into Los Angeles the day before and checked into a hotel on the beach in Santa Monica.

"Keara, let's all go for a walk on the beach," David said over his shoulder. He was standing on the deck looking out at the Pacific Ocean.

"Can we go on that Ferris Wheel?" Tabitha asked, pointing to the pier.

"I hate to disappoint you guys but I promised to meet the other artists tonight at the gallery and hang our paintings. It's kind of an artist's ritual tonight, you know, we are going to just hang out and probably get some Chinese food, too."

"What about tomorrow then, Keara? Will you have time to go to the beach then?" David asked, his arms folded across his chest.

"Yes, how about we rent bikes and ride down to Venice?"

They both nodded.

I climbed into the black rented Mustang convertible. It felt like old times behind the wheel. Palm trees. Top down. Cool ocean breeze. My senses immediately filled up with Nick, of course.

223

As I headed towards Beverly Hills, I spotted a phone booth. Just like the old times, I fished through my purse for change.

"Hello," he answered sadly.

"Nick, hi, I was just thinking about you."

"Oh, Keara, I am so glad you called. I wrote you a poem for your special night."

"That is so sweet."

"Do you have time? Can I read it to you now?"he asked anxiously.

"Yeah, well, I only have about ten minutes, okay?"

"Yes, I'll read fast."

* * *

Opening night David had rented a big white limo for me. I poured myself into a leopard print long slinky Betsey Johnson dress. Tabitha wore a long black dress and David was swathed head to toe in Ralph Lauren. I did my breathing exercises the whole ride.

I stepped out of the limo into the chilly night air. I felt like a movie star. I took a deep breath and walked regally inside. Ian greeted us at the door.

"Keara, love the dress, give me a hug," Ian smiled, his eyes crinkled in pleasure.

"Ian, this is David and Tabitha."

"Tabitha, you look absolutely stunning. David, a pleasure, I'd like to talk to you about investing sometime. Keara tells me you're the best." Ian walked away with his arm around David.

"Tabitha, come on, I'll introduce you to the other artists. Isabel should be here any minute, so you stick by her side because I'll have to mingle, okay?"

She nodded happily.

I glanced around at the gallery. There was some wine, cheese, fruit and small Perrier water bottles out on a small table in the center of the room. In the middle of the table was a small ice sculpture of a lion. Ian was expecting about two hundred people.

I was standing by my favorite painting remembering what I was feeling as I did each stroke when two hands came from behind me and covered my eyes.

"Guess who," the voice said in a deep growl.

I spun around to Taylor's radiant smile.

"Taylor," I screamed. "I thought you were leaving for Paris tomorrow."

"I am but Daddy let me fly in for the night. He couldn't stand my bitching another minute. I have to fly out of here at six in the morning but I just couldn't miss your big night."

"Oh God, Taylor, I'm so happy you're here."

"Me too. Mommy, there's Courteney Cox over there. Do you think Ian can introduce me. This is so cool. Oh my God, look who is coming in, Claudia Schiffer."

Ian strolled over to us grinning from ear to ear.

"Ian, this is Taylor."

He kissed her hand. "Pleased to meet such a beautiful lady."

"Keara, brace yourself. You just sold a painting," he smiled proudly.

"Oh, Mommy."

I swallowed hard but couldn't say a word.

"Come with me, Keara and I'll introduce you to the buyers."

The glittering evening went so fast. I felt myself glowing inside and out. My cheeks hurt from all the smiling. It was time to gather up my family and go off to a celebration dinner.

"How are you feeling, Keara?" Isabel asked, gazing into my eyes.

"I feel like Cinderella. You are my fairy Godmother."

"I didn't wave any wand though, you did it all yourself. You are the magic."

"You brought me to Ian."

"You are very talented, Keara. I knew Ian and you would be a perfect match."

"Thank you," I whispered, tears filling up my eyes. I quickly dabbed at the corners, hoping to keep them at bay.

* * *

February was rainy and gloomy. We had moved into a house in the city. David had opened a branch office there, too. Tabitha was excited about her upcoming trip to Hawaii with Isabel. Taylor was in love with Paris. Tara and Bruce were becoming plump indoor city cats. I was hunting around for my own studio to paint

225

in.

I peeled off my yellow rain slicker and slipped out of my wet sneakers. I padded barefoot across the living room and decided to start a fire. I was happy to have the house all to myself. David was putting in late hours. Tabitha was on the basketball team at her new school and would be late. As I was igniting the fire, the phone rang. I hoped it was the real estate agent telling me she'd found a reasonably priced studio.

"Hello," I answered, picking up a rubber band and twisting it around my long wet hair.

"Keara, I'm glad I didn't get your machine," Ian said cheerfully.

"I just got in. I'm trying to get warm from all this wet weather. Is it sunny in L.A.?"

"Uh, no, it's kind of cloudy today. Keara, I'd like for you to come in and have lunch with me tomorrow."

"Mmm, what's up, Ian?"

"I don't want to tell you over the phone. It's supposed to be sunny tomorrow."

"Okay, I guess I could use the break."

"Perfect. See you then."

I hung up and called United shuttle. I made a late reservation going home. It was the first time I had been able to act on my own without fearing David's interference. Also, I hadn't seen Nick in months. Maybe we could meet for coffee at the airport. Funny, how this time it really would be coffee. Painting was my new addiction now. I dialed him collect.

"Keara, what do I owe this honor to?" His laughter crackled over the line.

"Oh, Nick, don't make me feel bad for not calling often. Listen, I'll be in L.A. tomorrow and thought we could meet at the airport for some coffee."

"I remember meeting you a long time ago for supposedly coffee at that same airport."

"Very funny. This time we really will have the coffee, wise guy."

"Okay, Keara, you know I never could say no to you. I guess you have been just as much an addiction to me."

I hung up with a tingling sensation around my heart. I wondered what Nick would think of the silver in my hair and my brown eyes. I no longer wore color contacts.

The next morning I dressed in a navy blue pin striped double-breasted blazer with matching trousers. I pinned up my long chestnut hair and slipped on my Kenneth Cole's navy blue pumps. I paced back and forth in front of the bay window waiting for the cab. David was too busy to take me to the airport. He left the house at four in the morning and didn't return till ten each night.

I arrived at Ian's Gallery promptly at one. He rushed to greet me as I entered.

"Keara, so good to see you. You look wonderful." He kissed me on both cheeks.

"Thanks, Ian. The suspense is killing me. Tell me."

"Don't you want to go to lunch first?"

"No," I screamed. "Out with it."

"Okay, there is this prestigious art school in Paris and well I sent some of the slides from the show because they were offering this scholarship, you see, and well, it's yours if you want it."

"What? What are you saying, Ian?" I asked, falling down into his leather chair.

"It's located in the heart of Paris, on the Left Bank. The courses are held in French so you would have to take a French crash course for two months. That should be enough to integrate you into the school."

"Ian, enough rambling, you're not putting me on, are you? I don't know what to say or think."

"I think you should say yes. David is busy building up his business. Tabitha is going into high school and Isabel is there for her. Taylor loves being in Paris. It's your turn, Keara."

"Oh God, Ian, do you mind if I took off for the beach, maybe do some meditating down there. I'll call you from Santa Monica before I go to the airport with my answer."

"Sure, but I have to know today. There's a lot to be done to get you over there."

"Okay," I mumbled, rising slowly up and hugging him tight.

I jumped into a taxi and had him drop me off in Santa Monica at the pier. I stumbled out of the cab in a complete fog. I kicked off my pumps and strolled barefoot in the sand. I found a quiet place on the beach and plopped down to meditate. Two hours later as I rode in the taxi to LAX, I knew my answer.

I paid the driver and slid out of the cab. I raced over to the first phone I saw and punched in Ian's number.

"Yes, Ian, yes, yes, yes," I cried. "Yes."

"Great, Keara. I'll fly into San Francisco next week to go over everything. You made the right decision."

"I don't know how to thank you, Ian."

"Your charm and talent does the job, Keara."

I hung up and ran for the gate. Nick was already there looking handsome as ever. He was wearing beige trousers with a crisp olive green shirt. I hurled myself into his arms. Tears started streaming down my face.

"Keara, what happened? What is wrong?" he asked soothingly. He pulled me towards a chair. I curled up in his lap.

"Oh, Nick, these tears are happiness, frustration, goodbye, growing up, everything all at once. I am going away, Nick. Far away."

"What are you talking about?" he asked, squirming in his seat. "Did you and David split up?"

I peeled myself off him and plunked down beside him, holding onto his hands.

"Ian managed to get me an unbelievable scholarship for painting in Paris. It is an opportunity of a lifetime," I cried, a fresh wave of tears streaming down my face. I buried my head in his chest.

"I can't believe it. When are you leaving?" he asked, his voice trembling.

"I don't know exactly but probably soon. What do you think?"

"I'm so happy for you. This is a great learning process. Hey, phone cards go to Europe," he laughed softly, his eyes misting. "I've been thinking about taking up French, too."

"Would you visit?"

"Maybe. But now you should put all you energy into painting."

"Oh, speaking of painting. You have to go over to Ian's now.

There is a special painting waiting there for you. You just had to have a Keara for your wall."

Tears started racing down his cheeks.

"Now, don't you cry, Nick. I am crying enough for us both."

We collapsed into one another arms.

"Thanks. I'll cherish it always."

"I love you so much, Nick Bartoli," I sobbed.

"I love you so much, Keara Fitzgerald."

"Do you mean that, Nick?"

"Yes, I do. I love you, Keara."

The announcement that my flight was going to be boarding in ten minutes came across the loud speaker.

"Nick, if you told me that a year ago, I'd come flying back to San Diego but now. Do you understand why I have to go?"

"Yes. You have to follow your dream. Maybe while you are there, I'll be strong enough to follow mine and go to Chicago or just move out."

It was time to board.

"Oh, Nick, I love you," I whispered softly, as I took my right hand and laced my fingers around his shirt pocket and ripped it off.

"What was that?" he asked, totally surprised.

"I wanted a souvenir," I grinned wickedly, running my hands through his hair.

"Wait. I have one more souvenir for you."

He pulled me into his arms and kissed me on the lips. His lips felt like velvet on mine. His tongue silky as it darted into my shocked mouth. He tasted like a mixture of salt and tic tacs. I could almost hear angels singing. They were singing in French. I was deliriously dizzy. The stewardess was tapping me lightly on the shoulder.

"Miss, you have to board now," she said clearing her throat.

We pulled apart. I looked deep into his eyes.

"Goodbye, Nick. Thank you. Your kiss will stay on my lips forever," I cried out. "I'll write." I gave him one last hug and dashed off for the plane.

Oh my God, Nick Bartoli kissed me. Somebody, shoot me now.

The End.

ABOUT THE AUTHOR

Mary Dempsey currently lives in San Francisco where she is working on her next novel, "Before Lunch." Before her writing career began, Mary owned a Stable of race horses, ran her own public entertainment company, and was a prominent disc jockey in New York.